Education for a Multicultural Society
Case studies in ILEA schools

Edited by
Martin Straker-Welds

Bell & Hyman · London

First published 1984 by
Bell & Hyman Limited
Denmark House
37–39 Queen Elizabeth Street
London SE1 2QB

© The contributors

All rights reserved. No part of this publication may be reproduced, stored in a retrieval system, or transmitted in any form or by any means, electronic, mechanical, photocopying, recording or otherwise, without prior permission of Bell & Hyman Ltd.

Education for multicultural society.—
  (Modern teaching series)
  1. Minorities—Education—Great Britain
  I. Straker-Welds, Martin   II. Series
  371.97′0941   LC3736.G6

ISBN 7135 2460 X (cased)
ISBN 7135 2371 9 (limp)

Typesetting by MS Filmsetting Limited, Frome, Somerset
Printed in Great Britain

Contents

Introduction   1

Playgroup and nursery
Introduction   8
1 Working with under-fives: a multi-ethnic approach   9
   Chris Tibbetts
2 St Anne's Nursery School   22
   Pauline Walsh

Multicultural education in the primary school
Introduction   25
3 The impact of an anti-racist policy in the school community   27
   Mike Mulvaney
4 Childeric School: developing a multicultural policy   34
   David Milman

Multicultural education in the secondary school
Introduction   43
5 Developing a whole-school anti-racist policy   46
   Peter Mitchell, Maura Healy and Liz Lindsey
6 Geographical education for a multicultural society   58
   Dawn Gill
7 Integrated studies at William Penn School   71
   Paul McGlyn, Bruce Gill, Brenda Downes, Richard James
8 Humanities in Hackney Downs School   78
   Peter Traves
9 World History in Tulse Hill School   84
   Nigel File and Donald Hinds
10 Developing a multicultural science curriculum   91
   Jenni Newnham and Sue Watts
11 Multicultural mathematics   97
   David Gilbert
12 Peace studies: an active approach to tutoring   108
   Peter Davies
13 The role of the Languages Department in a multicultural school   117
Sol Garson
14 Drama for a multicultural society   124
   Elyse Dodgson

Resources and teacher training
Introduction 135
15 The Whites of their Eyes: a case study in responses to educational television   David Buckingham 137
16 Library resources for a multicultural society
   Helene Fawcett 144
17 Teaching resources
   David James and Garner Griffiths 157
18 Racism and literature: a case study in responses to a short story
   Michael Simons and Paul Ashton 165
19 Combating institutional racism – a training course for experienced teachers   Tuku Mukherjee 180
20 Bilingual resources in secondary schools
   John Wright 189
21 Anti-racist approaches in London Colleges
   Susi Rice 199

Anti-racist teaching
Introduction 213
22 Anti-racist teaching policies
   Shaun Doherty 215
23 Anti-racist teaching in the primary school
   Martin Francis 228
24 A course on racism
   Ilona Aronovsky and Carolyn Sikorski 235

Conclusion 245

Acknowledgements

The editor would like to acknowledge the help given by Mike Hussey in the early stages of planning and in particular his work on Chapters 1, 11, 14, and 16.

He is also grateful to the following for their constructive criticisms: Antonia Murphy of Bell & Hyman, Chris Tibbetts, Mike Mulvaney, Shaun Doherty and David Buckingham and also to Philip Boys, Pimlico School, Virginia Fields and Louise Aylward for their editorial help.

The editor also wishes to thank Annette Horan of the ILEA Multi-ethnic Inspectorate for her help in typing, organising meetings and in general.

Introduction

Martin Straker-Welds

In the beginning
The idea for this collection of case studies came out of a conversation between Mike Hussey (ILEA Inspector for Multicultural Education), Peter Davies (then Principal Deputy Head of Pimlico School) and myself in Autumn '81. During the previous summer, widespread dissatisfaction with institutionalised racism and unemployment created unrest in many cities. This served as a reminder to teachers who had already begun work on multicultural/anti-racist education that they had to continue to search for ways of developing anti-racist studies – a process which had already begun before ILEA first circulated its initial papers in 1977 on Multi-ethnic Education. Although there is no obvious consensus amongst the contributors to this volume, some agreement is currently emerging about what we are aiming towards. For example, it is important to establish that racism has given rise to the idea that 'race' can be used as a categorical division between human beings. We do not believe that this is a scientific category and deplore the use of this term in any attempt to discuss racism. Racism itself has generated the concept of 'race'. This operates at several levels. Societal racism, feeding on the historical legacy of imperialism and colonialism presents a 'natural' view of certain ethnic groups as biologically different and therefore inferior or superior. Structurally this appears to be borne out by the position of certain groups in the social division of labour. Institutional racism perpetrates these social disadvantages through processes and procedures which place minority ethnic groups at the bottom of the list for housing, employment, education and other life chances. At this largely invisible level detailed analysis alone can provide evidence for unintentional racism. Individual racism is therefore the tip of the iceberg. To treat racism as simply a problem of the individual disguises the racism operating at the other two levels.

Anti-racist education means tackling racism at all of these levels through the school curriculum. In doing this educationalists have to be sensitive to the existence in schools of both the 'overt' and 'hidden' curriculum. Through the 'overt' curriculum subjects and courses can be utilised to explain historical, social and economic forces which operate locally, nationally and internationally to foster oppression. The 'hidden' curriculum operating through institutional procedures e.g. primary/secondary transfer, options grouping, setting and banding determines the ethos of the school. The 'hidden' curriculum also confers values, status and worth to the pattern of interactions between students, staff and even parents within the school, supporting some and excluding others.

If we accept that racism is damaging to the dignity of human beings in general then its eradication is of the utmost importance. All educationalists, students and parents by working together can begin to set about eliminating patterns of exclusion which set groups whether based on sex, ethnicity or class at a disadvantage.

We wanted to provide some guidelines for teachers, based on good practice, so as to encourage world and international studies and social education across the curriculum. We have therefore asked a number of individuals to record their experiences as teachers writing for other teachers, rather than experts speaking from the safety of ivory towers. It seemed important to demonstrate that all schools and teachers and subjects had a contribution to make to the development of a multicultural/anti-racist curriculum and that this process involved a commitment which all areas of the education service could undertake. The case studies are not meant to be definitive statements but are addressed to all educationalists: teachers, students, administrators, inspectors, counsellors and community agencies who are involved in education for personal and social development in a rapidly changing society. We hope that these accounts will encourage student teachers and experienced staff alike, whether they are already developing courses or are about to begin the process, to participate in innovation and to record their own experiences and share them with others.

Background

Readers will find in this volume that there is no homogeneous world view or coherent blueprint which can be used as a model for multicultural curriculum development. The examples outlined in these twenty-four chapters describe developments which are responses to local situations on the part of educationalists who share a commitment to education for a multicultural society. As such, they are not the result of directives from an education authority or central government but based on a resolve to innovate which acknowledges debts to students, parents, community agencies, teachers' centres, advisory staff and members of the ILEA Multi-ethnic Inspectorate. These examples illustrate limitations and possibilities, and although they describe case studies in ILEA, they offer insights which could be of value to educationalists throughout the country, particularly in those local education authorities where attempts are being made to promote whole school policies for curriculum development.

During the last five years a number of education authorities have issued statements on multicultural education: Avon, Berkshire, Brent, Barnet, Bedfordshire, Bradford, Cambridgeshire, Croydon, Coventry, Derbyshire, Haringey, Hounslow, ILEA, Kirklees, Leicestershire, Manchester, Newham, Sheffield, Walsall, and Wolverhampton ([1]Andrew Dorn, 1983). These policies are locally rather than nationally inspired and vary in status, commitment to implementation and community support from minority ethnic groups, but all share a view that curriculum development is necessary.

The publication of Berkshire's policy was followed by ILEA'S statements during Autumn 1983. These have laid down a timetable for implementation of whole-school policies in schools and clarified ILEA's aims and methods. In a lengthy analysis of reasons for its change in perspective ILEA has set out some of the issues which have created problems for ethnic groups who have borne the brunt of racism. Black people who migrated to Britain during the labour shortage in the 1950s were very easily identifiable in a way which other migrant workers were not. Government legislation to curb immigration following disturbances in Notting Hill and Nottingham culminated in the 1981 Nationality Bill. These forms of legislation accompanied an increase in overt and institutionalised racism which more recently has assumed hostile proportions, with racist political groups attempting to gain a following by distributing racist leaflets to schools, and inciting racist hostility.

ILEA, drawing on the Berkshire policy, now states that it is no longer enough simply to base education on the principle of assimilating pupils into a predominantly 'Anglo-Saxon' curriculum, nor to integrate different ethnic groups into schools where cultural pluralism is encouraged by token respect paid to certain marginal but visible features of minority group cultures. A number of LEAs now call for an anti-racist stance to inform both the development of the curriculum and the schools' ethos and organisation. This raises significant questions concerning curriculum development, particularly in secondary schools, as to whether the existing subject curriculum should be adapted or whether whole-school innovation indicates changes in the structure, courses, subjects and teaching methods. Equally, discriminatory practices which exist in schools are one part of a wider web of practices in society over which schools exert little influence. Examples of different kinds of developments are to be found in this volume, all of which can play an important role in the development of whole-school policies, particularly if there is a commitment to community and political education and cross curricular collaboration. The editor of this volume views the most effective stance as one in which schools adopt a code of practice which promotes anti-racist education for a multicultural society, rather than the more piecemeal approach, often identified with 'multiculturalism', which seeks to alter parts of the subject curriculum without changing the ethos of the whole school.

The case studies

This book is divided into five sections: playgroup and nursery; primary; secondary; resources and teacher training; anti-racist teaching. Each section has an introduction written by one of the contributors and the case studies follow. These are examples of practice which are situated in a particular context. Many of the examples will have changed since or been modified as a result of evaluation over a period of time. By the time this reader is published there may be substantial differences as a result of changes in LEA policy etc. Nonetheless we would defend the approach we have chosen because it is based on practice and focuses attention on to real teachers in real situations.

Playgroup and nursery
In her introduction to playgroup and nursery school, Chris Tibbetts makes a strong case for intervention in early play experiences which tackle the negative aspects of racism by a positive acknowledgement of ethnic differences. Crucial to this is the involvement of parents in playgroups and the promotion of bilingual learning for minority ethnic groups. If necessary, energetic attempts should be made to break down barriers which may inhibit parents from minority ethnic groups attending playgroups and nursery school. There are many important suggestions from both contributors about involving parents and community agencies in the process of learning. These have been written down in great detail because there are reasons why minority ethnic groups may find it very difficult to take part in their child's early educational experiences at institutions of all kinds (ranging from playgroup right through to secondary). There are also detailed ideas about materials for the playgroup ranging from books, music, clothing, dolls, games etc. which show how a range of activities can take advantage of a multi-ethnic community.

Primary
Mike Mulvaney draws attention to the norms which influence the assessment and profiling of pupils in primary school. A crucial test assigns pupils about to transfer to secondary school to one of three bands. The verbal reasoning test stands out as a particularly inappropriate test in view of the cultural bias built into the structure. If we are to be consistent in terms of multicultural/anti-racist curriculum develpment then the methods of assessment we employ and the norms which we expect ought to be appropriate to everybody. The uneasy role of 'half-way-house' between playgroup and secondary education presents primary schools with problems. In this section both primary articles show how staff have worked collectively towards whole school policy statements. Mike Mulvaney writes about the importance of tackling anti-racist issues which affect children and parents in the local community. David Milman writes about the development of a multiracial curriculum. Both articles show how the policy statement was produced by the collective action of the staff.

Secondary
Peter Mitchell introduces the secondary section and demonstrates both here and in the account of Quintin Kynaston's whole school policy development how an investigation of the learning process as it is affected by both the overt and hidden curriculum has to be carried out by staff as a whole as well as by departments and subject specialists. Secondary schools with their divided and

fragmented systems, syllabuses and courses face particular problems over developing consensus about aims.

In this book you will find four descriptions of whole school policies (Chapters 3, 4, 5 and 22). Although individual teachers and subject departments can innovate in the imaginative way demonstrated by this collection of articles it is an advantage particularly for secondary schools to develop a coherent approach so that all departments are supported by staff consensus. The position of the head is crucial in supporting such developments although styles of leadership vary enormously; in some cases heads see innovation proceeding from the top downwards, in other cases the head devises a management structure which supports innovation from the grassroots; Some policies stress multicultural curriculum development while others have taken a more directly anti-racist stance.

Many teachers try to involve either their parents or local community both in the development of policies and in the curriculum. Elyse Dodgson (Chapter 14) shows how creative drama can use personal testimony of both students and their parents to bring alive experiences which are now historical. Paul McGlyn and his colleagues (Chapter 7) use the community as a base for local studies in their first year integrated humanities course. Nigel File and Donald Hinds (Chapter 9) make a plea for wider use of oral history to supplement other resources. Teachers in this way can demonstrate not only that they value the experiences which pupils bring with them to school but the community in which they have developed those experiences. Valuing the community languages and the mother tongues of bilingual students is crucial for all school and multi-ethnic communities. Sol Garson shows how a whole school policy on language, coupled with the Languages department's concern for the development of world languages, can help to provide for the special needs of all pupils, drawing on the experiences of bilingual students and teachers. Once again, this example shows the advantages of a whole school policy which can support language across the curriculum and clarify the aims for staff, community, pupils and parents. Such policies should also take account of both Science and Mathematics: subjects which may appear to be isolated if attempts to collaborate with other areas are not carried out. David Gilbert provides us with an example of work in Mathematics which could usefully be tied in with integrated humanities and other courses. Some schools also run social education courses based on 'active tutoring' or Health, Social and Political Education. Maura Healey and Peter Davies both give accounts of work that tutors can develop to produce the 'socially educated person' (Chapters 5 and 12).

Resources
In this section, David Buckingham introduces articles on learning resources with a warning that they are not neutral artefacts which well intentioned staff can use without clarifying their own situation. Learning resources depend for their impact on the context in which they are used. Staff have to face up to their

own attitudes individually and as members of institutions collectively to clarify the relationship between individual and institutionalised racism. This is a rare occurrence when resources are being discussed as David James reminds us in Chapter 17. Resources for anti-racist/multicultural education do not fall neatly into subject areas, nor should teachers concentrate purely on vetting the libraries, important though this is in the context of learning resources for whole school development.

All areas of the curriculum can innovate – this is best done through a process which involves collaboration across subject boundaries and using resources positively rather than hiding behind them. Sensitive approaches to providing resources for bilingual pupils and courses for FE colleges students are outlined in this section.

Anti-racist teaching
Shaun Doherty and contributors to the section on anti-racist teaching remind us of the possibilities and limitations of any school policy, faced as teachers are with economic, social and political divisions outside their school. Anti-racist education is political in its commitment and teachers who are committed to striving for equality in school and society must be prepared to change their style to one which is non-authoritarian.

These three articles take an interventionist stance of the kind advocated by the Rampton report in attempts to examine the roots of racism. They demonstrate that children are constantly making sense of a world which they perceive to be divided by class, sex and racism. Avoiding these issues by adopting an 'innocents' approach to younger children or attempting to separate racism from wider social injustices ignores the fact that there are structural as well as individual forms of racism. We are not simply protecting children from the views of individual racists. British society itself has a historical past steeped in imperialism and colonialism which has contributed to racist attitudes. Without a historical understanding of racism it can, as Ilona Aronovsky and Carolyn Sikorski (Chapter 24) point out, be reduced to a purely psychological phenomenon in which white racists are to be persuaded to relinquish their prejudices. Ideas of racial superiority dating back to slavery have been used to justify imperialism and the exploitation of black people. These ideas still persist in a divided society and anti-racist teaching therefore involves looking at the social, political and economic aspects of British society and international relations with the Third World.

Summary
These case studies provide some examples of initiatives which signal important directions for curriculum development in schools during the 1980s. Such initiatives rely heavily on individual teachers and subject specialists

librarians, media resources officers and staff from teachers centres. The common factor which unites them is the realisation by the individuals concerned that education for a multicultural society is an important dimension in the progress of schools towards a curriculum which offers all pupils the broadest educational opportunity possible. We are under no illusions about the complexity of the issues involved nor do we feel that schools can single handedly alter or compensate for social disadvantage. Challenging racism in school does not of itself guarantee a transformation of the outside world. The very insulation which some schools have traditionally used to protect their environment from outside influences inhibits the capacity of staff to understand the social pressures which face pupils and their families. They may include, for instance, the effects of class disadvantage and institutional racism which may affect health, housing, employment and leisure facilities and relations with the police. These articles have been collected together in the hope that initiatives of the kind outlined here may ignite a spark of recognition in the minds of other teachers and educationalists who are sharing similar attempts to innovate since they appear at a time when an increasing number of local education authorities are asking schools to move in the direction of policies across the whole curriculum.

Reference
1 Andrew Dorn *LEA policies on Multiracial Education* ILEA Multiethnic Review, 1983, Vol 2, No 2.

8 Playground and nursery

Introduction
Chris Tibbetts

While the need for developing a multi-ethnic approach has been fairly widely accepted in most areas of education, there appears to be a general, but largely unexamined, consensus of opinion which reasons that there is little need for any intervention during the pre-school years. It is frequently believed that as long as young children are merely enabled to mix freely together this will create a social climate in which they will develop complete tolerance to ethnic differences.

This section of the book argues that to subscribe to such a notion is to be gravely in danger of 'missing the boat'. Intervention in later school years cannot be entirely effective when there has been little recognition of or response to the profound and far-reaching effects of early childhood conditioning in a society in which racism is largely covert and institutionalised. No educationalist would argue that the first six years of life are not crucial to the development of social attitudes, yet this maxim seems rarely applied to an examination of the roots of racism.

Both articles in this section examine the need for pre-school workers to assess and adapt their existing practice in order to develop a more appropriate and sensitive approach to multi-ethnic education, and both give practical suggestions on how to do this. A growing number of pre-school workers are trying to develop programmes to effect change and alter attitudes and it is hoped this section will support them and encourage others to debate and initiate more change. The Commission for Racial Equality is at present producing a booklet with an accompanying resources file which aims to identify the issues needing to be considered in the formation of an anti-racist strategy for under-fives. There appears, unfortunately, to be relatively little direction or support for these individual workers from either national or local authority level, and little awareness of the need for comprehensive policy and planning changes.

Until the pre-school is recognised as the base from which change must begin and is seen as an integral component of a multi-ethnic approach, long-term fundamental attitudinal changes are unlikely to be effected. Instead, children will continue at first to absorb and later to learn how to utilise for themselves the double talk and covert prejudice which allows our society to suppress and deny both specific issues and its own general racism.

Chapter 1

WORKING WITH UNDER-FIVES: A MULTI-ETHNIC APPROACH

Chris Tibbetts

> Chris Tibbetts is a social worker working with under-fives and their families. While serving on a local and a National Committee of the Pre-school Play Groups Association she was involved in producing various pamphlets and articles. She has been a playgroup tutor.

There seems to be a wide-spread conviction in our society that young children have 'ethnic innocence' – that they are unaware of ethnic differences. In fact, a wide body of research (see bibliography at the end of this chapter) has proved the opposite to be true and has established that, as a result of the young child's need to order and categorise the physical world and personal experiences, an awareness of ethnic differences can exist as early as the age of $2-2\frac{1}{2}$. Studies have shown that the stage at which this development accelerates most rapidly is when the child is developing greater social awareness, often in about the fourth year.

The acquisition by young children of racist attitudes, while popularly believed to happen simply because parents teach their children such feelings, can more accurately be seen to result from the far subtler and complex process of socialisation. Consider the situation when a small child on a bus says loudly 'Look at that black man, mummy.' Most people freeze with embarrassment and the mother desperately attempts to quieten the child. The child almost certainly senses the tension of the mother and probably of the group on the bus, and so is made aware of an unspoken attitude – that this is a negative and taboo subject.

Unfortunately many pre-school workers reinforce this conditioning by behaving as if ethnic differences did not exist. Standard comments are: 'But the children all play so nicely together,' and 'We treat them just the same.' The question is on whose terms are the children playing nicely together, and being treated just the same? If the play activities and the general ethos in the school project only the values and attitudes of the host community, then all children, irrespective of their own cultural backgrounds, are channelled to play in a way which conforms to a 'white' ethnocentric view of the world.

This process is frequently unrecognised by the staff. Many, confronted with the idea of encouraging the development of positive awareness and attitudes, find it distasteful, feeling such practice could be very divisive or could create a harmful awareness in the children where none existed previously. Often, children's questions about ethnic differences receive an evasive response or no answer at all, and their comments are ignored. They are led to recognise that ethnic difference is a sensitive subject that is somehow 'taboo'. While continuing to observe, think and feel they cease to talk about these issues. Both pre-school workers and parents, greatly relieved about this, use the fact that the child almost never mentions colour to reinforce their wish to believe that young children are ethnically innocent. The fact that children are picking up subtle messages about ethnic differences, and the reluctance of pre-school workers to acknowledge this development leads to children absorbing the covert racist attitudes of our society.

Clearly, then, it is not enough simply to allow children to mix together and hope that they will as a result develop a natural acceptance of cultural differences and a 'colour-blindness'. A more positive multi-ethnic approach must be developed.

Parental involvement

It is generally accepted that working with the pre-school child should be seen in the context of working with the child's whole family. If in addition to this there is a commitment to develop a multi-ethnic approach, then the need for involving parents and other relevant adults is doubly important. Yet many pre-school workers seem to find it difficult to involve minority group parents, and question whether these parents feel less able, less motivated, less confident about being involved. However the real questions might be 'Why do pre-school establishments find it more difficult to involve minority group parents? Is it necessary to adapt our traditional methods of involvement?'

When indigenous white staff talk about involving people from the minority groups, this generally means involving them in something which is of the majority culture. Minority group members are frequently expected to conform to the indigenous group's standards when they come into the community at large – standards which they may not understand too well or do not accept. Because of their experience of both covert and overt racism, they may well feel that their ideas will not be understood or accepted. True involvement of minority group parents must be based on the concept of an exchange of ideas and values, rather than that of pre-school workers teaching parents to learn and accept the values and traditions of the host community. It is therefore essential that pre-school groups should recognise the importance of representation from the minority groups, and make it clear that parents are needed both for their personal, professional and parenting skills, and for the contribution they can make regarding their own culture. Rethinking traditional events with minority group parents can help to establish this approach – stalls at the annual fête or bazaar can be clearly billed as International; cookery sessions can be arranged as swapshops where parents take turns to demonstrate and exchange recipes; annual celebrations such as Dwali, Id, the Chinese New Year and Carnival can be celebrated as well as Christmas and Easter; and parents' committees and groups need to be made aware of, and encouraged to respond to, issues concerning all sections of the community. Independent projects run for and by the minority groups, while frequently seen as a threat to the established network of pre-school provision, could rather be viewed as an additional support to the community, and liaison with them as a valuable learning experience.

At the same time as acknowledging the need for parental involvement it is also important to recognise that minority group parents are individuals with different circumstances, needs and ideas. For example, while many minority group parents are personally suffering from the stresses of making the transition from one culture to another others, while still experiencing these stresses, will have found ways of coping with them. Others will have become acculturated. Some parents will consciously take the decision that they want themselves and their children to become fully integrated into the majority group's culture; some may choose to maintain their own culture by isolating themselves as much as possible from the host community; others feel that they want to acknowledge their identity by having their culture represented and valued in society.

Thus, not all individuals want or feel capable of the same levels of involvement. Those under stress may feel isolated and depressed and find it far more difficult to respond to requests to become involved. To help such parents pre-school workers need to establish a supportive and genuinely concerned approach which enables parents to express their feelings about themselves, their present circumstances and parenthood. Given this sort of encouragement parents may develop a greater confidence to contribute ideas and become more actively involved in planning and developing activities to be used in the pre-school setting.

Where workers make effective personal contact with families from the minority groups, they can develop a sensitivity and understanding which can never be learnt from books or lectures. However, having said this, it might be helpful to focus on some of the issues which have been regularly raised and to suggest possible ways of dealing with them.

1 Issue Many parents have to go out to work and so are unable to visit or help in the pre-school.

Suggestion Can someone arrange to visit the family at home? Find out what skills the parents do have, e.g. toymaking, repairing, and utilise them. Get away from the concentration on coffee mornings and arrange meetings and social gatherings that don't clash with work hours. Ask parents, including minority group parents, to offer hospitality.

2 Issue Grandparents, relatives, friends or childminders may care for the child during the day and bring her/him to the pre-school. It is not always the same adult who brings and collects the child, and this confuses staff and appears to decrease parent/adult involvement opportunities.

Suggestion Again, a home visit may help to sort out the family structure and who it is who brings the child. Adapt traditional ideas – need it always be mother on the 'mother rota'? Invite father, grandad, grandma or auntie to stay instead. And consider involving childminders who themselves could learn from and contribute to discussions on caring for young children in an ethnically mixed society.

3 Issue Parents may sometimes seem very unsure or hesitant about becoming involved. This may result from individual personal reasons, fear of racial hostility or cultural conditioning. They themselves may wish to help in the pre-school but other family members may expect or need them to stay at home.

Suggestion Is it possible to arrange a system whereby established parents take new parents under their wing – perhaps even call for those who seem particularly hesitant about coming on their own? Can the mother rota be made less intimidating by suggesting that two people do it together and giving clear instructions on what the expectations of this role are? It may be necessary to get the message of parental involvement across to the whole family to enable mother to stay, so encourage father, and particularly grandmother, to come along and help out too. Discuss with them all what contributions they feel they can make to the pre-school.

4 Issue Language difficulties create problems. It can be very difficult for staff to explain things like rules and regulations; and the limited language of some parents can lead to misinterpretation of their behaviour. A mother was thought rude when she said 'I take this boy home now,' rather than 'May I take him home now please?' In fact, she was having difficulties learning the subtleties of a new language.

Suggestion Obviously the best solution to this problem is to have members of staff who speak the same languages as the parents. It can be particularly comforting to parents (as it is to a new child) to find a member of staff who comes from the same ethnic group as they do. Such a person can give confidence and support to the family, and may be able to explain their particular concerns and problems to other staff. They can also act as interpreters and translators though these are skilled jobs and staff need to be aware of the limitations of using non-professionals to do this. However, such a person, if used properly, can help make staff more cross-culturally aware, and so help iron out the communication problems which frequently do arise in the pre-school, because of a lack of understanding of both language and cultural differences.

Local Authorities, Community Relations Councils, local religious bodies, community groups and minority group associations may be able to find funding to employ such staff. There are now many local organisations representing the different ethnic groups and it is important to make contact with them for information and assistance in advertising for and employing appropriate people. However, where it has not been possible to obtain such a member of staff, or where there are so many different languages represented in the pre-school that it would be impractical to employ enough staff to cover this, teenagers from your local schools can sometimes be used to communicate, and to assist generally.

5 *Issue* Parents from the minority ethnic groups may use other methods of child-rearing from those prevalent in many pre-school establishments and may have different perceptions of play. Like many parents, they may have expectations of the pre-school which are not in line with the ideas of the trained staff.

Suggestion Pre-school workers need to understand that different child-rearing methods and attitudes are not 'wrong' or 'bad' – merely culturally different. We in the West cannot claim to have discovered the definitive form of child-care. It is, therefore, important to adopt a positive and non-judgmental approach when explaining the aims and objectives of the pre-school to minority group parents, in order to avoid misunderstanding, hostility or withdrawal. The attitudes to play of parents brought up in a non-industrialised, rural society, may still reflect that society – where there is no pressing need for manufactured toys and organised play facilities, because natural play materials are readily available, there is plenty of space to play, and the young child can expect to be played with by many adults and children from her/his extended family and/or the village community. Giving parents an opportunity to talk about their own childhood memories of play and to link these with what goes on in the pre-school and the need for play provision in an urban society is generally very productive. Where there are language difficulties, a leaflet, translated into the relevant mother tongues explaining the value of play, might help – though quite a high proportion of Asian women are not literate in their own language. Again, someone who can talk to parents in their own language about the role of pre-school education and the value of play is much more valuable.

6 *Issue* In a mixed group, people from minority groups may gravitate towards others who have the same cultural background or language as themselves. The pre-school may feel disturbed by having these cliques of parents, and feel they need to break them up if they are to involve the parents in the general activities.

Suggestion The confidence and security these sub-groups can give their members is valuable, so it is important not to feel threatened by them, but always to encourage them to take part in the activities and decision making of the larger group.

7 *Issue* Parents often seem rather hesitant and unsure about bringing items from their own culture into the pre-school setting.

Suggestion Ask parents personally and request specific items at first – later they may gain enough confidence to offer things which they think may be of interest. And keep asking to ensure that there are items representative of all your ethnic groups. Countries like India and the West Indies cover vast areas and include many different ethnic groups.

8 Issue Introducing multicultural items and tackling ethnic and cultural differences in the pre-school will open up the sensitive area of racism which can create considerable tension and hostility.

Suggestion Make it clear to parents what your aims and objectives are and why it is important to provide an environment in which each child can develop her/his own positive ethnic and cultural identity. Once parents trust your motives their co-operation and appreciation is generally given. However, if you are faced with resistance and racism which you feel unable to handle, look to your local Community Relations Council or the National Commission for Racial Equality[1] for assistance. Many workers also find that in order to understand and cope with society's racism and their own racist conditioning, racism awareness training programmes can be very useful. Contact the Anti-Racist Committee[2] for information.

Having made these suggestions it must still be acknowledged that parental involvement is frequently hard work. Pre-school establishments are, often accurately, seen by the minority group populace as institutions in a position of power and authority, which represent and project the values and beliefs of the dominant culture. Thus finding ways of involving and working with parents and other adults from the minority ethnic groups may well take extra thought, time, sensitivity and understanding. But where pre-school provision has achieved this, it can provide an extremely valuable resource to a community.

Materials and activities

Playgroups and nurseries try to make themselves friendly and familiar places for the children that go to them. Pauline Walsh deals in the following article with the importance of the mother tongue in making a child feel secure. But children also need familiar *things* around them to make them feel at home and to stimulate their imaginative play. Children from ethnic minorities need materials and activities relating to their own culture. Indigenous white children are growing up in a culturally plural society and need to develop positive attitudes to this. It's important to show them that all cultures are equally valued.

Some children and parents may view the introduction of multicultural play materials with uncertainty, even suspicion. However, if you continue to use them in a relaxed and *undirected* way, i.e. waiting for the children's comments and then responding to them positively, most children will begin to enjoy playing with multicultural materials, and talking to you about ethnic differences they see in the world around them. Parents too will generally grow to trust your motives and start joining in the activities and provide many of the materials which are suggested in this section.

Books
More and more under-fives groups are using books for young children which reflect our multi-ethnic society. However, there are various important points to bear in mind when choosing books for this purpose.
1 Look for books where some or all of the main characters come from minority ethnic groups – too frequently they only appear in subsidiary roles.
2 Avoid books which portray minority group characters in a negative light, i.e., stupid, feckless, lazy, naive or wicked.
3 A great deal of material which is available has excellent pictorial value but the text is frequently far too difficult for the under-fives. By adapting and simplifying the text these books can still be used.
4 Children who are learning English as a second language may require books which use very simple and repetitive language, or to have those books you already use simplified for them (see *Story-telling in a second language*[3] by Eve Smith). Many of the materials that feature black children and have a simple text are early reading schemes.
5 Children's books are now available in a number of other languages and some of these could be provided, so that children could be read stories in their own language.

Story-telling
The general pre-school pattern appears to be that stories are told or read when all the children are together in a large group, generally at the end of the session, but this can be impractical, particularly where there are language differences. Frequent story-telling to small groups of children should be encouraged throughout each session. This is far more likely to stimulate conversation between staff and the children, and, unobtrusively, children of the same language level can be brought together, though not withdrawn from the main group. The following suggestions will help to make story-telling more effective.
1 Make sure there is always an adult in the book corner ready to read or tell a story – in whatever language is appropriate.
2 It is essential to tell simple stories with lots of repetition and opportunities for the children to join in with sounds, actions and simple phrases. Plenty of facial and vocal expressions and actions are necessary to keep the attention of most 3-year-olds, particularly where they have a limited understanding of English.
3 Telling a story is better than reading one – you can respond better to the children if you are not having to concentrate on the text.
4 Make up simple stories which use the experiences of minority group children. Use their names, familiar objects and situations which they can

identify with, e.g. shopping, cooking and special occasions like festivals, weddings, christenings and naming ceremonies.
5 Tell stories around the activities going on in the pre-school group and about visits to the park, shops, market, fire station, local building site, etc.
6 Use props to tell a story – they make a story more interesting and easier to understand. Have felt boards and magnet boards with pictures of characters and objects from all ethnic groups collected from magazines, catalogues, etc., or hand and finger puppets representing different ethnic groups. Children should be allowed to play with the puppets as this can lead to spontaneous story-telling, sometimes in their mother tongue. Knitting patterns for a family of West Indian finger puppets and a family of Asian finger puppets are available in the leaflet *Dolls and Puppets for the Multiracial Society*[4].

Action rhymes
These can be particularly useful when working with children who are learning English as a second language, because using actions with words may help promote understanding and, children who are too shy to speak on their own will often join in this group activity. However, rhymes should be chosen carefully and the following points given consideration.

1 Rhymes which relate to the child's own experience are very suitable. Pre-school children are egocentric and therefore relate everything to themselves – they particularly seem to enjoy and understand rhymes referring to parts of their bodies, e.g. 'This is the way we brush our hair', and 'Put your finger on your nose'.
2 Some action rhymes may confuse the child who is just beginning to learn English. If you hold up your fingers and say 'Five fat sausages' can you be sure the child knows they are called fingers and does not assume they are called sausages?
3 Part of the language learning process for young children appears to involve experimenting with sound patterns. Rhymes in which sounds are repeated and varied, and the main focus is not upon understanding, may help them to become aware of the sounds and rhythms of English which will be different from those of their mother tongue, e.g. chop, chop, choppity chop.
4 Try adapting or making up very simple, repetitive action rhymes. Help to reinforce language learning by using language that has already been used in the story or with some of the play activities, e.g.
'This is the way we play with the sand'
'This is the way we play with the bricks', etc.

Music and rhythm
Music is sometimes a rather neglected activity in pre-school groups but we suggest it should be emphasised because it provides excellent opportunities both for involving parents and helping children.

1 Ask parents from minority ethnic groups if they will come to sing and dance to their traditional music and demonstrate how to play their instruments to the children.
2 Incorporate some folk songs into your repertoire of songs and rhymes, such as 'Brown Gal in de Ring'.
3 Have a music table or music sessions so that children can handle and use instruments from the various cultural groups.
4 Many instruments can be too valuable to keep permanently for the children to use but 'play' instruments can be made to represent the real instruments. Suggestions for making some musical instruments are given in the pack *All Children Play*[5].
5 Use rhythm to help acquire the correct stress and intonation of language, e.g. tap out or clap the rhythm of the words and phrases like 'good morning', 'what's the matter?'.

Home corner
If the home corner is most rewarding when it is 'home in miniature' then it should reflect the mix in the pre-school group. However, where many different groups are represented this could be rather overwhelming. Rather than having all the cultures represented in one home corner, items can be changed from time to time, so changing the emphasis.

Items you can use to represent the various cultural groups
Empty tins and packets of food; papier mache or hard baked playfood. (Recipes for making playfood are provided in *Fun and Food for Playgroups*[6] published by the West Midlands PPA.) Cooking utensils (e.g. chapati rolling pin and board, tava (chapati pan)); Chinese wok and chopsticks; posters and pictures; calendars; ornaments and wall hangings; newspapers; birthday cards; record player (not in use) with record sleeves and dummy records; bedcovers, cushions and rugs; envelopes with stamps from various countries; small pieces of furniture, e.g. stools; small tables.

Two-way telephone and an old television case can also be put in the home corner and are valuable assets to language stimulation.

Many of these items can also be used in the play shop.

Dressing up clothes
Again, these should relate to the ethnic groups that are represented in your group. Obtaining and making dressing up clothes can provide a good opportunity for parental involvement. Possible items to request are:
jewellery; wedding and festival clothes and ornaments; hair ornaments and combs; scarves; slippers; embroidered jackets – Chinese, Indian, Cypriot, etc.; fans; hats; African print skirts and tunics; West Indian print skirts; saris (instructions on how to put on a sari are included in the pack *Dolls and Puppets for a Multi-Racial Society*); shalwar (Asian Ladies' trousers) and kameez (tunic) – these are not very difficult to make, so ask parents if they could give you a pattern or make them for you.

Dolls

Many black dolls at present available in shops are not lifelike – they are white dolls coloured black or brown, and black children may reject them. Galts and ESA do produce quite good black dolls and the black and brown, male and female Sasha dolls seem very acceptable, but these are expensive. Many groups have found that homemade dolls are often much more popular, and directions for making these are also included in the leaflet *Dolls and Puppets for a Multi-Racial Society*.

Staff, parents and students can also be encouraged to produce dolls dressed in traditional costumes, and the results are frequently very rewarding. Small pipe-cleaner dolls can be dressed to represent different ethnic groups, for use in the dolls' house, etc., and traditional dolls can be made such as the Indian bride doll which has two faces, back and front, one representing a bride in a traditional wedding sari, and the other in a modern wedding sari. A more comprehensive list of manufactured dolls and doll-making kits is given in HARMONY's multi-cultural toy list[7].

Interest tables and interest areas

Rather than using interest tables and areas to represent one culture on specific occasions, there should be multicultural items for every theme. For example, an interest table with the theme 'round' could include a chapati, a pancake and a West Indian bake or dumpling: West Indian maraccas, bongo drums, a recorder and a tabla (Asian drum); bangles and round beads from different cultures: and round slices of carrots and Indian radish (mouli); plus standard items like balls, a round mirror and a round bowl of soapy water with bubble blowers.

It doesn't matter if indigenous children or even the staff don't always recognise the objects brought by the minority groups. Let the children who do recognise them or the parents who have brought them explain to the rest of the group what the items are.

Table games

Jigsaws which reflect our multi-ethnic society can now be purchased but they are not always easy to find. Galts produce a series 'Just Like Us'. However, you can also make your own by using appropriate pictures mounted on stiff card and cut into simple three or four piece jigsaw puzzles. You can also make lotto games, simple domino games and snap cards in this way. Details of where to obtain pictures are given in the section on pictures and posters. Cheap paperback books like those produced by the New Delhi Children's Book Trust can be cut up and used to make these games.

Cookery

Making a simple foreign dish is one of the most effective ways of developing a more multicultural approach within the pre-school setting and of involving parents from the minority groups. Parents may agree to demonstrate where and how to buy certain foodstuffs, and how to cook them for you, or to supply a recipe and then rescue you when your chapati turns out triangular!

An excellent pack called *Cooking around the World*[8] gives over 90 recipes from all over the world which have been simplified to enable young children to prepare them. Cold cookery recipes are also included for groups with no cooking facilities. When making dough, use chapati flour for a change – it makes a long-lasting, stretching dough.

Painting and collage
When you mix your paints try to produce a selection of realistic skintone colours so that the children, if they choose, can paint themselves and their friends in the colours they see themselves. Such things as black-eyed beans, macaroni, rice, lentils, seeds and spices can be used for collage work. However, some people do feel that food is such a precious commodity that it should not be used in this way, and staff should be sensitive to these feelings.

Festivals
Where many different cultures are represented in one group it would be difficult to celebrate every festival. However, the staff should still know something about each of them, so they can talk to the children about the events. The Commission for Racial Equality's publication 'Calendar of Religious Festivals' gives quite a lot of useful information and all the dates.

Where there is a large group of children from one culture in a group, festivals can be celebrated very successfully. Cards and decorations, traditional food and sweets can be made, and parents encouraged to come into playgroup to tell the traditional festival stories, and dance or sing.

Pictures and posters
Pictures and posters depicting different ethnic groups can have an immediate and colourful impact in a pre-school setting but the choice of pictures should be carefully made. Ensure that they depict minority groups positively and in everyday normal situations. Avoid pictures that promote a human suffering-image, press problem-image, or tourist fun-image. Suitable pictures for the under-fives are those the children can identify with, e.g. pictures of babies, children, families, people in different occupations and activities, and whom they recognise from the society in which they live. Pictures can be used to make scrapbooks which illustrate the multi-ethnic nature of our society.

Sources of pictures and posters
local shops
local cinemas
airlines
government High Commissions and Embassies (there is a list of their addresses in London telephone directories)

Oxfam, Education Department, Oxfam, 274 Banbury Road, Oxford
Health Education Council
magazines and newspapers published for minority ethnic groups
ordinary newspapers and magazines – colour supplements, fashion magazines, women's magazines, mail order catalogues. These are now beginning to reflect more positively our multicultural society

Methuen have also produced a series of four posters showing families in an ethnically mixed urban setting.

Photographs
Photographs are particularly useful aids – children identify with them and chat about them very easily. A variety of albums can be made using playgroup photographs and pictures taken in the pre-school group or brought from home, e.g. families, babies (the children themselves when they were babies), children on outings, children at special events, festivals, etc. If secondary school students are involved with your group, perhaps producing these albums could be a project for them.

Conclusion

One of the main aims of those working with the under-fives should be to help children come to a clear and positive understanding of the world in which they live, and an understanding and acceptance of the different cultures in our society should be an integral part of this. Providing young children with an environment in which different ethnic groups and ways of life are represented, discussed and valued may initially be a difficult and controversial step but if we are properly to prepare children for adulthood in a multi-ethnic society, it must be a necessary aim of all pre-school provision.

References

1 Commission for Racial Equality, 10–12 Allington St, London SW1
2 Tuku Mukherje, Anti-Racist Committee, Southlands College, Wimbledon Parkside, London SW19 5NN
3 Smith, Eve, *Story telling in a second language*, Commission for Racial Equality
4 Tracey, Angela, *Dolls and Puppets for the Multiracial Society*, 7 Heathway, Southall, Middlesex
5 *All Children Play*, Fair Play for Children, 248 Kentish Town Road, London NW5
6 *Fun and Food for Playgroups*, West Midlands PPA, 6 Princes Chambers, Corporation Street, Birmingham B2 4RN
7 HARMONY, 22 St Mary's Road, Meare, Somerset

8 Tracey, Angela, *Cooking Around the World*, 7 Heathway, Southall, Middlesex

Bibliography
Milner, D., *Children and Race*, Penguin, 1975
Milner, D., *Children and Race, 10 Years On*, Ward Lock, 1983
Goodman, M., *Race Awareness in Young Children*, 1952

Chapter 2

ST ANNE'S NURSERY SCHOOL

Pauline Walsh

> St Anne's Nursery School is in Kensington and caters for children from various ethnic backgrounds – including a number of children of Embassy staff. There are about 16 full-time places available to children who have English as a second language or need help with speech. A mother and toddler group meets on Wednesday mornings. The teaching is organised on a team basis.
>
> Pauline Walsh is Head Teacher at St Anne's. She is on the committees of the Roundhouse Community Centre in Highbury and the Afro-Caribbean Resource Project. She is also a member of the Caribbean Teachers' Association and on the Advisory Panel of Nursery Headteachers for outdoor nursery equipment.

People involved in education have to be aware of the needs and characteristics of the children they deal with and this means understanding the cultural background of the children. For teachers in inner city schools it is particularly important, as a high proportion of their pupils will come from different ethnic groups. Travel and telecommunications have expanded horizons for teachers and the children they teach. People from all parts of the world visit England, temporarily or permanently. We should help all children to understand and appreciate the diversity of cultures that surrounds us.

Contact between staff and parents

One of the best ways to learn about the cultural background of the children we teach is to get to know their parents. The pre-school teacher has the opportunity of almost daily contact with child and parent. This contact can be used not only to inform parents of school policy but also to involve them in it – so that staff, parents and children are a mutually supportive group within the community. If this is to happen, we must make these first contacts with parents informative and satisfactory in order to gain their confidence.

Headteachers of nursery schools and nursery class teachers in primary schools (with the co-operation of their headteachers) should try to get out into the community to meet parents of under-fives. The Health Service and the Social Services are our greatest allies. We can have informal talks with groups of parents at Child Care Clinics, 'One o'clock Clubs', when they bring their children to play, and mother and toddler groups which can be set up in a nursery providing there is accommodation available and staff and volunteers to organise. These facilities offer contact with a group of adults with whom staff can have frequent discussions about the aims of the school. Regular meetings with potential parents help teachers to learn more about the cultural background of the child and parent. In some instances, this may help a parent to understand why it is important for them and their children to maintain their cultural identity. Many of our new parents are second and third generation who have lacked the opportunity to know anything about their own cultural roots and they may be willing to remedy the situation.

Most importantly, the staff must be familiar with different ethnic groups in order to understand the ways of parents and children. So as well as going out into the community to meet the parents, at St Anne's we invite the parents into the school. When the child starts school, the parent is encouraged to stay with her/him until s/he settles. This gives parents an opportunity to help their children to learn about their cultural inheritance. Very young children can learn songs, poems and folklore from their ethnic background and this increases their sense of well-being. The best source of this knowledge is the parents.

Parents can find out a lot about school policy from the booklets that schools provide. These should be on show at divisional offices, Child Care clinics, libraries, Mother and Toddler groups and the Parent Association. But even more valuable than this sort of dissemination of information is the actual presence of the parents in the school.

It gives them an opportunity to see how things are done to help the child learn. Parents who have not been to school in this country may not appreciate the significance of play in a young child's learning experience. Role play, for example, is not just 'dressing up' – it has sound educational concepts behind it. By wearing clothes signifying different male and female roles or people from different countries the children are putting themselves in the positions of others.

Mother tongue

One of the major concerns that parents have is that their children will not learn English quickly enough. It is in fact very unusual for a five year old to leave nursery school without a command of English – even after just one year in the nursery. Children love to communicate and very soon acquire the tool for communicating with their peers and teachers. Teachers help them to acquire a use of the second language. But fluency in the mother tongue is also important to the child's confidence. Children need familiar sounds and objects about them. What is more, bilingualism is an advantage.

It is sometimes hard to get parents to see this. When a French father brought his non-English speaking daughter to school he insisted that no French was used when we communicated with her. We have a fluent French-speaking teacher on the staff who tried unsuccessfully to explain to him that speaking French to the child would help her initially to understand the routine of the school. We reluctantly complied with his wishes knowing full well that the child would take longer to settle. One day she was looking so bewildered that I gave her an affectionate greeting in French. When she smiled and threw her arms around me I had to call my deputy to the rescue because I could not cope with her stream of fluent French. She then used both languages, first French, then English. This little girl blossomed when we explained to her father what we were doing and he accepted it because he saw how quickly she began to learn English and how happy she was using her own language. At the age of five she left, speaking perfect English and French, to attend the Lycée Francais.

A child from an Urdu-speaking family was asked by her teacher if she spoke Urdu. Her reply was in English – 'Only grown-ups speak Urdu.' Her parents want her to learn English and her father told us that another family was always 'jabbering' in Arabic with the child so that it is necessary for her to attend a special language class in the primary school. He cannot see that she has an advantage in speaking two languages.

At our nursery, then, language development is encouraged in both English and the mother tongue. We encourage parents to allow the child to become fluent in the mother tongue at home where s/he is exposed to language and can absorb it quite easily. In the school, staff and children learn greetings in foreign languages. However little, this provides a point of contact and encourages the child. When one Gujerati child was told by her mother to greet me she said 'My teacher would not understand.' When *I* greeted *her* in Gujerati she was so astonished that she clutched my hand and jumped with excitement. A Swedish boy who has language and speech difficulties was very happy when we greeted him in Swedish. He is still having difficulty expressing himself in English but he feels loved and is loving. This is the important thing for all children.

Children for whom English is a second language are usually brought to school by a mother who speaks very little or no English. In the case of the latter, I arrange for another parent who speaks the same language or someone in the community to attend the nursery on a few occasions with the child and mother. This person can explain to parent and child what goes on in the nursery, school policy, and ways in which the school can help the child. Parents can then put questions to me as headteacher through the interpreter. When parent and child begin to settle we ask the parents if they can reproduce some of the familiar English stories in their language or dialect and put them on tape. The child can then listen to a story read in her/his mother tongue in a familiar voice. We also ask for tapes of folklore from their own culture. This, together with familiar music, pictures, ornaments, clothing, household items and food cooked by the parents helps to give the minority children a sense of identity. It also provides a unique source of educational interest and learning for all the children. We get the parents from the different ethnic backgrounds to tell us the names and uses of the items they bring in. We talk about them to the children. We also learn their games and sing their songs. In doing this we hope to teach our children an appreciation of other people's culture.

By establishing a warm relationship with the parents as well as the children, we learn to understand their customs and help them to understand ours. Let us begin to build a co-operative community through our pre-school institutions.

Multicultural education in the primary school

Introduction
Mike Mulvaney

One of the great obsessions of education and schools is that we are hypnotised with the twin ideas of norms and measurement. The norms are necessary to make the measurement satisfactory. A reading age or quotient is a measurement against a norm. If it scores above the norm we feel some sense of satisfaction, but below the norm brings pressure (often from ourselves) which leads to stress and the familiar self-flagellation, self doubt and guilt that primary teachers suffer from.

Many of these norms have been invented by teachers, others have been adopted from other 'professional' groups, and yet more from society generally. The latter is frequently delighted to impose norms upon children and schools which have no other logic than the maintenance of a conservative tradition or, the 'it never did me any harm' syndrome. Therefore, as teachers, we tend to accept norms in the school that we would probably question under any other circumstances. We adopt them partly because they help to create a comfortable distance between us, the children, and the community. Many of the norms against which we measure children are imposed upon us by a hierarchy which had to conform to specific norms in order to achieve their present positions. Where children do not, will not, or cannot conform to the norms that we promote, then we invent categories into which they will neatly fit, such as ESN(M), ESN(S), maladjusted, physically handicapped, delicate, etc. etc. Having defined their variance to the norm, we can tuck them into appropriately labelled boxes with a clear conscience. Once they are parcelled in this way we can then invent a fresh set of norms to suit the package.

Over the last twenty years, in schools serving areas of cultural diversity and in working class areas, many of our norms have been challenged by children who do not share them with us. There are now many schools where English is a second language for most of the children, or where real communication takes place in dialect. Equally the white protestant ethic is unacceptable for many of our children and their parents. All too frequently, we have attempted to reinforce our norms and imposed them upon the children. English has been taught whilst the childrens' own languages have been ignored and frequently lost. How many Muslim, Sikh, or Hindu children have been forced to put their hands together, or to sing hymns in assembly? When, as a result, they become alienated, and reject school, we have been able to measure their variation from the norm and place them in those appropriate boxes.

An example of racist measurement in primary schools is the verbal reasoning test used to band children prior to secondary selection. If it is necessary to band children at 11, which I question, then it should be possible to do so without cultural or class bias, and without handicapping children. Nevertheless, year after year, we teachers collude in subjecting children to a verbal reasoning test which is loaded against many of them. Also in a good primary school, the subject matter of the VR test would not be part of the childrens' normal classroom experience. Despite this, we use the test to assist us in classifying the children into groups 1, 2 or 3 which, despite our pleas of innocence, are a summation of the child's success or failure in the primary school to child and parent alike. Too much of primary education is spent preparing children for the next stage rather than considering to what extent they are meeting their present developmental potential. There are many great issues facing primary education today. Racism, gender and class have been considered in the same way that Colombus discovered America – as though it didn't exist before he found it. At 11+ we know how well our children read, write and calculate because we have measured them and grouped them in relation to a norm called '2'. We transmit that information to secondary school. Do we know to what extent they have internalised racism or have been damaged by it? Have we tried to discover if they accept or reject sexual stereotypes? Could we even consider to what extent the child's naturally enquiring nature has been blunted by environment (political as well as social) and school? It has taken more than 100 years of public education to make clear to us that racism causes far more damage to children than eating peas off a knife. Hopefully the process in terms of gender and class won't take so long.

This section has two chapters on primary practice which, unfortunately, are both written by headteachers. The second by David Milman outlines the type of process that many schools have embarked upon over the past few years to develop a policy on multi-culturalism and racism. My own chapter extends the theme into the community that the school serves by taking the principles in the policy to directly challenge racism outside the school walls. It is interesting that two schools, Childeric and Gayhurst, from largely different starting points have developed policies which are almost interchangeable.

Chapter 3

THE IMPACT OF AN ANTI-RACIST POLICY IN THE SCHOOL COMMUNITY

Mike Mulvaney

> Gayhurst Infants School has a roll of about 200. It is in Hackney and its intake reflects the multicultural character of the area.
> Mike Mulvaney, formerly Head Teacher at Gayhurst School, is now Head Teacher at Laburnum Infants and Junior Mixed School.

I was once told, by someone who should know better, that schools in poor areas should provide a haven for children to escape the poverty of their environment.

That environment for many children is the inner city, and, for the majority in my present school, includes either: unemployment or a twelve hour working day in sweat shops; overcrowded, cold, damp housing with many of the surrounding flats boarded up; a denial of basic rights through DHSS benefits; inadequate health care resulting from lack of interest and random cuts in the health service. For black people (I use the word in its widest possible sense) this common experience is compounded by overt and institutional racism.

It is tempting, and easy, to withdraw into the school and use it as a fortress against a hostile environment. It is possible to make the school comfortable, warm, and beautiful. We can use textiles and teasels, stuffed owls and soft lighting, double mounting to really magnificent effect. We can isolate our schools completely until they look as though they had been lifted directly from rural Lincolnshire, Berkshire, or Oxfordshire. We can even have an anti-racist policy that operates fairly effectively in the school. However, we only have the children for six to seven hours a day. The rest of the time they must function within the environment that we successfully shut out or disregard.

Educational isolation is not a new phenomenon but an ongoing experience that only changes in the way in which it is achieved. Between the wars, in the East End of London, it was the Jews and working class activists that suffered the worst persecution. They experienced fire bombing, children were beaten up on the way to school, they were denied job prospects, and were the objects of hostility of the establishment. The majority of the Jews handled such racism by moving out of the area and losing their language and cultural identity – otherwise known as integration. The discrimination against activists resulted from their conscious political choice, a declaration, and despite the injustices committed against them, their political awareness led them to expect it and to cope with it.

The response of schools to this, and the general appalling poverty of the area, was to home in on the 3Rs and to impose a rigid discipline and authoritarianism similar to that which imposed the conditions that children were suffering in their homes.

The modern black experience has been, and is, that despite political inactivism they have still been bombed, murdered, discriminated against, and harrassed because, whatever their attitudes, political philosophy, income or adherence to culture, they are a recognisable minority.

Over the past ten years, the education service has been involved in a game of liberal educational semantics. In multiculturalism we (teachers) have passed through a number of stages from viewing cultural pluralism as a problem, through celebration, to affirmation, which is where most of us have rested. Many of us have briefly turned our schools into Hindu temples or Gudwaras. We have, every other year, celebrated Id or Diwali, or laid on the odd carnival with colourful costumes and a steel band borrowed from another school.

There are enormous spin-offs from this hierarchical form of culturalism. The 'minority' parents turn out to provide food, costumes, artefacts, etc., and appear to be eternally grateful. At the end of all such events staff and parents say 'namaste' to each other, and the school reverts to its celebration of white, male, middle class experience. The parents return to their own experience.

Multicultural policy at Gayhurst Infants School

At Gayhurst Infants School the staff group developed a policy on racism and cultural pluralism that was based upon experience and practice. It reads:

> The school is multicultural, and all that goes on within it must strive to reflect and build upon this basis.
>
> Culture is central to a child's identity, and the learning environment must reflect the cultures of those learning within it and within society at large.
>
> Teachers must become aware of the cultures from which children come, and the customs and attitudes within them.
>
> Teachers can encourage positive ethnic/cultural self identity by initiating activities which reflect a multicultural society. They should aim to give broad-based information and images about each cultural group, drawing as much as possible from the childrens' experience in a way that avoids the risk of stereotypes.
>
> Questions about racism, name-calling incidents etc., should never be side-stepped or over responded to. Children should be given appropriate information when and where situations arise. Teachers must avoid the denial of differences that do exist between groups and cultures because these act as a cover for racism.
>
> It is important for teachers to be sensitive to the feelings of parents and children where these relate to cultural conflict.
>
> Teachers must be aware of the racist connotations in language, and avoid such language personally and discourage its use at all times.

Recognition must be given to the positive value of mother tongue and dialect. Different languages should be shared and given positive images in the classroom. Labelling, letters home, etc., need to be comprehensible to all children and families.

The school as a body should form the closest possible links with organisations and groups representing minorities, and bodies which seek to further the aims of multicultural education. In the same way the school should dissociate itself from, and condemn, any group that is overtly racist or indulging in racist practice without self-examination.

The school as a body will condemn and oppose racism in all its manifestations wherever it occurs, and particularly in the school community and the community it serves.

At best, such a policy can only be a compromise between existing staff views and attitudes. There is much that could be added, and words that should be omitted. The policy is only valid at the time that it was written (1980) and for a short time afterwards. Given changes in staff, children and parents, levels of awareness, and the community it should be reviewed and modified annually. Most importantly, a policy should be an affirmation of practice and not an unrealistic list that can never be achieved.

When the draft statement was completed by the staff, it was taken to the parents for any discussion and amendment they thought was necessary. Generally they were supportive when each point of the policy was discussed. At the end one parent said, 'It's just as well it was explained to me because I couldn't understand a bloody word of it.' This made us realise that the policy is very jargonistic, and a group of parents and teachers offered to rewrite it in a more understandable form. It read:

> This school is multicultural. Religion, language, and custom make children what they are, and the children know about themselves and each other. Therefore, we as teachers must know about, and understand, the children's backgrounds to help them feel good about themselves, and to make them sensitive to how others feel and live.
>
> Questions about racism, name calling, etc., should never be side-stepped or over-responded to. Children should be given appropriate information about racism when and where situations arise. Teachers should avoid denying differences that do exist between people because this acts as a cover for racism. Teachers must be aware of the racist meanings that can be in language, and avoid its use at all times.
>
> Sometimes parents and children grow apart because parents expect the children to keep their religion, language, and customs when the children feel under pressure not to. We must be sympathetic and sensitive to both parties. The school must help children to keep their mother tongue which should be seen in notices around the school and in letters home.
>
> The school must work closely with organisations and groups that represent people of different religions, language and customs.

This now appears in the school booklet, but the original remains the school policy.

School and community

At Gayhurst, there were some good examples of anti-racist teaching, teaching of mother tongue, books and materials that reflected the ethnic mix of the school, ESL teaching integrated into the day to day curriculum. Racist and imperialist books were removed from the library, the developing racist attitudes of children were generally, but not always, challenged, and important letters home were translated. The practice and policy were, to some extent, effective within the school, but in the normal course of events would have had little impact upon the immediate or wider community.

It is only possible to bring community issues into the school, and *vice versa*, if time and space have been created for parents to feel comfortable there. They need to feel that their doubts and worries will be heard sympathetically, and that there are structures through which they can make an impact upon the curriculum and organisation. For a number of years, the school has systematically worked at methods of building a partnership between home and school which included casework on welfare rights and housing.

The Nationality Bill is a piece of racist legislation that, for the first time, provides a tiered structure of British citizenship. It discriminates against black people living here and abroad. It made many, who have lived here virtually all their lives, feel anxious about their future. It was obvious that a large number of children and parents would be affected by the bill. Several parents approached the school seeking assistance in understanding the implications for them and their families. We were not able to offer a great deal of help because the bill is a complex piece of legislation. The problem was taken to the Parent Teacher Association which organised a meeting with representatives of the Hackney Council for Racial Equality and the local law centre. At the meeting it was impossible to understand all of the implications of the bill and to answer, in detail, the concern that many parents had. The law centre offered to organise a series of evening courses for six parents who could act as counsellors to other parents and members of the community. After training, the counsellors offered a series of day and evening clinics to advise parents and families on how the Nationality Bill would affect them. They had the continuing support of the Law Centre for any enquiries they had difficulty answering.

This was a good example of how a school can be a catalyst to effective community action. It achieved the twin objectives of organising opposition to the bill, and enabling local people to cope with its effects. An additional spin-off was that prompt action allowed parents to register before the government increased the registration fee.

In 1980 two Sikh children transferred into Gayhurst from a local school. Their father explained that the move was necessary because the children had suffered racial harassment on the way to school, and the mother had twice been assaulted whilst accompanying the children. The journey to Gayhurst was shorter, and the children could be watched from the house all the way to school across a public open space. The father apologised that the mother had not come to school with him. She had stayed at home because the parents could not leave the house unoccupied since the property had been damaged by attacks in the past.

That evening two teachers visited the family and found them living, eating, and sleeping in one room. The rest of the house had been gutted by a fire that was caused by petrol poured through the letter box. Hackney Council Housing Department had refused to rehouse the family because they claimed, without a scrap of evidence, that the damage had been self inflicted. They had repaired the front door and put corrugated iron over the smashed windows, but had refused any other repair to the fire and smoke damaged interior.

The children were cowed and looked constantly terrified, and the parents were out of their mind with worry. Sympathetic noises between 9 a.m. and 4 p.m. would have done little to help the family or relieve their suffering. We had no option but to become involved in a campaign which was then being mounted by various anti-racist community groups.

A public meeting was organised at the Hackney Family Centre and was attended by the family, representatives of the groups, and parents and teachers from the school. At the meeting the parents and teachers, with others, organised to escort the children to and from school, to have at least two people in the house every night to allow the family to get some rest, to call the police whenever harassment occurred, and to put pressure upon the Council to rehouse the family in a less exposed position.

These objectives were achieved, but the Council consistently refused to rehouse the family. At a full Council meeting, attended by members of the campaign, a teacher from the school sat on the floor of the chamber and refused to move until the council made a commitment to rehouse the Singh family. At first the council members refused to acknowledge her presence and then they adjourned for an hour. At the end of the adjournment, it was announced that the question of rehousing would be reconsidered. The family were rehoused as a result of community, parental, and school action. As a result of these measures the local community was left in no doubt about the position of the school in opposing racism, particularly as we had responsibility of co-ordinating coverage in local and national press, and on television and radio.

Unfortunately, this is not a fairy story with a happy ending. Shortly after moving into new accommodation in Clapton, Mr Singh responded to some youths offering racial abuse outside his house. He was hit across the head with a cricket bat, and the resulting fractured skull and brain damage will be a constant reminder to him, and his family, of the racism in our society.

In 1982, the teaching staff voted that the police should not enter the building except in an emergency. The decision supported a Hackney Teachers' Association policy that members should not invite the police into their schools until the Hackney police had seriously examined their racist practice and established a dialogue with the local community.

It was a particularly difficult and controversial decision because the local beat constable was well liked and respected in the local community. The children related to him largely because of the accoutrements of his office – the uniform, radio, etc. However, in discussions with the children a very different perspective emerged, particularly from the black children. Many could give examples of parents, friends, and sisters and brothers who had been mistreated at the hands of the police. At five, six, and seven years of age, the children understood that a black person was more likely to be stopped on the streets, or to be pulled over when driving. Hackney Council for Racial Equality have an alarmingly thick dossier on racial harrassment by the police in Hackney – a notorious example is the mishandling of the Colin Roach affair. There must be many children, who given their knowledge of family and community resentment against the police, feel threatened by their coming into school. It could also be a barrier to establishing good relationships between children and teachers.

The parents were anxious to discuss the staff decision, and a well attended meeting was organised by the PTA. Representatives of the police, the black community, the union, and an ILEA member were invited to speak – only the police declined. After a full, and sometimes heated, debate where the ILEA member was the main speaker against the decision, the parents voted to support the school policy.

The PTA was at one time organised by a large committee elected at the annual general meeting. Some time back, a parent was elected who was known to have extreme right wing views and was suspected of being a racist. Shortly after he was elected, I was informed that he was to stand as a candidate for the National Front in the local council elections which were due soon. The teaching staff met to discuss the situation, and the majority felt that we should ask the committee to vote him off. There were three main reasons for this decision. The first was the constitution of the PTA, which was quite clear that its aim was to support the educational advancement of all of the children in the school. An avowed racist would find that impossible to comply with. The second was that the teacher members felt that sitting on a school committee with a member of the National Front might destroy their relationship with black parents, and would certainly raise serious doubts about their anti-racism. Lastly, we were seriously concerned that he might use his membership of the committee to advance his cause at the election hustings.

The proposal in favour of his expulsion was put to the committee and was passed by a narrow majority with most members abstaining. The decision caused a serious split in the PTA from which it took a long time to recover, and the school was accused of having a political bias. Such a stance is political. We could also have been accused of being humanitarian and just. Schools presumably would not back away from a principled position on being accused of the latter two, nor should they on the first.

There is little doubt that schools do not have a high standing amongst the black community despite the thirst that it has for education. There are a number of reasons for this, but one of the most important is the overt and institutional racism that black parents and children have suffered in schools over the past twenty years. Naturally they now regard schools as racist and with great suspicion.

I suspect that all the anti-racist policies that schools are preparing will have very little effect upon the alienation that that community feels. The possession of a policy and its operation within the school will not have a great impact upon the community at large. Unless the school is overtly anti-racist, and taking a principled position on these issues in the community, it will, despite the best intentions, be regarded as racist. Eventually, we must recognise that racism is a black issue that the black community must struggle against and find solutions for. As white middle class teachers, the best that we can do is to examine ourselves, our practice, and support them in that struggle.

Chapter 4

CHILDERIC SCHOOL: DEVELOPING A MULTICULTURAL POLICY

David Milman

> Childeric School is a primary school in Deptford with about 200 on the roll. A wide range of different cultures is represented in its pupils, including large groups of Afro-Caribbean, Turkish and other nationalities, and pupils from Chile, Sri Lanka, Bangladesh and West Germany. Over thirty have English as their second language.
>
> David Milman is Head Teacher at Childeric School. He is author, with Tina Milman, of a series of topic project books called *Take a Look* and a book on moral education called *What do you think*, both published by Blackies. He is a member of NAME.

For generations Childeric School has struggled to provide an education for local children. After a recent Harvest Festival assembly one of our guests, a senior citizen, wrung my hand, 'Do you know,' she said, 'I was here in 1913; it's changed so much. I've been sitting looking at all the little black and white faces.' She had pinpointed the latest and perhaps most dramatic change in the neighbourhood and therefore in the school, the change in the ethnic composition of the local population.

Childeric is a special priority area school. As such we receive extra allocations of staffing and money to help us try to meet the needs of children from a wide variety of ethnic origins and social backgrounds. There is massive unemployment in the area. About half our children come from one parent families and well over half qualify for free school meals. About a third of our children are either on the child abuse register or have social workers attached to their families.

The staff is, on the whole, a young one but the majority of the teachers have taught in the school for over ten years. When I was appointed to the school in January 1981 the previous head had been there for many years. His deputy and another male teacher had served the school since the war. In September of 1981 I was lucky enough to be able to appoint my own deputy.

I found Childeric was a school organised on traditional, formal lines. Discipline was highly structured and authoritarian as was the organisation of the school. I felt that parents were treated in a reasonably friendly way but somehow kept at a distance. In terms of multi-ethnic education it was clear that the leadership in the school favoured an assimilation approach. There were however among the teaching staff notable individual exceptions to this attitude. There was also quite clearly a level of concern to meet the individual needs of children and an awareness of the sorts of problems which mitigated against success in the school context. However in my opinion the approach was not uniform across the whole school. The school roll was falling and this created problems and challenges of using space in an interesting and creative way.

The tragedy of the New Cross fire happened during my first term at the school. While we collected money for the uncle of one of our pupils killed in the fire, and as the marchers set out from the park opposite the school we could hardly help but reflect again on the nature of our job serving a multi-ethnic community.

Developing a multicultural curriculum

As a new head I had my own list of priorities for the school. At the top of this list was the need to develop the curriculum and this of course included the development of multi-ethnic education. I was clear that I wanted this to be a whole school development. It has always seemed to me that any development has greatest value for those who are actually involved in initiating and planning the change and that working parties had great value for those members of staff involved and far less for those who received documents from afar. It also seemed to me that the development of a multicultural curriculum could only proceed in an atmosphere of frank discussion, of honesty and commitment to change. As a teacher aware of the seeds of racism in myself and of the conditioning I had received from my own upbringing and culture I knew how difficult it could be when one's own, often unrealised, prejudices are exposed. I also felt that the only climate which would properly nurture such joint development was one of democracy. Imposition from above and authoritarian directives seem to me to be both anti-educational and antithetical to the development of multi-ethnic curriculum.

The first task then, for myself and my deputy Brenda Taggart, was to signal to the staff that the approach of the new leadership team in the school was going to be different. As a staff we started to take joint decisions about almost everything from discipline to how we should allocate our resources. We viewed curriculum development as a whole school concern and were involved in a continuous process of evaluating where we were and which major initiatives we wished to tackle next. None of this was as easy or painless as it sounds but it was generally welcomed. As we moved forward it became plain that people were relaxing and gaining confidence in the new atmosphere. Brenda and I made sure that our doors were always open and that we were around after and before school. Gradually, on an individual basis or in staff meetings, people began to come forward with their concerns. Clearly there was a range of these about multi-ethnic education, including the lack of it. Clearly there was no school policy on racism and there was a growing demand from the staff that we should do something about it.

I signalled my commitment by redesignating the home–school liaison post holder, Nina Hurst, as a teacher with special responsibility for multicultural education. We initiated a course of staff meetings and started by examining our attitudes. We used the services of outside speakers, notably Ruth Ballin of the BBC and Iris Morrison of Lewisham Teachers' Centre. Nina herself, and for much of the first two years, Juliet Bartlett, who took over Nina's post while the latter was on confinement leave, took a prominent part in discussions.

Our growing awareness led us to examine our curriculum provision. It was becoming obvious that what we were engaged upon was an enterprise that affected the whole life of the school as well as the curriculum. We realised that multi-ethnic education was not a new subject on the curriculum to be timetabled among the humanities – rather there was a need for us to examine all of our practices with the multicultural dimension in mind.

We grew to feel the need for some sort of statement of our aims and beliefs. Our discussions had also led us to become more aware of racism – both the institutional racism inherent in any Eurocentric primary school and racism in our pupils and the wider community. It was clear that we would also need some sort of policy and a sensitive uniformity of approach in combating this racism.

The examination of our curriculum practices can best be illustrated perhaps by looking in more detail at the library development. I had widened the scope of Enid Pheasey's post to embrace both the Junior and Infant libraries. The Infant library had been newly created as a large room became vacant. Another large classroom was turned into a maths and science room with a staff workshop and school artefacts collection attached. We had also developed a school dark room and a parents' room. One of Enid's first jobs was to draw up a school policy document on sexism and racism in books and to examine and revitalise the library stock. In this we were much helped by one of ILEA's advisors, Janet Holman. Enid, helped by the staff, drew up a policy document. We weeded out the library books which we felt were sexist, racist or misleadingly Eurocentric, as well as many that were just old and tatty. At the same time we committed ourselves to an expenditure of many hundreds of pounds on replacing books. Staff were fully involved both in the process of weeding and reselecting. We spent time and effort trying to find books which presented positive black images that reflected the nature of a multi-ethnic society and which accurately portrayed the contributions of all societies to our world. Anybody who has undertaken this sort of exercise will know how difficult it can be to find the right kind of materials. We found ourselves writing off for catalogues, trying to locate minority bookshops and contacting embassies and multi-ethnic centres round the country.

Staff discussion as we weeded out the books and selected new ones was at times intense and heated. For example did we approve of *Robinson Crusoe* or *Epaminandas*? Did the bland illustration and story line of the *Seven Chinese Brothers* convey an unfortunate stereotype? What was wrong with Kipling's poems of the British Raj? Should we have a reserve shelf of books which were racist and sexist but which raised interesting points for debate? At one point in a session with Ruth Ballin, a teacher threw up her hands in despair – 'Honestly I sometimes feel frightened to open my mouth.' We were beginning to come to terms with our own social conditionings and educations.

Of one thing we were sure – that however difficult the task may be, we were not going to accept unthinkingly outside, expert prescription but choose and decide for ourselves. Advice and sympathetic help was welcomed but we were the ones who knew our own children best and who ultimately had to live with the consequences of our choices and take responsibility for them.

I proposed to Enid that she might present a report on her work to the governors and that part of this report should include the book policy document. By now we had all become so absorbed in our activities that we were a little taken aback by the reaction of some governors. However I had taken the precaution of inviting Mike Hussey of the Multi-ethnic Inspectorate and Janet Holman to the meeting and we survived some quite strong negative reaction.

The next step in our development was to prepare a further document for ourselves and then for the governors. This comprised an aims statement, 'Aims for Education in a multi-ethnic society', a job description for the multi-ethnic post holder, a policy statement on racism and a headteacher's statement and introduction. We felt this would begin to signal to all those working in the school, to the governors and through the parent governors to the parents exactly what our attitudes and beliefs were.

At this point it may be helpful to quote from a discussion document which we presented to staff and subsequently to the governors.

1. The pupils at Childeric School come from a variety of cultures, all that goes on should reflect and build on this. Recognition of the cultural diversity should also go hand in hand with the recognition of cultures not represented by the school population, including Vietnamese, Greeks, Bengalis and children from travelliing families. This should not only take the form of having brown faces on the wall, but there should be recognition of the positive value of mother tongues and dialects. Different languages should be shared and given positive images in the classroom and school generally. Labelling and letters home need to be comprehensible to all children and their families. Differing life styles should be understood and brought out.
2. We must all look at our own prejudices and realise that we see things from a point of view influenced by our own culture, by the media, by what we were taught. We must question the assumptions we make about the children, their families, their environments – are we influenced in our approach by what we think, not what really exists? Class, sex, age, as well as race, come into the sort of judgements we make.
3. We must be aware of the racist connotations in language and avoid such language personally and discourage its use at all times, e.g. talking about black looks, black marks.
4. We should be aware of stereotyping, whether of class, sex, age or race, and challenge it.
5. We should be aware of the ease with which prejudice can be taught and reinforced.

6 We must encourage positive racial/cultural identity by initiating activities which reflect a multicultural society. We should aim to give information and images about each cultural group, drawing as much as possible from the children's experiences keeping in mind point 4.
7 To extend point 6, the school should make as much contact as possible with parents, community groups and organisations and bodies seeking to encourage and foster aims of multicultural education.
8 Any form of racism should be tackled, never ignored. It should be dealt with by giving the children any appropriate information necessary but care should be taken never to over-respond. There are ethnic differences which cannot be ignored but from children of the age we teach much of the racism is regurgitated from the parents and the children are often ignorant of the significance of what they are saying. This ignorance should not be left uncorrected. Racist remarks from parents should not be ignored either, since inaction can be taken as a sign of agreement. Hopefully once the stance of the school is recognised, then parents will realise it would be inappropriate to voice them. Ancillary staff should be made aware of the non-racist stand the school is making.
9 We must be sensitive to the cultural conflict some parents and children have. We should recognise that to encourage all our children to reach their full potential, they should be helped to fully develop their social growth. All our children should have this opportunity, equally, to be equipped to live harmoniously in our multi-ethnic society.

Nina Hurst, 1982

We presented our policies to the school governors with a certain amount of trepidation and were delighted to find that they were accepted with enthusiasm. About this time we had a reconstitution of the governing body of the school. A black parent governor and a black non-teaching staff representative were appointed. I also suggested the co-option of Sandra Fuertado, who runs the young mothers' project at the Pagnell Street Centre.

Parents
We also addressed ourselves to the parents. A room with attached toilet became available on the ground floor of the school. Maureen Harniman, teacher in charge, lower school, and Anne Arnott, the reception teacher, were very keen to have a parents' room. We furnished and carpeted the room and moved in a kettle, toys and books. Maureen and Anne instituted a series of Wednesday morning meetings and a mothers' club was born. A substantial number of mothers began to turn up on a fairly regular basis. We were delighted that these represented an ethnic mix and that the mothers all seemed to get on extremely well. We ensured that there was always at least one teacher present.

There was an obvious demand for some specific event each time. Besides teachers talking about various areas of the curriculum we have invited in outside speakers. We have had nursery and school nurses, welfare rights workers and others. Maureen made films about reading and play activities throughout the school. The reading film was used to launch our own version of 'pact'. The play film gave rise to much interest. It was our experience that many parents were puzzled that what they saw as nursery play activities continued in the Infants department. We were concerned to try to explain what we thought was the central importance of educational play in the primary curriculum. Anne was completing a diploma in Early Childhood Education at Goldsmiths' College. As part of her special study she interviewed a cross-section of parents about their attitudes and expectations with regard to play in school.

On the surface much of our work with parents is not specifically concerned with multi-ethnic education. However there are obviously as many views of education as there are parents and cultures. We feel that it is our job to find out what these expectations are and to explain what we are trying to do. We see education as a partnership between home and school. All this is essential if we are to provide a climate of frankness and co-operation in which barriers can be broken down and multi-ethnic education can flourish.

Ancillary staff
The other group whom we wished to reach and with whom there can be problems of resistance to change was the ancillary workers in the school. Lunchtimes and playtimes are parts of the day when young children are at their most relaxed and most vulnerable. They are also outside the protective umbrella of the teaching staff. Ancillary staff often know the children well and live in the neighbourhood of the school. We needed to open up channels of communication with our ancillaries; we needed to cash in on their knowledge and experience and to get our messages over to them. We also felt that, traditionally, their status was low in the school. They had to feel that their opinions and feelings were valued. We placed a notice board in the ancillary staff room on which the day's events were written, just as they are in the teaching staff room. The deputy meets them daily. Maureen arranged to have some meetings with them. I now meet them regularly for half an hour a week. At the moment we are working our way child by child through the class lists. Within this somewhat informal context I have ample opportunities to reiterate the messages we want them to consider. We seem to have moved on from the 'you'd understand if you had to live with them' syndrome and to have begun to notice an increase in the sensitivity with which they handle children. We have managed to recruit one Turkish helper – little enough, but every little bit counts.

It ought to be obvious that intentions need to be translated into actions. It would be quite wrong to assume that the staff of the school were not already aware of many of the issues which we had raised. I was lucky in serving with a staff of dedicated and extremely hardworking professionals. Management teams cannot change schools single-handed. They can, at best, inspire, encourage and support. What we had talked about as a staff, indeed still do, was the need to be sensitive to the needs of individual children. There has always been value in starting our work from the rich variety of experience, cultural and otherwise, which children bring to school with them. Respect for persons – all persons – has always underpinned good work in the primary school. If we observe our children carefully and try to respond to their varied and changing needs, then we are half way to providing a broad and stimulating curriculum. If we teach children to observe closely, to question, challenge and hypothesise then they will reject stereotypes and dead received knowledge. In some ways good primary practice and good multi-ethnic education can be seen as synonymous. We feel as a staff that what really matters is the curriculum offer we make the children and our own attitudes and beliefs as they are manifested in our everyday encounters with them.

Resources
As a staff our preliminary work led to the feeling that we needed many more resources, as well as a deepening of our own understanding of the complexity of issues involved. Nina, Juliet and the rest of the staff have worked on building up a bank of resources. These range from puzzles, toys and books that reflect the multicultural nature of our world, through films, slides and posters to other learning resources such as those produced by ACER.

We decided to try to build a collection of artefacts, including multicultural artefacts. We begged, borrowed, scrounged and bought. Parents and teachers brought us things from their holiday visits. We bought materials from Ujamaa in Brixton. We commissioned a doll-maker to make us dolls that were sensitively ethnic. There is a range of resources in the community as well as in the school. Our celebration of the festival of India illustrates our use of these. We decided that our contribution to the 1982 National Festival would take the form of a school week in May. For a fortnight before, classes undertook preparatory lessons and went on a series of visits. The theme for the festival carried right across the curriculum, including not only geography, religious studies and history, but also claywork, fabric printing, painting, drama, creative writing and mathematics.

One group of children studied the ritual of a Hindu wedding, and performed the ceremony at one of our special assemblies. Another group worked on a class drama and produced the story of the Elephant and the Seven Blind Men from the Pali Canon, another item shown in an assembly. Yet another group of top juniors and first year infants made puppets and gave an enchanting rendering of the old woman and the rice thief – a nice example of co-operative teaching.

Most of the children produced some written work, many classes produced books looking at different aspects of life in India. Some of the children had an opportunity to wear Indian clothing. Everyone sampled Indian food one lunchtime, when our cook produced a chicken curry and Indian sweet.

Classes visited the Vasna exhibition at the Museum of Mankind and the Commonwealth Institute festivities. We also turned over one of our school halls to our own exhibition. The exhibition included a display of costumed dolls, on loan from the Ujamaa centre, and books borrowed from our own library, local libraries and from ILEA. There was a display of Indian clothing and ornaments (borrowed from children, parents and other sources) creative writing, painting, fabrics, a history of numbers and many photographs. The exhibition provided a platform for displaying the childrens' work and a means of sharing information and gaining a wider experience of the many facets of India. Care was taken throughout not to show an Oxfam or deficit model of the Indian sub-continent.

Future developments.

Our work on enriching the curriculum is ongoing. We have a teacher, Beti Camp, working on ESL work across the school. Much of her work is done in the classroom alongside the class teacher. Madeleine Clark, our Maths post holder, is looking at ways of increasing the multicultural component in our maths teaching. Where we have not been able to find appropriate materials we have tried to create them. Maureen was helped by parents to make a set of bilingual language master cards, each card has posted on to it a photograph, many of them of our parents and their homes.

We have looked hard at the images around the school, the notices we put up and the types of letters we send home. We have regular festivals and events. Our Christmas festivities, for example, have become much more international. Some of this could be dismissed as 'tokenism'. Bilingual posters, celebrations of Diwali and the Chinese New Year do not necessarily imply fundamental change. I take 'tokenism' to imply an outward gloss without any real inner meaning. However, we felt that we should take every opportunity to 'signal' to children and parents what we were about. I feel that this 'signalling' goes well beyond tokenism if it is seen by staff for what it is – not an end in itself but a public commitment to a set of shared ideals and purposes which need to be underpinned by real and sustained curriculum work and commitment to the life of the community.

The future seems to be full of promise and challenge. The staff has been joined by a full-time teacher of Afro-Caribbean origin and we have a Commonwealth Exchange teacher from Jamaica for the year. We have also been joined by Basil Morgan of ILEA's Primary Curriculum Development Project (for pupils of Caribbean origin). He will be helping us to look not only at our curriculum offer but at the hidden curriculum. This is exactly what we need to be doing at this particular stage of our development.

I am aware that this account has been very much from the personal perspective of a headteacher. Perhaps this is as it should be. Changing is a very personal matter. A head is after all in the position to have an overview of the life of a school. Perhaps change is most fruitfully initiated from above. However change only happens if everybody wants it, or comes to see the need for it. In the last analysis everybody concerned with the school is equally important to the process.

There are still so many things to be achieved at Childeric. However, we have made our own small beginnings. We have moved forward cautiously, questioning and arguing as we go. This cautious approach is not born of indecision or educational doubt, but rather of our determination to get things right. Above all we have tried to take as many people with us as possible. Development has to be by the whole school and not just by parts of it. This is the importance of having a whole-school policy which is a living reality and not just an empty phrase. Our next step will be a greater movement out to support the community.

Multicultural education in the secondary school

Introduction
Peter Mitchell

For over five years the ILEA has been encouraging schools to take initiatives to combat racism and to review the curriculum. In recent months there has been a move towards a more radical stance by the Authority emphasising more clearly than ever before the need for anti-racist teaching. Schools have been requested to produce policy statements which make clear their opposition to racism in all its forms.

Producing policies which are influential in the daily life of a school is far from simple. Quintin Kynaston saw its policy as one example, amongst many, of the school giving expression to its aims as a comprehensive school. Those who resist the need for the school to declare its position on such issues usually show little concern for the values they themselves give expression to in their work. (Schools need to make their concern with all children explicit, particularly at a time when society seems to be making it clearer than ever that some children are valued less than others). A school policy needs to be negotiated over time and, when finalised, should draw on the commitment of staff, children, parents and other members of the community. Written policies which are in any sense imposed are not passive documents, they are counter-productive and may lead to cynicism and apathy. A weakness in the development of some policies is the tendency for schools to operate as closed communities and to fail to recognise the importance of their relationships with communities outside school. These relationships become particularly important when a school is coming to terms with issues which are controversial in the community at large. These articles are concerned with education for a multicultural society.

Multicultural education however, is a complex idea and all we can hope to achieve is some clearer understanding of how it might be interpreted in a school. There is no doubt that sometimes teachers believe that multicultural education is solely about putting multicultural content into their lessons, about reviewing the curriculum for bias and finally about seeing that the library reflects the multicultural character of the school. While all of these initiatives are important they do not add up to an adequate consideration of the breadth of understanding we need to develop. Schools which are actively turning towards their communities are able to make clear the fact that they value cultural diversity. Sol Garson's account of language teaching at North Westminster Community School exemplifies this type of productive working relationship.

Within the school the overt organisation and relationships, together with the hidden curriculum, should add up to an atmosphere which is clearly enriched by the diversity of cultures. Staff and students should be constantly working for cross cultural understanding through collaborative work and decision-making, at all levels of school life.

Multicultural education which relies exclusively on changes in content is often no more than tokenism. Giving confidence to students as individuals and as members of different cultures is a necessary precursor to all students sharing in studies which extend their skills and understanding. Multicultural education must clarify the learning processes which students need to experience if they are to manage their own learning. Emphasising the importance of looking at how students learn is not meant to detract from the importance of teachers providing students with knowledge which extends their common sense understanding of such terms as culture and racism. These articles present ample evidence of teachers searching for ways in which their course can embrace content from outside Europe and give students active collaborative learning experiences.

It is important that content is selected on the basis of its appropriateness for developing conceptual understanding. (There are so many cultural perspectives represented in schools that the criteria used for selecting content must be thought through carefully.)

These articles display some of the tension that must exist from time to time in all schools, between critical curriculum analysis and straightforward change of content, as the quickest way to meeting an urgent need for multicultural relevance, and the careful course planning which structures experiences and selects content to illuminate concepts.

It is inevitable that some teachers will see the need for multicultural and anti-racist teaching more clearly than some of their colleagues. This fact may lead to some subjects making claims to being value free and therefore unaffected by talk of prejudice and bias; the history of subjects must lead us to question this assertion. Scientific enquiries may form a universal currency which moves easily across cultural boundaries, nevertheless it is possible to give the impression that the only science, both past and present, is carried out by Europeans. Jenni Newnham and Sue Watts show how science at Catford County has attempted to give a broader cultural emphasis to science teaching. David Gilbert's work at Battersea County shows how mathematicians can develop their work by studying mathematics in other cultures. Work in Drama and Humanities is, however, often more at ease with multicultural perspectives. Elyse Dodgson at Vauxhall Manor, and Donald Hinds and Nigel File at Tulse Hill, illustrate how ethnic minorities in the local community can work with a school broadening the experiences of the students and staff through sharing their adult knowledge. The theme of teachers learning alongside students is taken up by Peter Traves at Hackney Downs. Teachers involved in multicultural education quickly recognise the problematic nature of their work.

The work of the team of teachers at William Penn draws on the experiences of students; their work has reinforced the need for a continuous commitment to questioning the many different aspects of their courses. The influence of multicultural education is thus particularly in the areas of using students' own knowledge to build on confidence and broaden cross-cultural understanding; encouraging collaborative working between students; opening the school to work in a more responsive way to the community; planning courses which structure students' learning in order to build in cross-cultural content aimed at deepening their understanding of concepts; encouraging teachers to reflect on the way they handle controversial issues in the classroom; giving emphasis to learning experiences which involve students in active enquiries; being anti-racist.

The inclusion of the account by Peter Davies of active tutorial work in Peace Studies illustrates how important it is for teachers to consider the range of learning students experience. Topics like peace studies and racial prejudice are bound up with people's feelings; students need, therefore, to discuss and exchange ideas if they are to come to terms with these issues. Multicultural education can thus be seen as a stimulus to resolving the question of what makes a comprehensive school comprehensive.

Dawn Gill's article illustrates teachers' growing awareness that subjects have a positive potential for engaging with social and political issues. It also shows that subjects can no longer be regarded as politically neutral or free from ideological assumptions which underpin a curriculum based on separate disciplines.

Maura Healy's account of the social education programme at Quintin Kynaston and Liz Lindsay's account of her work illustrate the importance of schools moving forward in a coherent fashion. It is difficult to see how multicultural education can ever be sustained unless it is pursued consistently across the school. The current trend towards whole school policies on learning gives some hope for teachers concerned with the cross-curriculum messages students receive from courses. The teachers who have prepared these accounts have ideas which are of universal significance; to isolate their work is to be anti-comprehensive and by implication antipathetic to the development of pluralism in our society.

Chapter 5

DEVELOPING A WHOLE SCHOOL ANTI-RACIST POLICY

Peter Mitchell, Liz Lindsay and Maura Healey

> Quintin Kynaston is a mixed comprehensive school with 1050 on the roll. It is situated near Swiss Cottage in North London. Its intake is drawn from a wide area, from all social classes and many different cultures. Its teaching is organised on a mixed ability basis.
>
> Peter Mitchell, formerly Head Teacher at Quintin Kynaston is now Visiting Professor of Education at the Institute of Education. He has lectured at several NAME conferences.
> Maura Healey is Deputy Head at Quintin Kynaston. She is author of *Your Language*, (Macmillan) and co-editor of *Pastoral Care in Education*, the journal of the National Association for Pastoral Care in Education.
> Liz Lindsay is Head of Biology at Quintin Kynaston, and convenor of the multicultural and anti racist working party. She is convenor of the ALTARF secondary workshop, a member of Camden CCR Ed. Committee and of the GLC Ethnic Minorities Unit educational working party and Ed. Committees.

An overview: articulating a policy
(Peter Mitchell)

Developing a school policy on racism in a secondary school.
The cultural mix in Quintin Kynaston is not exceptional for a London school but nevertheless there are over forty first languages spoken in addition to English. Over the last four years we have become more acutely aware of the need for a school consensus, amongst staff and students, on matters relating to racism. Pressures on pupils from political groups outside school have attempted to exploit the uncertain economic future faced by many adolescents. Racism as represented in the political ideas of these groups strikes at the foundational aims of comprehensive education. It is because of this that we believed we should develop a coherent policy on racism which made our position explicit to everybody connected with the school.

To be effective any school policy has to be thought through in relationship to the school as a whole and teachers and students have to become personally committed to the policy. This is particularly the case where a policy is giving expression to moral values held by the school.

The aims of the school
Thinking about aims is often caricatured as a self-indulgent exercise which

bears little relationship to the practical issues involved in making schools work. At Quintin Kynaston we have tried to use aims to give direction to our work and to guide actively curriculum and pastoral policy decisions. They are certainly not enshrined in the staff handbook and kept separate from actual policy making.

The four most important aims are:

1 to demonstrate that all students are of equal value;
2 to give all students access to the main areas of knowledge;
3 to value the students' own knowledge gained through their common sense learning;
4 to see learning in school as essentially a preparation for continuous learning in the years beyond school.

Racism impinges directly on the first and third aims. It seeks to promote the idea that children from certain races and cultures should be provided with an inferior education because they are of less value to the community than other pupils. It denigrates the culture and perspectives of these groups so that a feeling of inferiority is generated amongst them.

Giving all students the confidence to learn is central to the purpose of comprehensive schools. The multicultural aspect of schooling is another dimension to being comprehensive which begins with embracing pupils who have different achievements and social backgrounds.

Whole school policies

The idea that the school should have a policy on racism is in keeping with the school's general emphasis on whole-school policies. We attempt to bring coherence to students' learning by focusing on the learning process in all our courses. Learning is thus reinforced from course to course as we attempt to meet our aim of preparing pupils to continue learning beyond school. A process curriculum also forms a basis for school policies on language and numeracy development.

All courses in the first three years are taught to mixed ability groups. This type of grouping supports the idea that students are equally valued. It also draws staff together in the joint planning of courses.

The school's commitment to mixed ability teaching and cross curriculum learning provided a sympathetic context for the discussions we held on the school's attitude towards racism. Where the curriculum is organised as a collection of disciplines it is probably more difficult to promote dialogue across the school. If this is the case then there is a possibility that a school policy will make no significant difference to the life of the school.

The procedure for school policy making

For a number of years we have made decisions on all major school policies at full staff meetings. Establishing the school's policy on racism has thus followed the same procedure as that used for all other policies. The setting up of the multicultural and anti-racist working party resulted in part from the Authority's initiative in putting forward its own thought on the importance of multicultural education to schools.

Each year we decide on major areas of concern which need to be reviewed. The subjects chosen are then posted in the staff common room so that any member of staff may join the working party. The groups then meet on average five times per term.

Before making recommendations on school policy, they will normally report to staff meetings so that staff are kept in touch with how their findings are developing. This was a particularly important part of the development of the school's policy on racism. The multicultural and anti-racist working party drew together a group of staff with a particular interest in the subject of multicultural education of which the issue of racism is only a part. Through their reports to staff meetings they were able to make the whole staff aware of the issues involved in such a sensitive part of school life.

We ensure that all staff attend staff meetings which are chaired by a rotating chairperson selected by departments. The agenda for staff meetings is organised by the agenda sub-committee which is made up of representatives of teaching and non-teaching staff. Each time the working party wished to report back to staff they had to put their request for time to the agenda sub-committee, who would allocate them a place on the agenda and a time to make their presentation and, if necessary, to answer questions.

This pattern of work gave an immediate legitimacy to the working party's deliberations and helped reinforce the idea that the commitment of all staff is needed if a policy on racism is to have any significant influence on school life. The working party was convened by Liz Lindsay, who has taken an active part in the work of ALTARF. It is inevitable that some staff will be quicker to sense the urgency of an issue like racism than others. The subject matter of some disciplines is a constant reminder of how easy it is to slip into the stereotyping of groups. Particular tutor groups may manifest prejudices which alert a teacher to the extremes of thinking which may be commonplace in the everyday experience of some adolescents. The working party drew together staff who were prepared to give their own time to making the school as a whole more aware of how racism could undermine the very principles with which we worked as a comprehensive school.

Setting out to raise the consciousness of one's colleagues is no easy task. Nobody wants to be told that they are insensitive to such issues as racial prejudice whether directly or by implication. It has been important for the working party to make full use of the opportunities to keep staff informed of how their findings, and possible recommendations, were developing. Report-back sessions were an important way of preparing the school for the publication of a policy on racism. A policy statement cannot be an effective influence on school life unless the time is taken to patiently build the context which will support it.

An important contribution to the continuity of the working party's efforts was the detailed minuting of their meetings by Liz Lindsay.

The policy
The policy statement agreed by staff falls broadly into three parts.

Part 1 deals with comprehensive school aims and racism and attempts to make explicit the way racism is antithetical to the aims which guide our work as a school.

Part 2 covers the curriculum content and processes which relate to learning about race, culture and racism. The content areas include the characteristics of race and culture, the historical study of migration and the political and economic sources of racism. (In support of this work the working party has undertaken a survey of curriculum content across the school.)

All the studies recommended for inclusion in the curriculum are to involve active research and participation in discussion by pupils. The teacher's role in these discussions is to facilitate a climate in which reasonable discussion can take place. Expanded guidelines on the ground rules for discussion have been prepared for staff by the working party.

Part 3 of the policy concerns the needs of staff to be vigilant over matters relating to racism. Any racist behaviour must be reported immediately to the head or deputy head and it will be dealt with as a matter of priority. The policy makes it clear that all staff are responsible for transmitting school policy and there must be no ambiguity in the way the school reacts to racist behaviour.

Assemblies are used for explaining school policy. They are also used to introduce studies which may be controversially included in the curriculum. In the past eighteen months two such topics have been covered. A march through Paddington by an extreme political group led to a letter going to all parents which expressed the school's opposition to the march. The reason for our attitude was explained in assembly and the whole matter was discussed in social education period. We recently made a study of the Nationality Bill which followed the same pattern. We also invited the local law centre into school to advise anybody who felt they might be affected by the Bill.

The fact that social education is a 70 minute period each week, taken by the form tutor, has supported the work of the multicultural working party. The social education programme includes political, moral and religious education amongst its concerns. Both the content and discussion techniques involved in studying race, culture and racism are in harmony with social education. Form tutors remain with their forms from years 1 to 5 and have a responsibility for every part of the social education programme. Again, therefore, the majority of staff are involved in thinking out how to approach important issues raised by the working party and the social education course development team. The work I've been describing has been supported through INSET funds (see Liz Lindsay).

Conclusion
I am often asked if the policy makes any difference to the school. Having a clear position certainly helps minority groups to feel supported. It also helps those young people who may feel prejudiced to know where they stand in relationship to the school. If they have been disciplined for racist behaviour they are welcomed back to return to their studies. We have to assert that every student must be free to learn, irrespective of their social or cultural background, if we are to function as a comprehensive school.

Curriculum innovation: putting it into practice
(Maura Healey)

If you are starting from scratch in designing a course then it ought to be possible to get it right in principle and to 'design in' the flexibility to allow it to change in response to evaluation or to changed circumstances. At any rate there are precious few excuses for going badly wrong.

The social education course we run at Quintin Kynaston took a year of basic planning and is subject to regular review. For all its strengths and weaknesses it provides:
1 a vehicle for transmitting the 'values held by the school which are moral in character';
2 a vehicle whereby the 'common sense learning of students' can be enhanced;
3 a vehicle which allows the school to acknowledge and learn from the range of cultures and life experiences of its students.

Our brief was to develop a programme around the areas traditionally covered by titles such as religious, moral, health, political and sex education and to integrate it with careers, study skills and library-user education. The course was to be taught by over forty tutors to all students from first to sixth year.

We teach a twenty period week. One period a week is allocated to social education. The timetable is blocked so that a whole year group is taught SE at the same time. Each form is taught by its tutor. The head, all three deputies, the head of year and the deputy head of year are timetabled to be available for each year group's social education lesson. This facilitates team teaching and micro-teaching.

The course development team consists of the six deputy heads of year, the head of careers and myself. Right from the start, we have been given ample financing and a great deal of support and advice from inside and outside the school. That support has continued and several items of our programme have been developed by the school's mixed-ability working party and our multi-cultural and anti-racist working party.

The process of planning and writing the course began in earnest in 1979, although an embryonic course had been developed over the several previous years. SE was already timetabled before the course development team was appointed so our first year of operation was pressured. Fortunately we did not allow ourselves to rush into a premature use of commercial material or other easy ways of packaging social education. Rather we used the first year to pilot one or two ideas and most importantly to thrash out what kind of course we ultimately wanted. This lengthy process of discussion has stood us in good stead in that it allowed us to achieve a degree of understanding, consensus and commitment which has enriched the course and allowed us to make significant progress in the area of anti-racist teaching. Moreover it has given us some stable criteria for evaluating our work and helped us to define priorities for further development.

We were able to work effectively because the school's objectives in valuing all students and helping them develop autonomy had been fleshed out in its organisation. The mixed ability of years 1–3 continue in many subjects in the fourth and fifth year. The mixed-ability tutor groups are very stable. They have the same tutor, head and deputy head of year right through to fifth year. They spend two weeks with their tutor in our residential centre – one in their first year and one in their third year.

All the teachers in the school had had experience of co-operative course planning and development and there was commitment to the principle of social education and preparedness to work together through a process of innovation in materials and methodology.

The course development team's work involved making decisions, choosing this approach rather than that, this topic rather than another. We worked on the fundamental assumption that the 'socially educated people' can think for themselves, decide what value to give to the different kinds of evidence about the world that come their way, make decisions about their responses to that evidence which give proper weight to the consequences of those decisions on themselves and others, and finally accept responsibility for those consequences.

We never saw ourselves as being in the business of simply telling students what the 'socially educated' person ought to do in any given situation. That would be no way to develop autonomy. Rather we would focus on the process of making decisions – journeys not destinations.

This is not to imply that the school as an institution has no opinion as to what the socially educated person would do, should do in certain specific situations. Indeed the ways in which the school operates and the position it takes on various moral/social/political issues are part of the evidence s/he encounters about how people manage the world. Our stance against physical violence for example is clear and unswerving but it only makes sense if, in our dealings with the issue, we share with students the 'journey' of thought and experience we travel on the way to a destination.

We came later to plan content. We needed to define a series of 'arenas for debate' of value and relevance to our students. The task was to attempt to find ways within these arenas for the 'learning to be independent' to take place. We wanted to value, and exploit as a learning resource, that experience and knowledge of the world which students brought with them to school. We needed too, to anticipate their needs. We ended up with a spiral curriculum in which the topics and concepts are 'revisited' over five years and re-examined in the light of students' increased experience.

The 'arenas for debate' which emerged and the emphasis on journeys rather than destinations have implications for the role of the tutor in social education.

It means that tutors had to be explicit about the aims of the programme in helping students reach their own decisions. They had to become the enablers of reasoned discussion rather than moral/political arbiters. We have had to work hard to develop these kinds of skills in ourselves. It is not an easy role. It makes demands of tutors in terms of management of groups, materials and ideas.

We have attempted to build on, reflect and articulate a multicultural society in a variety of ways.

1 Our material is designed to promote talking and listening – and sharing of ideas.
2 A major study for all students is a lengthy unit developed jointly by the SE team and the multicultural and anti-racist working party with the help of John Wright. Its topic is bias and it aims to involve students in active research and analysis of bias in the media – particularly books and newspapers. One successful resource is a tape of three students describing different encounters with biased material and their response to it. One wrote to a publisher, one invited a journalist to school.
3 We have taken a stance on events which affect our students' lives. When the British Movement marched through Paddington, we redesigned the term's programme so that each tutor group discussed the implications of the march and the origins of racism. It was vital that everyone understood the school's sense of outrage and its values.
4 Similarly assemblies and lessons were designed to focus on the Nationality Bill. Work was done on immigration in order to dispel myths and to aid understanding of the politics involved. A surgery was held at the school over a period of time by West Hampstead Law Centre so that students or their families could seek advice.

These specific topics are examples of units in which anti-racist teaching is prominent among the learning objectives we would identify. However they can only work in a context in which they are supported by the rest of the course and by the whole school policies.

As far as the rest of the SE course is concerned we were paradoxically blessed by the poor quality of much of the commercial materials available. We had to write our own. We had to look beyond the basic schools TV programmes for our films and videos. Necessity was the mother of invention. We often make mistakes but our errors are quickly spotted and a thoroughgoing annual evaluation of the course identifies areas for rewriting and rethinking. We have not been lumbered with course books and expensive resources which can easily blunt criticism simply because it is so difficult to throw them out.

So throughout the course we have attempted to challenge stereotypes and prejudice and to develop in our students the skills of critical independent thinking. For example, much of our work on study skills taught as part of the social education programme focuses on the skills of gathering and using information, and emphasises the importance of active interrogation of texts. This reinforces work done elsewhere on bias.

The social education course is supported by whole school policies on racism and by the clarity of the school's aims. Because all tutors teach SE the planning of the course, the writing of materials, the in-service training we undertake to support it and the involvement of tutors in its evaluation offer a useful basis for discussion and development of those policies. It also offers tutors from all disciplines the opportunity to move from awareness of school policy to action.

Outward and blatant manifestations of racism have virtually vanished within school but there is much still to be done. We need to help *all* students develop the skills and strengths to fight stereotyping and discrimination. We continue to face the problems of the differing status accorded to different cultures. We need more and better resources. We will always need in-service training and support. We need to constantly evaluate this and other courses. Students participate in this process – but not enough.

Changing the climate – the process
(Liz Lindsay)

Formation of the working party 1978
As early as 1977, Peter Newsam issued to all schools a document on multi-ethnic education. The year 1978 saw the growth of organised overt racist activities in the community with the government immigration laws giving a certain respectability to racist prejudices, which were also becoming more evident within the school.

Protest movements such as ALTARF, which in March 1978 organised a rally attended by 2000 people, were formed to counteract racism and in 1978 a small multicultural anti-racist working party (MCARWP) was set up at Quintin Kynaston and was invited to present to the staff a paper summarising the Newsam document and attempting to make them more aware of the presence of and the reasons for racist attitudes. The small working party has continued to report the results of their research to staff meetings, has produced documents and initiated discussions on its numerous recommendations and has attempted to increase staff awareness with respect to issues such as:

1 political, economic origins of racist attitudes which result from ignorance and prejudice;
2 evidence of and methods of dealing with racist behaviour within the school;
3 liaison with parent and community groups;

4 the continued development of an anti-racist curriculum;
5 surveys to establish the linguistic diversity of the students at Quintin Kynaston and their needs as ESL students.

Recommendations of the working party accepted by the staff have been gradually incorporated into school policy so that decisions are seen as the responsibility of *all* staff and not a few individuals.

By 1980 with greatly increasing unemployment figures and economic gloom, fascist groups, especially the British Movement, gained greater support from students and there was an increase in grafitti and racial abuse in the school.

Adoption of Quintin Kynaston policy on racist behaviour 1980

In September 1980 the working party presented to a staff meeting an outline of a suggested school policy on racist behaviour, stressing that any successful policy required strong support from the hierarchy and a consistent approach by *all* staff to specific racist incidents. Appropriate school responses were outlined clearly to a checklist of racist offences. The working party recommendations were accepted by the staff and incorporated into the school handbook.

The effectiveness of the school policy on racist behaviour has been monitored by the working party. There appears to be a greater confidence in teachers and students in tackling any racist incidents and the number of these inside the school has decreased. However attitudes of the 'hard core racist' have probably changed little and their activities may now be confined to activities outside the school. This seemed to be confirmed by the number of Quintin Kynaston students who took part in a BM March through the Paddington area in late 1980. On this occasion the school made its opposition to the BM very clear in social education and assemblies and by letters to parents and the local press.

Programme to change attitudes

The working party has always stressed that the most important need is to change racist attitudes held not only by the extreme neo-fascist groups but unconsciously by the vast majority, who fail to recognise examples of racism and who may behave unintentionally in a racist manner.

Programmes which assist students to explore the full social and economic (as well as moral) implications of racist issues are urgently required. Any general programme must do more than 'teach respect' for other groups by moralising or by examining their cultures and must involve research and participation by students themselves so that students can understand the political and economic basis of racist ideas as well as of the more blatant neo-fascist activities.

ESL provision at Quintin Kynaston

The Quintin Kynaston intake began to change by 1979 as a result of the primary school link scheme, resulting in an increase in the number of ESL students with a mother tongue other than English and a decrease in the number of Afro-Caribbean students.

A survey carried out by the working party in 1981 established that 100 students must be classified as ESL students with 43 different mother tongue languages. With the help of the Netley Language Centre, a document was prepared by the working party on the implications of the presence of ESL students.

The working party stressed the need for at least one full-time ESL teacher on site to support students in the mainstream classroom and to advise teachers. Since then, our needs have increased and we now need two full-time ESL groups. The arrangement of ESL students travelling to a language centre was considered unsatisfactory socially as there was little interaction with English-speaking students. It was also considered unproductive not to learn English language in a context where learners are required to use the English language for a particular purpose.

Early in 1981, Quintin Kynaston was extremely fortunate to have John Wright appointed as 0.5 teacher funded by INSET to research the school's needs to develop some appropriate material for incorporation into school policy programmes. With co-operation from the working party, he produced some excellent documents containing a great amount of not readily available information and gave guidelines for teachers and tutors for class discussions. He also initiated work on ESL classes by setting up a Cantonese class. John assisted the working party unit's strong recommendations for an ESL teacher. In September 1981, Quintin Kynaston obtained its first full-time ESL teacher on-site.

Last year, an ESL teacher was appointed and despite very poor accommodation he has greatly assisted the introduction and integration of the new ESL students into school life and has greatly increased the confidence and their ability to learn. At the same time, we feel the school should review and ask for more resources for extra ESL teachers and for some mainstream teachers to be timetabled to prepare materials.

Liaison with parents and community
Parents are made fully aware that Quintin Kynaston, a comprehensive school respecting all students of equal value and importance, is intolerant of racist behaviour and aims to provide a secure environment where all students are free to learn. Leaflets are distributed at stalls at annual school fairs and surgeries are set up at some parent-teacher nights where specialists from West Hampstead Law Centre are present to provide on request information and advice to families e.g., regarding the recently introduced Nationality Act.

The working party considers that the school should gain sufficient credibility with the community on its anti-racist stance, so that families gain enough confidence to report to the school any harrassment suffered from racist groups.

Links have been established with the Camden CCR Racial Harassment Monitoring Group because one of the Quintin Kynaston students was identified as being a member of a gang harassing a Bengali family. Some members of the working party also serve on the Camden CCR Education sub-committee.

In-service conferences
In order to increase staff awareness and understanding of the racism experienced by students in the community, the working party organised a conference for Division 2 teachers. Workshops were led by members of the Law Centre, Camden CCR and the CRE. This was later followed by a conference on anti-racist strategies in the classroom. The response to both conferences was positive and we have since organised further conferences as requested by the participants using INSET funds.

Student involvement
During the past 12 months Quintin Kynaston students and the Students' Council have become increasingly involved in monitoring the effectiveness and helping to implement the anti-racist policy. Their interest was stimulated by their active participation at the end of 1982 in the production of ALTARF'S BBC Open Door Programme 'Racism ... the 4th R'. Students wrote scripts and interviewed the Quintin Kynaston head, Peter Mitchell, regarding the school policy and also Azim Haajee, from the West Hampstead Law Centre, regarding the work of the centre within the school. Some students were involved in a discussion about the way racist ideas are reinforced by some curricula which they considered should be revised. A poem and artwork by students were also part of the programme.

A video made at the school by a group of upper school students records a discussion by students of their experiences at the school. The working party intends to use this video to increase staff awareness of students' experience.

A number of sixth formers and a fifth year student who, as part of her English coursework, researched the effectiveness of the school anti-racist policy, concluded that the existence of the school policy was not made explicit enough, especially to incoming students. After a discussion with the school council, the students and the Council have together produced a leaflet to be issued to all incoming students in the new school year. The leaflet very briefly explains that the school has both an anti-racist and anti-sexist policy and that all students are equally valued.

The leaflet assures new students that the school will support them if any other student attempts to discriminate against them on the grounds of sex or ethnic origin.

Recently, some sixth form students addressed a staff meeting and were critical of the exclusion from the school policy of any mention of possible racist behaviour amongst teachers. The students wanted assurance that if necessary, action would be taken against members of staff who behave in a racist manner. They also considered that the school should be explicit on its anti-racist standard not only during interviews with incoming students but also in the recruitment of teachers.

Urgent provision for 1983–1984
While Quintin Kynaston's anti-racist policy (September 1980) has proved reasonably effective with respect to overt and intentional racism, there is an urgent need for further development of resources to attack 'prejudice and ignorance' among both staff and students in which unconscious, unintentional racism thrives. Many original programmes still need to be designed in all subject areas by people who have an awareness, understanding of, and insight into, not only racism, but also of the school and classes for whom they are developed. Members of the working party have not had the considerable amount of time for research discussion and production required to develop many of the ideas for appropriate resource material. All teachers are subject to tremendous pressure with their heavy teaching loads, meetings and extra-curricular activities.

ILEA, in its publication, *Anti-Racist Guidelines for Schools and Colleges* (April 1983) stresses the urgent need to encourage students to make an analysis of racism which must take into account economic and power relations, political, historical and cultural factors. Hopefully, the ILEA multi-ethnic staff will soon have prepared for issue to schools original material for all subject areas which will motivate and stimulate students' own research, discovery and discussion in the classroom. Such material can supplement but not replace the type of material best prepared by school working parties, appropriate for the classes for whom they are designed.

Chapter 6

GEOGRAPHICAL EDUCATION FOR A MULTICULTURAL SOCIETY

Dawn Gill

> Dawn Gill is Head of Geography at Quintin Kynaston School (see chapter 5 for details). She is currently on secondment to the ILEA Multi-ethnic Inspectorate as advisory teacher for antiracist strategies. She is a member of ALTARF and is co-ordinating co-editor of *Contemporary Issues in Geography and Education*, a new journal to be published three times a year.

The content of education is not politically neutral. In no subject area is this more obvious than in geography. An examination of the subject in relation to the needs of a multicultural society makes it clear that geography in the secondary school tends to support an inequitable status quo in both world affairs and British society.

Geography is a subject through which negative images of non-European peoples may be presented in textbooks. Explanations of poverty and underdevelopment have often located the cause of such problems within the individuals or nations who suffer from them. Studies of unemployment may fail to counter the commonly held view that immigration is somehow to blame. Inner city impoverishment may be studied in the context of immigration, and without reference to the unequal division of wealth in society.

The aims of this article are to outline a critique of geographical education as defined by secondary school examination syllabuses and textbooks, and to suggest classroom strategies which may heighten awareness of the political implications of curriculum content.

Research undertaken on behalf of the Schools Council in 1982[1] involved an examination of 20 O level and CSE syllabuses. One of the main conclusions of this research was that syllabuses and textbooks used in geography teaching are frequently implicitly racist. Readers may wish to familiarise themselves with the detailed reasoning which led to this conclusion. The research report is available free of charge from the education department of the Commission for Racial Equality.

The main findings of the syllabus analysis are as follows:
1 The importance of other countries tends to be seen in terms of what 'they' provide for 'us'.
2 The case study approach to a study of plantations can neglect their historical development and economic context.
3 The possibility of negative effects of western influence on Third World development tends to be ignored.

4 Failure is 'individualised' where there is a focus on people and their problems and a neglect of the economic and political aspects of these problems.
5 Poverty and lack of food tend to be linked explicitly with the rate of reproduction in the Third World.
6 The political and economic reasons for lack of food in Third World countries are given little consideration.
7 Migration tends to be presented only as a problem; the syllabuses and materials tend to link migration explicitly with urban problems such as inadequate housing and lack of jobs.
8 Population growth is presented as the main cause of migration. Other causes are seldom explored.
9 A focus on problems tends to deflect attention from cause to symptom in most aspects of teaching about Third World issues, in particular with respect to poverty and population growth.
10 Poverty for some countries and people is considered outside of a context which looks at wealth accumulation for others.
11 A western model of development is commonly put forward as the only model.
12 Many classroom resources are implicitly racist.
13 The content of urban geographical education tends to be presented in terms of theories and generalisations which are unlikely to help children to understand the processes which shape their lives.

The potential of geographical education

Geography is the study of spatial patterns. Until recently, however, at school level, the examination of spatial patterns has tended to focus on description while neglecting explanation. Thus global inequalities in the distribution of wealth may have been studied in terms of distribution patterns, while the causal mechanisms which determine the creation of inequalities have been ignored.

Geography O level and CSE syllabuses commonly focus on issues such as population distribution and movements, world problems, agriculture, urbanisation and world trade.

An understanding of important political issues must underpin geographical education if explanations of spatial patterns are to be meaningful. Colonialism, neo-colonialism, price fluctuations, reliance on primary industry, monoculture, plantations, poor wages, profit, tariff barriers, multi-national companies, transfer pricing, international finance, aid, destabilisation, élites, advertising, monopolies, corruption, planning and decision making in urban and rural areas on the part of private companies and governments: these are the kinds of issues which are becoming the focus of attention in geography as teachers and researchers seek to explain spatial distributions at scales from the local to the global.

Through a study of the localisation of disadvantage in inner cities, and a consideration of the inter-relationships between poverty and other forms of deprivation, geography may play a positive role in encouraging the recognition of forces which operate to the disadvantage of less powerful people in the urban system, black or white.

Through a study of the 'ongoing process of underdevelopment' in parts of the Third World, geography may also play a part in encouraging a recognition of the cause as well as the consequences of poverty and powerlessness on a global scale.

Through debate on development and urban issues it is becoming legitimate for geographers to raise questions about the ways in which political systems may operate to the disadvantage of some groups in society; it is also becoming legitimate to raise questions about the ways in which global political forces operate to the disadvantage of certain countries, and certain groups within these countries. These questions are becoming central to a curriculum which attempts to take into account the need for an *explanatory* spatial analysis.

A geographical education which engages with the kinds of issues outlined briefly here may play a part in fostering a more comprehensive political education which is part of both the rationale and the process of education for a multicultural society.

Raising awareness of the political content of geographical education: practical suggestions

These suggestions are reproduced by the kind permission of the Association of Curriculum Development in Geography. *Contemporary Issues in Geography and Education*,[2] the journal of the Association, aims to promote dialogue between people concerned with the ideological content and political context of geographical education, it facilitates the exchange of ideas on learning materials and classroom strategies. The suggestions presented here are for ways of using materials *already available* in geography classrooms in order to help children to recognise how attitudes are formed. The suggestions focus on an examination of racist attitudes.

1 'Brainstorming'[3]

Brainstorming is a useful technique when introducing any new topic. It stimulates interest by encouraging participatory involvement in the lesson; it provides a starting point because it enables the teacher to examine pupils' existing knowledge and ideas.

How does it work? Pupils sit in groups of three or four, or in pairs, and are given exactly five minutes to 'brainstorm' a topic – that is, to make a list of all the words and ideas that come into their minds when that topic is mentioned. Co-operative working has advantages in that children are less likely to be inhibited by the fear of making 'mistakes' if they are not individually responsible for an idea or a product; ideas are expressed more freely when one person's idea sparks off ideas in another person; however, brainstorming is a useful technique even in classrooms where children work alone. After five minutes – that is, before the ideas have run out, and while enthusiasm is still high – the 'brainstorming' is stopped.

Each group may then share its ideas with the other groups; the teacher may wish to compile a chart which records the ideas of the whole class. This chart forms a useful basis for later discussion; it may be better to put it on a large piece of card than on a blackboard.

Below is the result of brainstorming about Africa with a mixed ability, third year class. There is one contribution from an individual who did not want to work with others, and one from a small group. The childrens' images of Africa tend to reflect the stereotypes presented in the comics and the media.

Our images of Africa

(Brainstorming for 5 minutes)

African tribes	Wild animals	It's poor	Leather skinned
Gold money	Tarantulas	Tribes	clothing
Coffee Cocoa	War	Religions	Rain forest
Poor people	Gorillas	Music	Deserts
White people	Not very good	Dancing	Strange foods
Black people	schooling	They hunt	Tarzan Jane
Rich people	Sun	Live in huts	Mohicans
Fruit	Mosquitoes	Spears	Canoes
Rain forests	Sahara desert	Shields	Tools made by
Hot deserts	Not much water	Jungle	themselves
Starving people	No parks to play in	Swamp	Continent
Jeeps used	No king or queen	Wild animals	Hot climate
One big continent	But lots of freedom	Plains	Messages sent by drum

The next task is to encourage a recognition of how our images may be formed. A later task will be to examine whether these images bear any relation to Africa today. Do most people really run about in grass skirts and boil missionaries up for dinner?

After brainstorming comes a brief discussion of where we get our images from: comics, TV, films, textbooks, novels, aid posters. What kind of images are presented and why?

Each person in the class (or group, if people wish to work together) chooses a piece of homework, the purpose of which is to encourage a more detailed examination of images. Newspaper reports, comics, a book or books, a film or films, posters, TV, newsreel film, jokes about Africa are examined carefully for images presented of Africa or African people.

The pieces of work shown here are not very sophisticated. They are intended to demonstrate that children of 13, 'academic' or otherwise, can examine at some level the ways in which their images may be formed.

Where we get our images from? *(Nicky G.)*
I get my images about Africa from books, comics, TV, like if you see a comic with a black man in it. He would have a bone through his nose. And a wide mouth, and a big pair of rubberly lips. And a grass skirt. And the images on TV are Tarzan and Jane programme and the black people are always dim.

Images of Africa – Film *(Moses Blackman 20.9.80)*
Tarzan
I think that Tarzan gives us very bad images about Africa because it makes the people that live in tribes look so stupid and foolish and they make the countryside look so dangerous, plus I think that the images in Tarzan are bad because it makes the Africans look like savages and simple minded fools.
Roots
The part of the series about Africa in Roots tells us that Africans did have pride and that they are not savages and that they are a poor race.

Tarzan is fiction yet more people believe that it's true but Roots is much nearer to the truth, yet people don't want to believe it.

African Images *(Anna Grough-Yates)*
The media presents many different images of Africa, many of them incorrect. Some of them are also racist. The natives are always primitive, topless with grass skirts and a spear in hand. Jokes about cannibals are wicked and they're not often very funny.

Toys are made to represent Africans, the Golliwog is a good example. It is quite a racist toy, as it portrays Africans to have black skin, black spikey hair, red lips, etc. This toy often influences young children to believe that black Africans look like this.

I think that the media presents Africans wrongly which influences the public and gives them wrong ideas.

Images of Africa – Films *(Diane Larrington)*
In many films that involve Adventure they are set in the jungle. If it is an oldish film they are usually fronted by white men and women with large amounts of luggage, and require great numbers of black topless men to carry it over bridges and waterfalls. Tarzan usually goes to villages that have witch doctors and chiefs that wear nothing except feathers and bones. African people are thought of as primitive and speak in a funny way and are usually the butt of jokes. If you are African people immediately think your father's a chief and you walked around half naked, your name is pronounced in an African accent and your supposed to speak peculiarly. I'm not African but I sometimes feel sorry for African people. PS you never see South Africans in films.

Images of Africa (Robert Crusha 22.9.82)
The images of Africa that the media present are that Africa is full of cannibals, jungle tribes, dangerous animals and that only strong people can survive there. Also it shows that white people are captured and either burnt or boiled with tribes doing dances around them. Africa is also shown as it's got lots of temples full of gold. If I was asked to go to Africa then I may be put off by things like this.

2 Looking at films

In a sense this technique is a bit like brainstorming. The class is asked to list all of the *adventure films* they can think of which are set in Africa/India/South East Asia/Latin and Central America/Arabia. The teacher may wish to record the list on an overhead transparency, or a wall chart. Here is a part of a list produced by a third year class:

Tarzan	*Lawrence of Arabia*
Raiders of the Lost Ark	*Goldfinger*
Zulu	*Shaft in Africa*
Zulu Dawn	*Orient Express*
Flame Trees of Thika	*MASH*
Carry on up the Khyber	*Apocalypse Now*

The list is then examined: for each film, who are the most important people? Which people are doing the intelligent and heroic things – are they black, white, male or female? Letters are placed next to each film title (WM; WF; BM or BF). It quickly becomes apparent that white men are represented as the most important people in most of the films set in countries where black people live. In many films women, if they appear at all, do so only in the role of sex objects; they are subservient to the men, they may provide sexual gratification and often they are quite silly as well as physically rather weak.

It is useful to draw analogies between racism and sexism when analysing the images presented in films or books. Black people and women, if visible at all, are generally presented in a way which suggests that they are subservient and stupid human beings. It may be illuminating for children to speculate on whether or not their own attitudes may be affected in any way by what they see on TV.

3 Using Geographical games and simulations

Games and simulations were developed in the 1970s as a means of teaching ideas quickly and effectively. An examination of the kinds of ideas which were taught may give a valuable insight into the role of geographical education in fostering certain attitudes which are unlikely to be helpful to good race relations. Walford's *Games in Geography*+ serves to illustrate the highly political nature of the content of geographical education in the 1970s. For example, in the context of a discussion on racism it may be worth mentioning the 'Railway Pioneers Game' – a simulation in which players assume the roles of railway companies in the USA in the mid-nineteenth century. One of the objectives of this game is 'to help pupils' geographical and historical understanding of the USA through familiarity with aspects of its human and physical geography'. The indigenous population of North America who had occupied the land for centuries before Europeans 'discovered' it are mentioned in two sentences – one concerned with 'chance factors, such as the opposition of Indians, freak climate conditions, disasters, strikes, etc.' which pushed up the costs of railway building; and later in the game, companies building north-west of Minneapolis are 'hampered by attacks, and must repel Indian raiders'.

Walford makes the point that 'the profit motives which appear in some simulations do not invite judgement on the simulation itself, but on the particular set of circumstances which gives rise to it' (see p. 165 Graves' of *New Movements in the Study and Teaching of Geography*[5]).

4 Assignment: 'Do textbooks affect our attitudes?'

This assignment takes extracts from commonly used school geography books and from old books which have been kept in order to demonstrate bias in texts. It is not possible to reproduce the extracts in full here, but the brief quotations, together with the questions on the worksheet, give an idea of how similar assignments could be produced.

Do textbooks influence attitudes?
Objectives of assignment
1 To study information given in some geography texts.
2 To think about the ways in which we may be influenced by what we read.
3 To consider how attitudes may affect decision making.

Tasks
1 Study the extracts carefully. List the suggestions made about Europeans and non-Europeans. (A suggestion may be explicit or implicit. You have to 'read between the lines' for the implicit suggestions.) A list has been begun below to help you. All the examples are taken from the first extract. Use the other extracts to complete the list.

Europeans	*Non-Europeans*
Business people	Neglected their land
Efficient	Depended on Europeans
Scientific	Had houses built for them
Have organisational ability	Provided labour
Responsible for building roads and railways	
Provided clean water	
Started companies	
Planted crops	

2 When your list is complete, tick all the *positive* suggestions. Put a cross against the *negative* suggestions. Count the ticks for Europeans. Count the

ticks for non-Europeans. Count the crosses for each. Write a comment on this exercise.

3 Image that you are a European child, studying geography at school. All of the books describe Europeans and non-Europeans in the way that these extracts describe them. You have never met a non-European. What sort of ideas would you learn about non-Europeans? What would you believe to be true about Europeans?

'It is possible that some geography textbooks contribute to racial prejudice.'

Discuss this idea with a partner. List all of the arguments you can think of which *support* this point of view. List all your arguments *against* this point of view. Try to give evidence which supports the two sides of the argument.

4 Many Europeans work in jobs where they may influence what happens in developing countries. Their attitudes towards non-Europeans may influence the decisions they make. For example:
   a) Someone working for Brooke Bond in Kenya may make decisions on wages, working conditions and hours of work.
   b) A person working at the London Metal Exchange may help to fix prices for Zambian copper, Bolivian tin.
   c) A person in the British Government may argue *for* or *against* tariff barriers.
   d) A voter can choose between two political parties: one wants to increase aid to poorer countries; the other wants to cut aid.
   e) A Trade Unionist has to vote 'yes' or 'no' about action in support of South African black mine workers who want the right to belong to a union.

Write about each one of these situations. Explain how *negative* attitudes towards non-Europeans may influence the decisions made. Explain how *positive* attitudes may affect the decisions.

5 Study extract 5 again, carefully, then read the following:

'The idea of anyone owning a particular plot of land is strange to them...'

This extract is about Africa. But something similar could have been written about people in Australia, or North America at the time when Europeans first went there. The people believed that the land, like the air, belonged to everyone. To take land and say 'This is mine' would seem like stealing it from the rest of the people. It may have been unthinkable that anyone should *own* land, because the land was everyone's right, just like the air we breathe.

People do not all have the same ideas about right and wrong. In this country many people believe it is *right* for some people to own a lot of land, while others own none. In China, most people believe that this is *wrong*.

At first it may have been easy for the Europeans to take land from some of the North American Indians, the Australian aborigines and people in other parts of the world – if those people believed that the land couldn't be owned, only borrowed. Another thing which may have made it easy for Europeans to steal the land was that they had guns. The Indians, Africans and Aborigines could be shot if they fought for their land. Think of all the cowboy and Indian films; think of films like *Zulu* and *Zulu Dawn*. What happens to the Indians and Africans?

Extract 5 is written from a European point of view. Rewrite the extract from the point of view of a Masai person whose family have used the land in Kenya and Tanzania for many generations. How do you feel about the fact that Europeans have come and taken large areas of land?

Extracts

Extract 1
from Long and Robertson's 'World Problems' p. 73 (Hodder and Stoughton 1969 reprinted 1975)
This book is used in 44 per cent of schools which teach about the Third World, according to research by David Hicks. Hicks' work is published by the Centre for Multicultural Education, London University.

In the early days of plantations, the areas of land where they were started had been largely neglected for cultivation and had few inhabitants. Most plantations were started by companies, who not only planted the crops but were responsible for building roads and railways, providing clean water, setting up houses, schools and health services for their workers. Even now the social welfare of the people of Assam and Ceylon depends on the success of the tea plantations, that of the Cubans depends on sugar and tobacco plantations, while the cultivation of rubber enables nearly half of Malaya's population to have the highest standard of living in south Asia. The supply of products from plantations bulks large in world trade and in meeting the needs of countries of raw materials and food. Thus plantation agriculture is very important.

Extract 2
from the GYSL Resource sheet on Calcutta (Cities and People 4.3)

Calcutta is not a wealthy city and it has proved impossible to house and provide amenities for this great inward surge of millions. More than three-quarters live in slums or in tenements with one family to a small room. The problem is complicated because almost a quarter of the city's population lives a single life and two-thirds are male.

It is well known that millions have the pavement as their home. Streets are strewn with sleeping families at night. But the pavements also remain almost as littered during the day. It is evident that thousands of people either lack the energy or the need, because unemployed or unemployable, to move from their gutterside homes.

Extract 3
from D. Forde and D. Stewart 'This is Your Adventure' Book 3.
(First published, 1968, Johnston and Bacon)

It is very expensive to go on safari. That is why only wealthy men, film companies and scientific expeditions can afford it. The servants on the expedition are all African, called 'boys'. They are highly skilled men who prefer the free life of the bush to any other. Every white member of the expedition needs the following personal servants:
one lorry driver
two trackers
one skinner
two cooks
three camp servants

Extract 4
from H. R. Cain's 'Human and Economic Geography' (Longman) p. 175

Plantation Agriculture. In selected areas of the tropical regions which are capable of yielding commodities of value in world commerce, the business of cultivation has been taken over by Europeans. Land has been acquired and plantations set up for the large-scale production of such crops as rubber, bananas and sugar-cane by more efficient and scientific methods than those employed by the native farmer. These plantations involve a combination of European organisation, capital and skill with native labour. The peasant farmer thus becomes a wage-earner, buying the food and other things he needs with the money he receives for his work.

Extract 5
from Honeybone and Roberson, 'The Southern Continents', Third Edition, 1971 (Reprinted 1973)

The European-managed farms on the plateau in East Africa were very large, and trouble has arisen because many Africans consider that some of their grazing land has been taken from them. In the old days, tribes such as the Masai of Kenya and Tanzania used to wander with their cattle over very large areas in search of pasture. Some of them still do so today, and the idea of anyone owning a particular plot of land is strange to them.

Extract 6
from S. Crawford's 'The Developing World', Book 2, pages 20 and 21 (Longman)

Plantations. These are large farms, growing mainly one or two crops. The farmers had enough money to buy food supplies and pay wages until the first crops grew. Once the plantations were producing steadily the managers became rich men with well built houses. There were always plenty of peasants to work on the estates...

The men and women who work on the plantations do so because they cannot grow enough on their own farms to eat and sell. Most peasants have little plots of land less than one hectare in size.

References

1 Gill, D., Research Paper available free of charge from the Commission for Racial Equality (Elliot House, 10–12 Allington Street, London SW1)
2 Association for Curriculum Development in Geography, *Contemporary Issues in Geography and Education*, vol 1, parts 1, 2, and 3, available from Frances Slater, Association for Curriculum Development, London University Institute of Education, Bedford Way, London WC1
3 This and many other excellent teaching ideas comes from Richardson, R., *Learning for change in World Society; Reflections, Activities and Resources*, World Studies Project and World Trust, London, 1976, available from 24 Palace Chamber, Bridge Street, London SW1A
4 Walford, *Games in Geography*, Longman, 1977
5 Groves, N., *New Movements in the Study and Teaching of Geography*, Temple Smith, 1977

Further reading
A selection of short articles which may form the basis of staff discussion on the issue of geographical education for a multicultural society.
Association for Curriculum Development in Geography, 'Racist Society, Geography Curriculum' – a collective of readings (conference document 1983)
Carnie, J., 'Children's attitudes to other nationalities', Chapter 10 in *New Movements in the Study and Teaching of Geography*, Graves, N. (ed) London, Temple Smith
Hicks, D. W., 'Bias in Geography Textbooks: Images of the Third World and Multi-ethnic Britain', Working paper no 1, Centre for Multicultural Education, London University Institute of Education, 1981
Hicks, D. W., 'Two sides of the same coin: an exploration of the links between multicultural education and development education', *NAME Journal*, vol 7, no 2, Spring 1979
Gill, D., 'Secondary School Geography: contributions to Multicultural Education', Working paper no 2, Centre for Multicultural Education 1982
Geography and Change, Teachers' Guide for the GYSL Development Education project, Nelson (not a recommendation for the GYSL teaching materials – for reviews of these see *CIGE*, vol 1)
Marsden, W. E., Stereotyping and Third World Geography, *Teaching Geography*, July 1976
Sivanandan, A., 'Race Class and the State in *A Different Hunger:* writings on black resistance, Pluto Press, 1982
Worrell, M., 'Multiracial Britain and the Third World: Tensions and approaches in the classroom', *NAME Journal*, vol 6, no 3, Summer 1978
Contemporary Issues in Geography and Education, Vol. 1, Issues 1 and 2 (Autumn 1983 and Spring 1984) focuses on geographical education for a multicultural society. These two issues contain useful articles and practical suggestions in the form of lesson plans, syllabus guidelines etc.

Bibliography

Racism and sexism
Teaching and Racism, ALTARF, 1979
Race in the classroom, ALTARF, 1979
Baker, B., Bishton, S., Covett, D., Jennings, D., *Read All About It: a study of race reporting in the Media,* AFFOR (1 Finch Road, Lozzels, Birmingham B19 1HS), 1980
Cohen, P., Gardner, C., *It Ain't Half Racist Mum*, Comedia Publishing Group, 1982
CRE, *The Fire Next Time, The Urgent Need for Policies*, 1980
Downing, J., 'Now You Do Know' (An independent report on racial

oppression in Britain for submission for a World Council of Churches Consultation), War on Want Publications, 1980
Downing, J., Wood, W., *The Media Machine*, Pluto Press 1980
Morrison, L., *As They See It: a study of race relations from a black viewpoint*, Commission for Racial Equality, 1981
Smith, D., *The Facts of Racial Disadvantage: a national survey*. Political and Economic Planning, CRE, 1976
Rampton, A., 'West Indian Children in our Schools' – interim report of the Committee of Inquiry into the Education of Children from Ethnic Minority Groups, HMSO, 1981
Spender, D., *Invisible Women: the Schooling Scandal*, Readers and Writers, 1982
Tierney, J. (ed.), *Race Migration and Schooling*, Holt Educational Books, 1982
Wilson, A., *Finding a Voice: perspectives of Asian People in Britain*, Virago, 1978

Pedagogy
Brown, D., Pearson, J., Sinclair, S., *Priorities for Development (a teachers' handbook for development education)*, Development Education Centre, Selly Oak, Birmingham, 1981
Dore, R., *The Diploma Disease: Educational Qualifications and Development*, Unwin Educational, 1976
Fisher, S., Magee, W., Wetz, J., *Ideas into Action: a handbook for teachers by teachers*, World Studies Project (One World Trust, 24 Palace Chambers, Bridge Street, SW1A 2JT)
Fisher, S., Flood, M., Richardson, R., *Debate and Decision: schools in a world of change*, World Studies Project, 1979
Freire, P., *Pedagogy of the Oppressed*, Penguin 1972
Hicks, D. W., *Minorities: a teacher's resource book for the multi-ethnic curriculum*, Heinemann Educational Books 1981
Huckle, J., Geographical Education: *Reflection and Action*, OUP 1983
Richardson, R., *Learning for Change in World Society: Reflections, Activities and Resources*, World Studies Project, 1976
Searle, C., *The World in a Classroom*, Writers and Readers Publishing Co-operative, 1977
Stinton, J., *Racism and Sexism in Children's Books*, Writers and Readers Co-operative, 1979
Young, M. F., *Curriculum Change: Limits and Possibilities*, for the Schooling and Society Course Open University, Routledge and Kegan Paul, 1976

Development Geography
Bowles, T. S., *A Survey of Attitudes towards Overseas Development*, HMSO, 1978

George, S., *How the other Half Dies: the Real Reason for World Hunger*, Penguin, 1976

Goodenough, S., *Values, Relevance and Ideology in Third World Geography*, Open University, Units 27–28

Harrison, P., *Inside the Third World*, Penguin 1979

Hayter, T., *The Creation of World Poverty: An Alternative View to the Brandt Report*, Pluto Press, 1980

Hoogvelt, A., *The Third World in Global Development*, Macmillan, 1982

Lappe, F., Collins, J., *Food First: The Myth of Scarcity*, Souvenir Press, 1980

Moore Lappe, F., Collins., Kinley, D., *Aid as Obstacle: Twenty questions about our foreign aid and the Hungry*, Institute for Food and Development Policy

Rodney, W., *How Europe Underdeveloped Africa*, Bogle L'Overture Publications, 1972

Rogers, B., *The Domestication of Women: Women in the Third World*, Tavistock, 1980

Thompson, D., Larson, R., *Where were you Brother? An Account of Trade Union Imperialism*, War on Want Publications, 1978

Whittemore, C., *Land for People: Land Tenure and the very Poor*, Oxfam Public Affairs Unit, 1981

Chapter 7

INTEGRATED STUDIES AT WILLIAM PENN SCHOOL

Paul McGlynn, Bruce Gill, Brenda Downes, Richard James

William Penn School is a six form entry boys' comprehensive with a roll of 1000. It draws its intake from about 30 feeder primary schools in Lambeth and Southwark, areas which suffer from the traditional inner city problems. In the first year pupils follow a common core curriculum in mixed ability groups, except for maths which is set after half a term. One third of the timetable is devoted to integrated studies – English, history and geography. From second year pupils study these subjects separately and there is greater setting across the timetable.

Paul McGlynn is Head of Third Year at William Penn.

Bruce Gill, now doing research in Birmingham, was formerly Head of Fourth Year at William Penn.

Brenda Downes is Deputy Head of Second Year at William Penn.

Richard James is Head of Integrated studies.

The idea of Integrated Studies was very much in vogue in the late 1960s when there was an acute teacher shortage. By the early 1970s the Integrated Studies department at William Penn was well established but by 1976 it was apparent that the syllabus no longer met the needs and expectations of staff and pupils. A review of the course was therefore undertaken by the staff.

The development of the pilot course is best understood against the background of the factors which contributed to the evolution of the Integrated Studies course in general. The main factor in this process has been the need felt by staff to respond in the most positive and effective manner to the mixed ability composition of the teaching groups. In this respect the earliest existing syllabus was singularly defective. The problem was that although it acknowledged that the groups were of mixed abilities, its entire approach was based on the transfer of methods found successful with fairly high ability subject-based streamed groups. It was unsuitable and the task of preparing suitable materials and planning alternative approaches was formidable.

Group work was an obvious alternative technique but of itself would not solve the problem. New materials had to be prepared and in the summer term of 1976 a group within the IS department addressed itself to this problem. The solution that was advocated was to expand our local studies unit into a whole term's work. The emphasis was to be in research, first-hand experience, with as much work being done outside in the locality as in the classroom. The course looked into local building trends, street names, immigration patterns, land usage, services and amenities and as such was considered more exciting and relevant than its predecessor. Furthermore, it marked the first stage in the process whereby the urban environment began to assume ever-increasing importance as an immediate resource.

In 1977 the new syllabus – consciously devised to meet the needs of mixed ability groups and the resulting demands for resource-based learning – was in operation.

However, another factor was making its presence felt. During the 1970s increased attention was being paid to the multi-ethnic composition of British society. The plethora of multicultural/multiracial/multi-ethnic courses, seminars, conferences, discussion groups, etc., was such that even schools noted the development. The new syllabus took up this theme in a general way in its central aim which was to provide a course which reflected the experience and culture of pupils from many ethnic backgrounds and gave them an understanding and appreciation of the geography, history, literature and language which have shaped their own and other societies.

The content of the course

These aims effectively transformed the course content. Successive terms dealt with the environment, people's adaptation to the environment and their moulding of it. The topics covered in the first term included the earth and its relation to the universe, the formation of the earth, the evolution of human beings and the beginning of civilisation in Ancient Egypt. This was clearly an unrealistic schedule, the time available being insufficient, so that in actuality the course tended to culminate at the development of early human beings.

The second term's work continued the evolution theme with a discussion of the notion of ethnicity and a consideration of contrasting environments and their influence upon human lifestyles. The intention was to contrast a variety of lifestyles. The selection made for this purpose included mountain regions, frozen lands, desert lands, the tropics, and also contrasting environments within Britain, e.g. hill and dairy farming as opposed to cereal farming. Again the time factor proved a constraint. It became necessary to restrict the contrast to two areas. One hot and one cold were selected. The arctic regions were an obvious choice and consideration of the ethnic mix in the school suggested that the West Indies be the tropical region even though it was not a typical example. There were inviting possibilities of using the multicultural make-up of these islands to some advantage and general pupil interest in the topic seemed guaranteed.

The third term's work sought to investigate how people built and lived in communities, the local environment and the development of London. However, the tendency for the West Indies topic to carry over into the third term combined with the summer weather which encouraged outdoor work led to the situation where the local studies project grew to dominate all else. Thus after one year of operation a very large proportion of the course content was omitted because it was unrealistic to try to cover so much in the time available.

Methodology

The policy regarding methodology was positively to encourage group work and research; the teachers were encouraged to plan work together, share ideas and resources and contribute to an ever-increasing resource centre. Work booklets were prepared by either small groups or individuals. The function of the themes depended on the teacher's intentions. Most teachers used the themes to limit the area of study, thereby keeping it within the scope of available resource material; a few, however, experimented with using the theme occasionally as a trigger for free enquiry. The great problem was how to organise the time and materials in such a way as to achieve maximum flexibility, there being many possible directions that individual pupils might choose to pursue.

Class teaching was used to introduce themes and sub-themes whilst the worksheets, aids and tasks were intended to provide or supplement the variety of ways of looking at a topic. Very quickly though, the course became heavily orientated towards worksheets. This situation was considered most unsatisfactory but it was also difficult to avoid.

The course sequence presented problems. All teachers involved in the course agreed that the local studies work of the third term provided a more relevant and logical starting point. The argument was simple and forceful. Start with the child's own experience and move outwards to the wider spheres of influence and experience. This is the pattern characteristic of most inter-disciplinary humanities-based courses. One starts with the child and progresses through the family, home, locality, country, and so on. On this basis the existing course seemed back-to-front, starting as it did with the universe and gradually focusing inwards toward the local community. Inadequacies such as these led to the view that the course should be reviewed yet again. It was decided to switch the content of the first and third term. The first term now incorporated a booklet which dealt with the historical development of London. The accompanying notions of 'movement of people' and 'growth' provided conceptual tools for those of us who sought to use the theme both to trigger off free enquiry and to link with the West Indies topic which by now had come to comprise the content of the second term's work.

We had reached this position through observation of the classroom reaction of pupils and by questioning our concept of pluralism and how it related to unequal distribution of power. Being somewhat naive our perceptions were lagging behind those of the pupils who now regarded themselves as British. If every pupil was British why were people of different colours or countries of origin still regarded as outsiders? The idea that pupils could retain respect of their parents' culture on an equal basis with that of the host culture while still regarding themselves as British citizens, highlighted conflicts which could not be resolved in the multicultural objectives of the course. It was difficult to explain marked differences in experience for black and white as regards things such as unemployment, free dinners, grants, areas of poor housing, racial abuse and police harassment. The implications of these differences demanded that the pupils be presented with an opportunity to examine their own aspirations and the complex forces which conspire to thwart them. Pupils and staff were forced to examine their attitudes towards racism and its relationship to class and ways in which these attitudes are institutionalised within the structure of British society.

The task that faced the department by 1980 was to develop an anti-racist core to the course which was both academically sound and relevant to the experience which pupils brought to the classroom. However, it was only by working through the pilot course itself that we came to realise what was entailed. How did this transformation come about? Throughout the process of developing our courses we had to be aware of the conceptual complexities of integrated, cross-curricular and multi-disciplinary elements but the basic generalisation running throughout the course and embodying a range of concepts was that British society was and is a constantly evolving multi-ethnic society open to a wide range of influences. From the arrival of the first hunters from Europe to the most recent patterns of migration, British society and consequently the local area in which we live, has been subject to continuous modification. In collaboration with ILEA's multi-ethnic Inspectorate we drew up the following concepts:

Adaptation   Changes in the physical environment and social institutions, local needs in terms of housing, employment, education, transport etc.
Authority   Power, imposition of legal codes and effect on people.
Change   Patterns of settlement, migration and projections of future development.
Culture   Ways of living affected by environmental, social and economic circumstances.
Stratification   Social distribution of wealth and power in a local area.
Differentiation/interdependence   Examining effects of age, sex and ethnicity.
Conflict   Historical, social and economic aspects, racism and cultural diversity.

The results are set out in the description of our local community study which follows.

Local community study

We wanted to bring the children to an understanding of the community in which we live. As we had studied the history of London through movement of

people and growth of communities, it was decided to use these two concepts as a basis for the pilot course. We wanted the pupils to be able to answer the following questions:
What/Who do I see when I go out?
How has London become what it is? Is it static?
What kind of 'influences' are there in the community?
What is a 'Londoner'?

Week 1
A discussion was initiated about why people move. Pupils were asked to list as many reasons as they could think of – these varied from going on holiday to running away from a war. The second stage was to categorise these moves into the following:
   local
   national
   international
   permanent
   temporary
   voluntary
   compulsory
This was done by group discussions, after the teacher had ensured that pupils had a clear understanding of the words used. Some moves fell into more than one category.

Week 2
Later, using the same check list, the moves were placed into *different* categories:
religious   political   social
economic   geographical   educational etc.
We used pp. 12 and 13 of *Earth's People*[1] as stimulus. Group work again – attitudes and values emerged through discussion.

Week 3
At this point, the work was related to the class and the boys made bar graphs to record moves *they* had made:
1 local, international and national
Also their:
2 religions
3 birthdays
4 where they live
5 hobbies
Thus, we were able to discuss how *their* families had come to South London/or why they had stayed here/why some were about to move. They realised that even their class wasn't a 'static community'. (Again, attitudes and values.)
   We marked a local map to record where each pupil lives in the area.

Pupils were asked to speak to an older member of the community and to try to find out how things had changed in their area during the last few years – or longer if they could remember. Pupils took notes on conversations and then made an oral report to class. Also, we talked about things in which pupils themselves had witnessed change.

Week 4
We considered the facilities which are available in London today, e.g. utilities, public amenities, shops etc., and which of those things aren't available in smaller towns or the country. The groups discussed why this is so. We considered why such a range of amenities is necessary in a place the size of London. We considered supply and demand in relation to population. Are people manipulated to want things? These topics were discussed in class with notes being made on the blackboard, then the boys wrote notes to put in their folders.

We made a survey of the facilities available in Lambeth, especially those related to the young. We also had a traffic survey near the school and a shop survey in local shopping streets (Herne Hill). We concentrated on groceries. Boys were asked to make a weekly examination of a shop near home and to collect the following information.
1 How many 'new' things in the last 10 years?
2 How many groceries from other countries?
3 How much used to be imported and is now produced here?
We wanted to find out what is available and why. What, if any, conclusions could be drawn about supply and demand, i.e. what had the older established community gained from permanent and temporary immigrants from other countries or other regions of the British Isles?

Week 5
What of the problems of living in towns? The idea was 'brainstormed' on blackboard. See *Earth's People* p. 22 e.g.,

pollution	vandalism	loneliness
overcrowding	racism	poverty
aggression	boredom	
unemployment	crime	

We read the poem 'Sheet Gang' from *Black Ink*[2] as stimulus for creative writing – 'Imagine you're in a gang ...' or 'Imagine that you've witnessed ...', with an attempt to cover the following questions – who? why? how? where? Stories were read out in class and discussed, for content and possible improvements needed. This encouraged boys to listen to and discuss each others' work. We aimed to get the pupils to consider the causes of such attitudes and actions.

Week 6
We then discussed the types of people we see when we go out:
  gender
  class
  ethnic Group
  type of work/lack of it.
We used the 'People' page from the Oxfam booklet *Conflict*.[3] We discussed additions to the community
e.g. foreign food restaurants
  social events
  new words in the language etc.
This furthered the discussion of growth and supply and demand.

Week 7
Where does 'their' culture meet/come into conflict with 'ours'? How can we tell the difference anyway? Think back to grocery lists, for example. Don't new generations take things for granted as being part of our culture and tradition if they're there when they are growing up? We brought into the discussion previously studied history – where did 'our' culture come from in the beginning? Can it be truly said to be distinctive from all others, not influenced by them? What advantages does a community gain from multi-ethnic culture?

Week 8
Having spoken of empires which colonised England in the early part of the course, we considered the fact that from the sixteenth century onwards the development of mercantilism and the need for further sources of raw materials, expanded markets and cheap labour led to the European expansionism.

We started from the voyages of discovery, (reasons and results) and drew maps of the world with the main journeys marked on, learned the names of the oceans and continents and reconsidered the reasons that people might have for building empires.

Where do we go from here? The course grew out of questions and will remain relevant and educationally alive through further questioning. We feel that courses should respond to the needs and questions of pupils rather than prescriptive specifications by educationalists. But the common core of concepts will continue to provide a framework from which pupils can interpret an increasing set of personal, local, national and global perspectives.

References
1 *Earth's People* Macdonald Educational, 1973
2 *Black Ink* Black Ink Publishing Co-op; 258 Coldharbour Lane, Brixton, London SW2
3 *Conflict*, Oxfam

Chapter 8

HUMANITIES IN HACKNEY DOWNS SCHOOL

Peter Traves

> Hackney Downs is a boys' comprehensive school with about 920 on the roll. Its intake reflects the multicultural population of Hackney. Teaching in the lower forms is organised on a mixed ability basis, which in some subjects continues up to fifth form level. For the first five years boys are taught in groups of not more than 22.
>
> Peter Traves is Head of Humanities at Hackney Downs. At present he is seconded for two years as an Advisory Teacher with the ILEA.

In the early and mid-1970s Hackney Downs School was experiencing a number of changes that forced the staff to a radical re-examination of its work. It had changed from a grammar to a comprehensive in 1967 and the last of the 'favoured' intakes were now in the upper school. For the first time the teachers were faced with the problems and the potential of the range of ability of an inner city school intake. At the same time, and for very different reasons, the cultural make-up of Hackney Downs was in a state of flux. The school had drawn largely on the white working class of Hackney with a high proportion of Jewish boys from Stoke Newington and Stamford Hill. A change in the catchment area had greatly diminished the Jewish intake but the upper school was still predominantly white. A typical fifth form of twenty-two in the mid-1970s would probably contain no more than three boys of Caribbean extraction (often first generation immigrants themselves) and one or two of African or Asian origin. A first form of thirty, on the other hand, might well contain fifteen or sixteen boys from a Caribbean background (more often second generation). The intake of other cultural groups had not yet increased markedly.

It was, in fact, the change in the range of ability that attracted most attention from the staff. The need to re-examine and remodel the curriculum was accepted by most teachers. In particular the needs of pupils in the junior part of the school were seen to be pressing. One of the responses to this was the development of a humanities programme.

The idea of an integrated course for at least the first years had been debated within the school for several years before it was actually implemented in September 1975. It began with the new intake of that year and was gradually extended until in 1978 it took in the first three years. Humanities involves six departments working and planning together in teams – Drama, English,

Geography, History, Remedial and Social Studies. At present each class has eight lessons of humanities in a thirty-five period week. Reinforcement and team-teaching allow working practice to be flexible and have played a crucial role in the nature of the course.

Humanities has provided an invaluable forum for the discussion and examination of key areas of the curriculum and of classroom practice. This discussion has continued over the years, in team planning, fortnightly meetings and, at greater length, at the annual weekend conference. Discussion documents, videoed lessons, tape recordings and pupils' work have been some of the focal or starting points of our considerations. In our discussions we have looked at the role of subject specialisms, the move from primary to secondary school, basic literacy, the mixed ability classroom, language across the curriculum etc. Multicultural education rapidly became a central issue in the planning and building of a humanities programme.

As so often happens the initial pressure for the inclusion of multicultural education in the agenda for discussion came from a small group of teachers. Especially important was the role played by John Hardcastle who from the moment he came to the school in 1973 grasped the crucial importance of multicultural education. From the first we have received great support from outside agencies. In particular the help and encouragement we have received from Joan Goody, an ILEA Advisory Teacher, has been invaluable.

However, this group of teachers was not isolated and got a sympathetic hearing from all those involved in early humanities planning. The issue of multicultural education was fed into discussion at every level. The habit of thinking of the children in the class as a resource was well established in Hackney Downs and it led quite logically to accepting that the changed cultural intake of the school needed to be reflected in the curriculum.

Multicultural education has many pitfalls – not least the idea of being seen solely in terms of compensatory education. If it is to be a means of enriching the curriculum then it must be taken on by teachers at their own level. In an established course that is to be a long-term part of the school's education programme, it is not enough simply to offer materials that reflect a culturally plural society. Those teaching the course must have a realistic sense of the potential of the cultures they are presenting. Historians who teach the Romans to first years have at least some idea of the intellectual range of Roman history and culture. There is a danger that equivalent teaching of, say, the Caribbean might not be accompanied by an equivalent insight. I think it is fair to say that though we still have a long way to go the Humanities department has made a rigorous effort to educate itself in this respect. This was a formidable task and it could only be accomplished by sharing the work around. Over several years members of the various departments prepared and presented talks and papers on a wide range of topics. We did not restrict ourselves strictly to the subject matter we intended to teach. Our aim was to broaden and deepen our understanding rather than directly to resource our lessons. The effect on the staff was worth all the efforts it cost. Not only did it increase knowledge and raise the prestige of multicultural education but it also engaged the staff intellectually and provided enjoyment and stimulation. The staff involved in setting up the multicultural syllabus were actually learning a great deal themselves.

The syllabus

Although from the first we emphasised the need to widen the range of cultural reference as often as possible there has been a tendency to package the multicultural input into units of work. In the second year classes study aspects of the geography, sociology and history of India, West Africa and the Caribbean. The limitations of this kind of approach must be all too clear. It tends to isolate the multicultural content. It limits the pupils' experience of this work to one year and consequently to one stage of their intellectual development. Nevertheless there have been real achievements. The course stresses the variety of images available of these parts of the world and questions the simplicity of many models of third world countries. The history we teach helps to break down some of the cruder assumptions our children come with by presenting the richness of Indian and West African civilisations. We also try to teach about imperialism, hoping to indicate its economic foundations and the debt Western development owes to its ex-colonies. The Indians, Africans and West Indians are presented as being active participants in their own histories and cultures and not simply as poor victims. Consequently there is a strong emphasis on resistance.

The role of Caribbean history is particularly important in this respect. It is relatively easy to point to the past splendours of Asoka's empire, the Mughals, Rajput princes, Songhai, Mali or Ghana but the Caribbean seems at first glance to present an image of an oppressed and degraded people denied access either to their real cultural roots or to continued cultural achievement. Well-meaning teachers can do more harm than good by simply concentrating on the miseries of the Middle Passage, the treadmills of the sugar factories and the lash of the overseer's whip. The slaves were cruelly treated but they were not just victims. They brought with them rich and varied African cultures which they preserved, fused and metamorphosed into the culture of the Caribbean. The continued vast influx of slaves kept the 'African connection' very much alive well into the nineteenth century. Africa provided the base and the driving force of Caribbean culture. The story of harsh oppression needs the context of European political and economic development. More importantly it also needs the counterbalance of the unending resistance that took place in the Caribbean. Slave resistance, which developed into the West Indian drive for self-determination, and which was shaped by African culture, has become the centre of our studies in the Caribbean to show the way in which resistance became an integral part of a whole way of life. In particular we draw these themes together by looking in some detail at Toussaint L'Ouverture and the S Domingo revolution.

Though I think this course has achieved a lot and its general framework of ideas can be justified it is manifestly unsatisfactory in several respects. Apart from the objections already mentioned it crams too much information into too short a time. This means that lessons tend to be overloaded with fact and that there is less opportunity than might be hoped for of drawing on the knowledge and experience of the children and their families in a multicultural classroom. The pupils tend to become restless when too much time is spent on one topic. Boring Indian or Caribbean geography or history is as boring as any other, only potentially more disappointing and damaging. Partly in response to this it was decided at last year's conference to radically re-examine and revise the humanities syllabus. We are in the process of doing this right now.

Syllabus revision
We began by agreeing on concepts that would be fruitful for study from the points of view of all the disciplines involved. From these we agreed on themes that would best illustrate the concepts and then on topics that would embody the themes and concepts. The concepts and themes would run throughout the three years and would be returned to at increased levels of abstraction and complexity as the pupils developed in ability and understanding. We aim to begin more directly with the pupils' own experience – the move from primary to secondary school, what can be seen in Hackney, in London and, of course, in the multicultural classroom. In this way we hope to tap the resource of a culturally plural school effectively. We hope to be able to move in a more coherent fashion from direct to less direct experience drawing parallels and pointing differences but being able at key points to relate things back to their own developing view of the world.

A theme like *The Movement of People* can be tackled at many levels. It can draw on the experience of black and white, Asian or Cypriot children. It can be illustrated and explored through the Angles and Saxons, the nineteenth century Irish or through the continued and complex movements of the people of the Caribbean. It can be worked on by way of personal anecdote or by analysing the network of social and economic factors that push and pull peoples into emigration and immigration. A theme like *Resistance* is not culturally or racially exclusive. It can take many forms and has had a multitude of historical manifestations. By looking at Spartacus, the Peasants' Revolt, Toussaist L'Ouverture and Gandhi the theme is often handled more safely than by immediately plunging into the bewildering sense of oppression and desire to resist that many of our pupils experience. It also means that there is a broader and more intelligent context in which to discuss those feelings when the classroom relationships have matured enough to handle them constructively. We hope that multiculturalism will become a more fully integrated part of the course just as we hope that the separate disciplines will be brought more effectively together.

Literature in the multicultural syllabus

I would like at this point to talk about the role of literature in a multicultural approach to humanities. The literature does not have to be, and indeed should not always be, tied too closely to the context of the humanities course. Sometimes poetry or story can be used to illustrate or explore imaginatively the subject matter or theme of the rest of the lessons but there also has to be room for the study of literature for its own sake. In both cases there is a rich fund of writing from English-speaking cultures and also in translation. The literary quality alone of an anthology of poetry like *New Ships*[1] or a collection of prose and poems like *The Sun's Eye*[2] justifies its place in the classroom. Such books also serve to widen the children's idea of other cultures as resources for literay and imaginative stimulation. It is also possible to use literature that takes on issues like cultural conflict or cultural plurality. Some books do so in a direct and immediate form like the stories and novels of Faroukh Dhondy, others have a historical setting as in *Sixty Five*,[3] V. S. Reid, or *The Eagle of the Ninth*[4] by Rosemary Sutcliff. Literature often provides a safer and more secure context for pupils to handle difficult and potentially painful ideas.

Because of the team-teaching we are able to be flexible in the way in which literature is taught and this is especially valuable with regard to multicultural literature. Stories like 'An Honest Thief'[5] or 'Ohia and the Thief'[6] are accessible immediately to a whole class of first years. Other stories and poems are best handled first in small groups. This is especially true of literature that demands particular cultural or linguistic knowledge. For example a poem like 'No lickle twang',[7] which is in strong dialect is often most effective when a small group of pupils able to read and discuss the language with little difficulty are introduced to it first. They will then be able to bring it to the whole form, prepared to lead and direct the study of the poem. These children then, quite naturally, take on a role of linguistic and cultural authority that usually belongs to the teacher. Thus the linguistic and cultural richness that exists in the multicultural classroom is acknowledged.

One of the things we have found is that the resources available for multicultural education are excellent. Books, packs, tapes and videos are available and, in most cases, are thoughtful and well prepared. Publishers like Harrap and Longman have produced first class material on Africa, Asia and the Caribbean. By broadening the cultural range of our material we have radically improved the educational quality of our resources.

Assessment of the syllabus

The limitations of what we have achieved are a source of anxiety to us. Multiculturalism needs to be flexible enough to respond to the full range of culture in a school and beyond that in society in large. As yet, despite our efforts, our main response has undoubtedly been to the Caribbean, West Africa and Asia, in that order of effectiveness. Staff education needs to be continued and this places a very heavy demand on new teachers even though we do take into account candidates' attitudes and strengths with regard to multicultural education when making appointments. It is also true that multicultural education has not eliminated racism. Boys, both black and white, who have studied the glories of African culture and the depth of the Afro-Caribbean connection are still liable to use the word 'African' as an insult.

The achievements though, are real. The course and the resources are richer and more varied than ever before. Humanities has been part of a process in the school which has led to multicultural education becoming institutionalised in courses and examinations up to and including A level. The teachers involved in teaching the course number over twenty, and include the head, sixth form head and seven heads of departments. This has helped establish the issue of multiculturalism at the centre of curriculum and pastoral discussions throughout the school. The climate has changed and the onus is now on those who ignore multicultural education rather than on those who include it, to justify their actions.

Finally, while we have not eliminated racism (nor could we have expected to have done) we have created a more meaningful and intelligent context in which it can be discussed. The knowledge and ideas which pupils have access to in humanities provide a framework in which they can explore issues like personal and cultural identify. They also help provide ammunition for those who wish to fight racism and remove some of the foundations from under the structure of lies and myths on which racist attitudes flourish. If it is true that children do not simply take on board the values and beliefs of parents and adult society in general but attempt to assess and personalise them, then multicultural education must be able to play a role in making this mediation more informed and effective.

References
1 *New Ships*, OUP, 1971
2 *The Sun's Eye*, Longman, 1968
3 Reid, V.S., *Sixty Five*, Longman Caribbean, 1975
4 Sutcliff, R., *The Eagle of the Ninth*, OUP, 1962
5 Callendar, Timothy, 'An Honest Thief', (in *The Sun's Eye*)
6 'Ohia and the Thief' (in *Legends from West Africa*, Ginn, 1974)
7 Bennet, Louise, 'No lickle twang', (in *New Ships*)

Chapter 9

WORLD HISTORY AT TULSE HILL SCHOOL

Nigel File and Donald Hinds

> Tulse Hill is a boys' comprehensive school with a roll of 1000. Its wide catchment area includes Norwood, Streatham, Clapham and Brixton.
>
> Nigel File is Head of History at Tulse Hill School. His other publications include *Black Settlers in Britain, 1555–1958* (written with Chris Power), Heinemann 1981 and *Assessment in a Multicultural Society: History at 16+*, Longman, 1983 (for Schools Council).
>
> Donald Hinds is Deputy Head of History at Tulse Hill School. A past secretary of the Caribbean Writer's Association, he has contributed articles to the *West Indian Gazette*, *Flamingo*, *Joffa Magazine*, the *Observer* and the *Guardian*. He is on the editorial committee of the journal *Oral History* to which he has also contributed articles. His book *Journey to an Illusion*, Heinemann, 1966 is an account of the West Indian experience in Britain.

Whose history is it anyway?

In the early 1970s during a session at the Moonshot Youth Club, Deptford, a young black woman spoke bitterly about her experiences while attending school in London. She had been told that black people had no history! She naturally grew to hate the subject. To her, it was bad enough belonging to a people without a past, without being obliged to study other people's history. If her son is now at Tulse Hill, her experience will not be visited on him, for we teach that history is everybody's past. This, however, is easier said than done.

History as traditionally taught is elitist, sexist, Eurocentric and racist. One can swing through 300 years of history via Drake, Raleigh, Cromwell, Marlborough, Wolfe, Nelson and Wellington with only passing references to women, non-European peoples and countries. Queen Elizabeth I, perhaps the most often-mentioned woman in British history of the last 400 years, usually denotes a period or else is frivolously mentioned for her virtue (*sic*) or her vanity. Queen Boadicea of the Iceni is a shadowy figure from the twilight zone of myths and legends. There are more than 20 000 statues (in France alone) of Joan of Arc, but she tends to be regarded as an exceptional woman in a man's world.

If history is to be multicultural, certain questions must be asked. The fundamental question is 'What is history?' We must accept that it is much more than courtly intrigues and bloody wars. It cannot be simply the careers of leaders, kings and presidents. If history is 'social change through time' as the social historian Professor Arthur Marwick would have it, then everybody is involved. George Lamming's dictum about the writer and language, 'that they are all contributing as craftsmen to the still unfinished edifice of the language', can be adapted to suit our purposes. All of us are engaged as craftspeople on this vast edifice of world history. Perhaps not all the pupils in 2 Turner had an ancestor at the Battle of Hastings, but that was because they were otherwise engaged, perhaps in the Valley of the Indus or the Niger, or the Yangtze. One of the most fascinating facets of history is the knowledge that at any given time one's own ancestors were present. The challenge, no less fascinating, is to unlock the doors of the past and learn what they were doing. Such personalised history has given us *Roots*, and though few people will be sufficiently motivated to investigate their past as Alex Haley did, the awareness that one's ancestors were there instils in us a feeling of belonging.

Surely the most irritating question is 'Why should I do history? Will it get me a job?' The question arises because of the distance between the subject and the pupil. Take the Second World War, for example. It can be taught as the climax to the careers of Churchill, Roosevelt and Stalin, interestingly supported with films and slides. However, to the middle ability range pupils from a working class background, VE Day is a very long time ago. But what were their grandparents doing on that day? What can other members of their families tell them about their experience of the war? Oral history can play a significant part in the teaching of the subject at secondary level.

At Tulse Hill we have had two members of staff leading discussions on the Second World War with examination groups. One, now retired, was a Second World War pilot who was shot down over the jungles of Burma, and the other was just old enough to remember being evacuated from blitz-torn London. Oral history has its pitfalls. It should not be used merely to keep the lower ability pupils interested, or regarded as the poor relation of the written text based on official publications and war diaries of senior officers. But used as a means of examining history 'from the bottom up' – it is an immensely valuable teaching method.

If history is approached in this way the subject should shed its masculine and racist overtones. But be warned, history with a multicultural content brings with it other problems. Not least among them is language.

In the autumn of 1969, the West Indian Student Union invited Donald Hinds to be one of a quartet of speakers in a discussion of the position of West Indians in the United Kingdom. On the night, the Chair introduced the subject and the speakers to the audience which was made up mainly of West Indian students. When Donald spoke he was attacked by one of his fellow guest speakers for using the definition 'West Indian'. It was after all a mistake made by the colonialists. How could Columbus have sailed in a westerly direction reaching the Western Islands without first reaching the Eastern Islands and the Sub-continent itself? The person objecting claimed that by using the term West Indies and West Indian, Donald was submitting to European domination and colonialism. When the speaker went on to speak about *Trinidad, Dominica, St Vincent* and *Grenada*, no one pointed out that not only were most of the names of the Caribbean outrageously European, but that they were as Catholic as Ferdinand and Isabella of Spain. Indeed, there is scarcely any area of the world where Europe has stamped its image so heavily as it has in that archipelago from 10 degrees north to the Tropic of Cancer and Longitude 60 to 95 West. That encompasses the Caribbean, but would the Arawaks or the Caribs have called it by that name? The more fastidious one gets, the more difficult it gets to teach the new materials about the Caribbean, the Incas and North American Indians. Did I say American Indians? We have already said that Columbus did not reach India. As for America – Amerigo Vespucci lived from 1451 to 1512 and was honoured for guessing that the mainland behind the islands Columbus had claimed for Spain was big enough to be a continent, but he did not think there might have been two continents. So what do we call the land where the Mayas and the Aztecs built their temples, the land where the Crees, the Herons and the Seminoles lived, fought and died?

There were people on the further shores of the Atlantic before October 1492, the dawn of the Columbian Age. Once the term pre-Columbian is used, Europe again assumes the centre of the stage. There was history being made before the arrival of Columbus; but that is not as easily accessible as that of Renaissance Europe. The inaccessibility is increased by language. Carib and Arawak oral tradition came up against Renaissance Europe and was judged and dismissed as inferior to the Europeans' seemingly insatiable appetite for writing, painting and inventing and generally recording things. So for over 400 years the wholesale destruction of what was indigenous was to take place until a new world was to rise in the image of the old.

Another term which raises hackles, is the verb 'to discover'. Did Columbus discover the West Indies? If some bookish pupil should reply 'No, it was Roderigo do Triana, the lookout who shouted 'Land oh! For Captain Columbus was asleep below' then s/he deserves a commendation, but that is all. The reply one would get at an ethnic meeting, like that one in 1969, would be a firm 'we were not lost'. So when do you discover a people? Is it when you have the power to dominate, to change customs? If that is so the West Indies were discovered, but not so India, China and Africa whose people did not experience destruction as the Caribs and the Arawaks. In Africa, China and India at least their people survived colonialism and in the age of nationalism generated a renaissance.

We are still some way from teaching history from the bottom up. The concept of all people contributing to history – all groups, men and women, rich and poor – is a sound one. It is difficult because for centuries we have been going in the wrong direction. There is a lot of work to be done. The history of the area which supplies our pupils must be exploited. Residents with knowledge of the locality must be encouraged to share it. Pupils must be urged to see the First World War propaganda poster, 'What did you do in the war,

Daddy?' as something more – a lever to prise open the memory to older relations, neighbours and friends. Pupils and teachers working together could add a new dimension to the multicultural curriculum, not only from the bottom up, but sideways as well.

Developing a multicultural syllabus at Tulse Hill

In the light of all this, we became aware that, at Tulse Hill, the syllabus needed fairly drastic revision. Specific criticisms of the history syllabus had been made at the Eastbourne Conference of 1973. This was one of the first whole-school conferences supported by the ILEA. It looked at the school and its relationship with the community, and parents, senior students and members of the community were well-represented, as well as Inspectors and other local authority workers. It was alleged that the history syllabus did not cater for the interests of black pupils and that it did not provide enough working class history. So the department decided to review the syllabus and teaching materials.

The most pressing need seemed to be the infusion of world history into the syllabus, as British social and economic history was already well-resourced. Individual members of staff were already experimenting with different materials – e.g. work on the West Indies and slavery, on Great Zimbabwe and a CSE project on black soldiers in the First World War. But a more defined structure was needed. People were aware of their own ignorance – most of us had studied only British and European history. The course was necessary as a counterweight to challenge the widespread misapprehensions held about virtually every other part of the world.

We decided to present a view of seven different parts of the world – Europe, Africa, India, China, North America, South America and the Caribbean – as they existed around 1400 AD. This timespan saw mature African Kingdoms, the rising Mughals, the Ming Dynasty and the Inca Empire. It was also the last time that those areas would remain unaffected by the age of European Encounter.

Little resource material was then available so we undertook to research and write our own. Some of the ILEA's World History Project materials were used, including their ETV programmes; the Inspectorate gave help, as did the Warden of the History and Social Science Teachers' Centre and the School of Oriental and African Studies extramural department. The School media resources officer was very keen to be involved with the imaginative production of the learning materials which took the form of information booklets incorporating original source material and original line drawings wherever possible. The booklets also had study tasks which were designed for mixed-ability use. It became clear that the content would have to be circumscribed because of limited time available (currently two 45 minute periods in the second and third years) and a series of concepts to teach around emerged. We aim to get pupils to understand something of the social organisation of the societies, rulers and ruled, justice and what passed for crime; economic organisation, food and trade; the influence of religious thought; and the beauty and magnificence of material objects within the culture. The unit on Africa makes reference to the West African kingdom, the Ethiopian Empire, Great Zimbabwe, the Trans-Saharan and East Coast trading networks and Islam. In India we examine both the Moslem Mughal Empire and the Hindu Vijayanagar Empire. China involves the Sung and Ming Dynasties, South America the Inca Empire, Europe is focused mainly on Britain, the Caribbean on Arawak and Carib histories and North America on the Pueblo and the Kwakiukutl peoples. Film and video material for this remains woefully scanty.

That was the easy part. The problem of accounting for the changes that took place between AD 1400 and 1900 both in terms of syllabus and pedagogy remains very difficult. From the outset we were agreed that we wished to get away from a Eurocentric view of the 'voyages of discovery' and the 'carve up of Africa'. Insofar as European expansion was concerned, the impact on the 'objects' was as important as the doings of the 'subjects' and whilst we wanted students to understand the full impact of European colonisation we did not want to create new myths or a simplistic oppressed/oppressor category. This led us to view *contact of peoples* through a series of analytic concepts. This provided a satisfactory historical explanation and also a useful way of teaching. These ideas were worked out at a series of department working weekends at the school's residential centre.

The concepts for the contact themes were as follows.

Co-operation Where contact is on friendly terms with mutual respect, as in the case of early Portuguese and West Africa. The results were mutually beneficial.

Exploitation In Eurocentric histories this is often avoided and in liberationist mythology the uneven relationship where there is an unfair exchange of a country's resources or labour with the use of superior force is stressed to the exclusion of all else. Exploitation is the hallmark of much European contact between 1400 and 1900 (and beyond) and it is important to understand the plight of the people contacted, to see that it is not totally the prerogative of European peoples and to see which Europeans benefited.

Rejection European domination, though overwhelming, was not total. The Ethiopians and the Maoris were able to reject the Europeans. The Japanese rejected both Chinese and European imperialism.

Settlement This phenomenon, also taken up as an important part of British history, is here related to all voluntary movements which involve groups putting down new roots – the British in America and the Caribbean, Afro-Caribbean peoples in Britain, Asian peoples in the East and Africa – the list is endless.

Mission The element of contact coming from religious motives in the worlds of Christianity and Islam.

Forced movement This is used to cover all peoples who were moved against their will, including, in economic reality, indentured 'servants' and transported criminals, as well as the overwhelming category of victims of the Atlantic slave trade.

Refuge People who have moved to avoid persecution, Europeans to America, runaways from slavery.

Resistance Unsuccessful but significant attempts at rejection, the many African wars of resistance, the North American Indians and slave revolts are obvious but also resistance at the cultural level, particularly on the slave plantations.

The vastness of this project led us initially to produce many resources and let pupils plot a path through some of them on the basis of area or concept and time-span. This required both excellent classroom management and enterprising groups of pupils. Present practice is to study an area as it was in 1400, then to select appropriate themes through which some of the changes that have taken place up to the twentieth century can be traced. For the Caribbean this would typically include (in the time available) the peopling of the West Indies, settlement, forced movement, mission, and exploitation; slavery, exploitation, resistance and refuge, and the Haitian Revolution, rejection. Finally, two or three lessons are devoted to an aspect of that area in the twentieth century so that some link between the history and the present is made.

The final section is a term's work on industrialisation. This treads the familiar path focusing on Britain but it tries to link industrialisation with imperialism in terms of investment and markets.

Curriculum change has also taken place within the disciplines of geography and religious studies so that a world view is built up geographically and aspects of culture and religion are approached through world religions. A first year humanities course, which integrates English, geography and history, was also revised. The important history input posits the question 'Who are the British?' and examines the settlement and contribution of various groups to British society. The first year course looks at population movements involving the Celts, Romans and Anglo-Saxons. This is continued in the second year with a similar examination of the Vikings, Normans, Jews, Afro-Caribbeans and Huguenots. The list is not complete and good material is still being sought on the Irish, Asians and other Europeans. Key concepts include what makes identity, cultural contributions and material survivals. Part of this has been developed into *Black Settlers in Britain, 1555–1958* by Nigel File and Chris Power.

For the examination classes it was felt that twentieth century history was relevant in absolute terms and also because of the wealth of primary sources, especially audio-visual. A particularly multicultural view informs parts of the course. The two world wars are looked at globally so that non-European theatres are included and the contribution of colonial peoples to the British war effort is given proper credit. Studies of fascism include the domestic variety of Mosleyism and its anti-semitism, and resistance to it. The post-war settlement of colonial peoples in Britain and the consequences of living in a racist society can be studied. A special feature of the course is the opportunity to do coursework for both CSE and O level and, as part of this, to make a personal study about a topic which the student thinks is of relevance to him or which could be termed 'my history', though not necessarily family history. In order to achieve the flexibility that coursework gives we have had to choose an O level syllabus, JMB's 'Britain and the World', which does not contain reference to the Caribbean, Africa or India in any detail. Study of black history of the United States is possible.

There are a number of problems which are yet to be resolved. Brevity in the world history course is the most obvious. We still think it necessary as a matter of policy to give institutional parity of esteem to the major world areas. There might be a time in the future when a less racist society will make this less necessary. In a mostly white school introducing a multicultural syllabus, a more representative approach could be taken. Also our approach is rather mechanistic as one society unrolls after another. If we were starting again it might be possible to design a course which is much more conceptually based and chooses its examples from the fund of world history. Another problem is that of levels of abstractness. Although we deal with real people, the approach lends itself to general characterisations, even if supported with concrete examples taken from primary sources. The problem of non-written sources has also been referred to. Compared to British history the number of textbooks and similar books is fair for most parts of the world except India, but slides, films and video, which can bring concreteness and liveliness to history, have yet to be produced. The BBC, for instance, makes good programmes encouraging teachers to adopt a multicultural approach but produces very little for Schools TV.

From what has been written, we hope the reader has got some idea that our approach to multiculturalism is not steel drums and saris but attempts to get pupils to engage with weighty and difficult concepts and issues. We have not underlined that is is anti-racist; we hope that aware people will see the potential in our work. We do think that students should have opportunities to study what they see as part of the history of their culture in a culturally plural Britain. We also think that stereotypes and erroneous views of Britain and the World mislead white and black pupils in our schools and that the power knowledge has should be used to open up alternative views which our pupils may be able to make use of.

Chapter 10

DEVELOPING A MULTICULTURAL SCIENCE CURRICULUM

Jenni Newnham and Sue Watts

> Catford County School is a girls' comprehensive school with 900 on the roll. It has a balanced intake from Lewisham which fully reflects the borough's multicultural population. The school is organised on a mixed ability basis; English, maths and science are compulsory curriculum elements for five years. Class sizes are favourable – science groups rarely contain more than twenty-three pupils.
>
> Jenni Newnham is Head of Science at Catford County School. Sue Watts is an advisory teacher from the Secondary Curriculum Development Unit working for the ILEA Multi-ethnic Inspectorate.

This account attempts to describe the work we have been engaged in at Catford County School in developing a lower school science curriculum for a multicultural society. We have not ignored issues relating to other areas of the work of the department but have chosen to concentrate our efforts on the first and second year science curriculum.

When we started working together in September 1980 the department was using a new lower school syllabus developed by Jenni Newnham after consultation with the other members of the department. Sue Watts worked with science teachers in the classroom, looking at the curriculum in action. We made tape recordings of children working together in science lessons and listened to the tapes, making transcripts of some sections. Some interviews between Sue and small groups of first and second year pupils were recorded. We gradually learned a great deal ourselves about what the children were doing in science lessons, how they felt about science and how we might be able to assist them to learn more effectively. Most of our pupils believe that science as done by 'scientists' means discovering new things all the time and that science produces answers that are always 'right'. They also had many suggestions to make regarding their own learning. These included more opportunities to read about what they are doing.

We began our development of the lower school science course with these aims.

1 To give a wider social perspective to the work, particularly a multi-ethnic one.
2 To include more reading.
3 To update the view of technology we give in our applications of science.
4 To show science as an activity carried out by people everywhere.
5 To attempt to correct the view of science as pure research.

6 To show how science and technology change the world we live in.
7 To show how we make use of technology.

The curriculum

The most useful resource in our work has been the units from the *Third World Science Project*.[1] These were received as we began considering where to begin with our development of the curriculum.

1 Fermentation and distillation

Drawing extensively on material from two of the *Third World Science* units, 'Fermentation' and 'Distillation', we wrote a topic reader for second year pupils to use with a section of work on microbes. The booklet contained the following topics:

General information on wine and beer making
Description of brewing 'Pito' in Northern Ghana
The distillation of 'Enguli' in Uganda
Extracts from writing by pupils in Zambia about the production of a drink called 'Kanchine'
The use of alcohol from sugar cane as a fuel to replace petrol in Brazil
Questions were included at the end of each section.

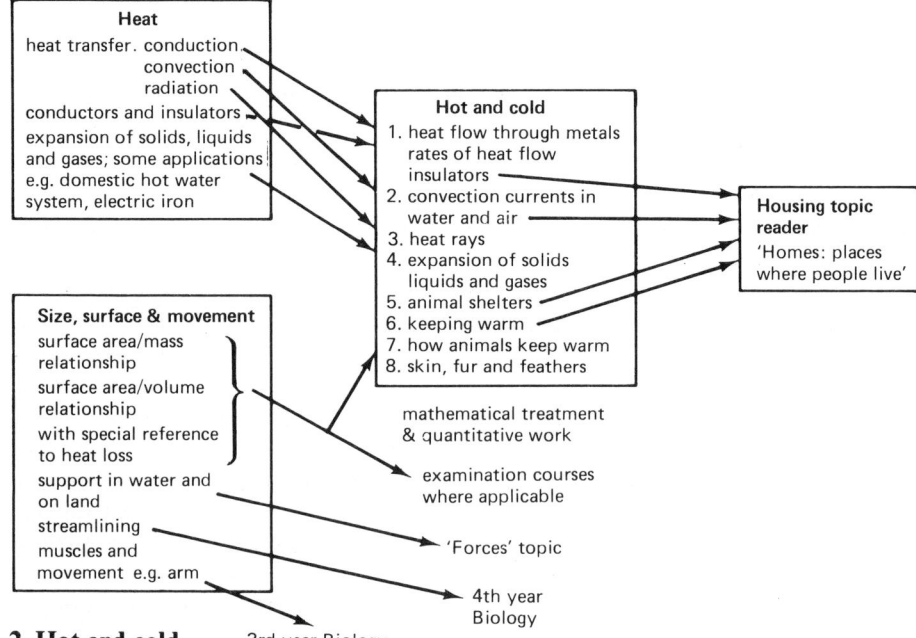

2 Hot and cold

We next looked at two of the topics which were covered in the second year syllabus and which we had found to be unsatisfactory. Figure 1 illustrates how we went about changing 'Heat' and 'Size, Surface and Movement' to form a new topic – 'Hot and Cold'. Some of the ideas and concepts were moved to other lower school sections or were felt to be more suitable elsewhere in science courses. However, the fundamental difference was the inclusion of the topic reader – 'Homes – Places where people live'. We have called it a topic reader as we see the materials it contains not as peripheral, background matter but as an integral part of the course.

In the introduction we develop the idea that all people need some means of shelter regardless of where they live. However, the form that this takes will depend on a variety of factors including climate, materials available, cost and convenience and the life styles of the people. We then have four case studies which we chose to illustrate all the factors mentioned. We try to emphasise the concepts which link with the practical work involved in the topic like insulation, conduction of heat and convection currents. The first two case studies are taken from a *Third World Science* unit called 'Housing'. The first contains materials written by third year pupils in Zambia about different types of housing. The second is an edited version of an account of an intermediate technology township in Ghana which we have called 'A New Town in Ghana'. This account should prove interesting as it counteracts stereotypes of all people in Africa living in mud huts or jungles. The third case study is written by relations of one of the teachers in the department about their timber house in Canada. We decided to call the fourth section 'Living in South London' and plan to include some accounts written by our pupils in this section. However, until the materials have been used for the first time, these are not available. We therefore wrote about our own homes emphasising the links with ideas of energy or heat conversion, materials etc. This booklet, like the first we wrote, also contains questions and ends with the suggestion that pupils should write about their own homes. In this way we hope to be able to produce a second edition of the reader with contributions from our pupils.

3 Salt

The next area we decided to develop comes in the first term of the first year. We considered what we could use and develop from the *Third World Science* unit 'Salt'. We tried to get salt from plant materials, using banana skins and grass, and we had an entertaining session heating the materials strongly to make ash (making the whole science corridor smell rather unpleasant), mixing the ashes with warm water, filtering and evaporating the filtrate. We did end up with something which contained salt so we were able to write a worksheet for practical activities for our next group of first years. We have now written another topic reader, this time called 'Salt'. It deals with salt in our diet; where people get their salt from; salt from underground; salt from the sea; salt from swamps; salt from plants; uses of salt and salt and health. One of our major sources of information was the *Third World Science* unit 'Salt'.

4 Shops

In our most recent piece of work we have moved away from the pattern of writing booklets. We wanted to develop some resources about the uses of plants to go with practical work about seeds, plants and plant growth. After much discussion we came to the idea of constructing four 'shops':

A DIY shop
A grocery shop
A sweetshop and newsagent
A fruit and vegetable shop

Each 'shop' is a display of pictures, photographs and information about items to be found there which are plants or directly derived from plant materials. With the 'shops' we have a booklet of information and questions. This is used to raise a number of issues. These are just a few examples:

1 Where does the timber we use come from? Very little comes from Britain. Many of the hardwood doors, window frames etc. to be found in DIY shops are of wood from West Africa and South America. Hardwoods take a long time to grow. We try to get over the idea of the destruction of forests and some of the effects that this has.

2 People in other parts of the world grow plant materials to sell to us rather than growing food for themselves. We introduce the idea of cash crops like tea and coffee.

3 We also introduce a number of health education issues. These arise because we include tobacco and sugar as things which come from plants. Also we consider the importance of fibre in our diet which, of course, we get from plants.

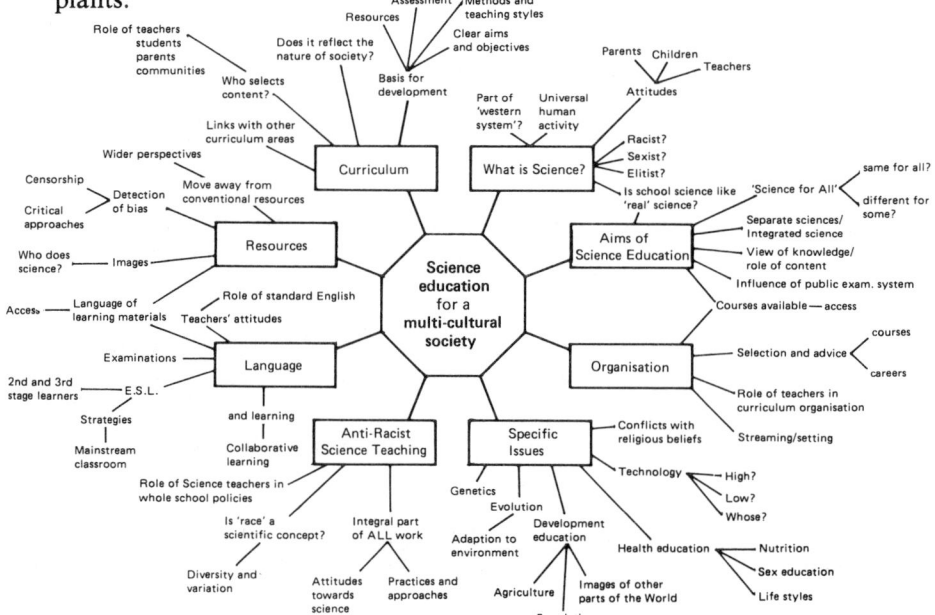

It is not possible in this type of account to give an analysis of all the issues which need to be considered in discussing science education for a multicultural society. Figure 2 gives a diagrammatic representation of what many of these issues are. It will be obvious that the work we have done so far has not considered anywhere near all of these issues. This is because we have chosen to describe our work on the first and second year curriculum. This should be seen as part of a continuing process of curriculum evaluation and development in which we try to give wider perspectives to all our work – we do not see multicultural education as a separate study. A list of some discussion starters for a science department in considering education for a multicultural society is given in the appendix to this section.

Another teacher from the department attended a course run by the Secondary Curriculum Development Unit earlier in the year. The teachers present wrote a report for ILEA *Science News*. We would like to quote from that report:

> Part of the course raised issues concerned with institutional and unintentional racism. As with any other activity in society it was found that the science curriculum was culturally biased towards a European/North American viewpoint (ignoring, for example, the contributions, both current and historical, of Arabs, African, Chinese and Indian science).
>
> Some time was then spent on discussion of teaching practices sensitive to these issues and to the development of resources for teachers and pupils. As teachers we cannot ignore outside influences upon the attitude, motivation and self-image of our pupils. Rarely are representatives of ethnic minorities shown or perceived to be in positions of power or authority.
>
> The oft heard and expressed phrase 'I am not a racist, all children are the same to me,' is a good example of unintentional racism. This sentiment completely ignores the multiplicity of values, backgrounds and experiences of our pupils. Not to recognise this diversity is to deny the value of their heritage. This in turn leads to negative feelings towards peoples from certain ethnic groups.
>
> Some people argue that in schools with few or no ethnic minorities, multi-ethnic education is irrelevant. We would answer this by pointing out Britain is a multicultural society and that children from these schools are part of it.[2]

We have plans for extending our work in the future. We hope to set up links with science departments in two neighbouring schools where Sue has also done some work.

In addition we have become sensitive to the way we consider books for use in the classroom. We have found a number of old and extremely biased books in the science department but we were also pleased to find a new series which served our purposes in many respects. This series is *Reading About Science*.[3] It is attractively produced, contains reading sections about most lower school science topics and also has illustrations of people which counteract sexist stereotypes and include people from a variety of ethnic backgrounds. We have found these very useful in providing reading and extension work to go with our syllabus and materials development.

References

1 *Third World Science*. Prepared by a team at the School of Education, University College of North Wales, Bangor. Director: Professor Iolo Wyn Williams. Available from Centre for World Development Education, 128 Buckingham Palace Road, London SW1W 9SH.
2 'Science Education for a Multi-Cultural Society', *ILEA Science News*, March 1983.
3 *Reading About Science*, Heinemann Educational, 1982.

Appendix: Science education in and for a multicultural society

Some questions and discussion starters for science teachers to consider.

1 What is science? Is it part of 'Western culture' only or a universal human activity?
2 Is science in school like 'real science' as done by scientists?
3 If we concentrate on the processes of science, what is the role of content?
4 What science courses are available in the school? Are different courses designed for some groups of pupils? Why?

Anti-racist teaching
1 Do science teachers have a role to play in anti-racist teaching?
2 How do science teachers fit in with whole school policies?
3 Is 'race' a scientific classification?
4 What should we teach about race and related issues in science courses?

Some issues for science teachers
1 What is taught about genetics and evolution? Have you considered that many approaches to these topics in textbooks and teaching materials are from a white perspective?
2 Are all science teachers in the school aware of possible areas of conflict between the religious beliefs of their pupils and the content of their science lessons? How are these handled?
3 How are areas of health education considered? For example, is a sufficiently wide range of foods used to illustrate nutritional principles?
4 How is sex education approached? Are the parents consulted?

Resources
1 Are teaching and learning materials assessed for bias?
2 What images are presented in the resources used (a) Who does science? (b) What are other parts of the world like?
3 Have you considered non-science and unconventional science resources to support wider perspectives to your work?

Chapter 11

MULTICULTURAL MATHEMATICS

David Gilbert

> Sydenham School is a girls' comprehensive with a roll of 1750. It has a multi-ethnic intake from the area around Lewisham. The teaching is organised on a setting basis.
>
> David Gilbert, formerly Maths Teacher at Sydenham, is now in charge of Computer Studies at Battersea County School.

Mathematics has traditionally been perceived in schools as a subject isolated from the major portion of the curriculum. Linked to the sciences via calculation and manipulation of formulae, its connections with other subject areas are often regarded as tenuous. At best, other subjects, for instance the social sciences, use mathematics as a statistical tool of analysis.

For many years the subject was taught in a very traditional manner in British schools. It had intrinsic appeal to a minority of pupils, while for the majority it consisted of the dutiful learning and application of routines. In recent years attempts have been made to break out of the 'traditional' mould of mathematics teaching in secondary schools, and to include topics which were previously studied exclusively at more advanced levels. This area has been dubbed the 'New Maths', although the ideas which it incorporates were often investigated long before the start of the twentieth century.

As society in the UK has in recent years begun to evolve in an increasingly diverse way both ethnically and culturally, educators in all subject areas have started to recognise a need to reflect this in the curriculum. Those engaged in the teaching of English, the arts and the social sciences have on the whole found the task easier than have teachers of science and mathematics. This has been because these latter subjects, especially mathematics, have been seen as neutral and only concerned with 'impartial truth'. This attitude can lead to the exclusion of mathematics from the attempt to make the curriculum more ethnically and culturally diverse. The tendency is to assume that maths, being a neutral subject, does not need to be multi-ethnic. Pupils may absorb this attitude from teachers and come to regard mathematics as a subject set apart from the real world in which they themselves are involved.

One of the first things that struck me as I began to teach maths was the way that pupils perceived its relevance or, more often, irrelevance to their needs. Often the 'useful tool' aspect of maths is stressed by both employers and teachers. This can be broken into two parts. First of all there is the concept that an ability with maths is in fact a necessary skill that members of our society need in order to survive and cope with their lives. Secondly maths is seen as a 'testing ground', and a facility for the subject on the part of an individual is often taken as a more generalised mental capability for logical reasoning.

Pupils often perceive the subject's usefulness in terms of the numerical manipulations which they will encounter outside school, mainly to do with money. In this respect, the ability to use a calculator for manipulations involving the 'four rules' is perhaps the most highly prized skill to be acquired. Perhaps it is natural that many pupils see the employers' view that skills in mathematics indicate a logical and able mind as far less relevant to themselves.

Furthermore, maths often does not find an integrated place within the school curriculum – it can be taught in isolation from other subjects, even the sciences. As the rest of the school curriculum becomes more orientated towards studying society and reflecting its changes, maths may become even more separate from the mainstream curriculum. Maths teachers must avoid the pitfall of developing an isolationist attitude.

It was with these thoughts in mind that I decided to look at the possibility of expanding the Maths curriculum to include some multicultural input, and at the same time to investigate inter-subject links within the school curriculum. Broadly speaking the topics that I and other teachers have been investigating are the following.

1 The use of multicultural illustrative material in examples, topics and projects.
2 Cross-cultural approaches, such as comparing number systems.
3 Mathematics connected with the art and religion of different societies.
4 An historical approach tracing the development of mathematical thought throughout the ages.

These areas allow the possibility of linking Maths to the other subjects in the school curriculum in a wide variety of ways. Perhaps one of the most comprehensive approaches has been that developed by the maths department of Saint Veronica's school in Peckham. The teachers in this school used the idea of multicultural topic materials based on India in order to broaden the base of their syllabus.

My own work has concentrated on the study of number systems among different peoples, using this to illustrate the concept of bases to pupils. This involves some aspects of historical and sociological study which help to make this topic more realistic and meaningful to the pupils. As an example of a people who used a different number system from that developed by the Hindus which the West has adopted, I chose to look at the Maya of Central America.

The Maya and their counting system

Historical background
The Maya are an indigenous Central American people who live today in an

area which is contained by Belize, El Salvador, Guatemala, Honduras and Mexico. They are descended from people who crossed the Bering Straits from Asia over 25 000 years ago in search of game animals for food. Hence they are related to the other members of Amerindian peoples who stretch from Alaska to Tierra del Fuego.

As the supply of big game animals began to dwindle about 10 000 years ago, seed planting and small game hunting replaced the hunting of big game as a method of survival. Following this, farming developed from seed gathering so that by 3400 years ago cultivation based on maize, beans and squash was firmly established in Central America. The Amerindians were great pioneers of agriculture, and the maize plant as we know it today was developed in the region of what is now Mexico. Farming tools included the wooden digging stick, the stone axe and fire which was used to clear ground for planting. Houses were constructed of wattle, daub and thatch, and the people made simple pottery.

Shifting slash and burn agriculture, still practised today, was refined into a two-field system which allowed the development of permanent residences and kitchen gardens on the valley floor whilst slash and burn was used on the hillsides. The clusters of houses which were established in the more fertile spots developed into villages and communities; as the society began to coalesce, religious ideas also took form, often centring around the cultivation of maize and its preparation as food.

Approximately 3000 years ago food surpluses increased and became more dependable, due perhaps to an increase in the variety and types of food available. This meant that the population could support some individuals who used the surpluses for purposes other than subsistence. Thus it became possible for a priest class to develop whose activities were supported by the labours of the peasantry. With the passage of time, the priest class became hierarchical in form itself and grew to wield great power in the society.

Diverse architectural styles developed in Central America and, associated with them, a distinctive art emerged. The running of such a complex society which was heavily dependent on its agricultural base required accurate and detailed astronomical observations, especially since the religion was closely connected with the planting cycle.

The precise astronomical data required by the religion was gathered at elaborate religious/ceremonial centres which were often astronomical observatories as well. They were usually examples of sophisticated sculpture and architecture whose magnificence is deeply impressive even today. The Maya developed a very precisely worked-out number system, working with place values in base 20 and a sub-base 5. In order to make the system work they invented and regularly used a symbol for zero, the first people in the world recorded as having done so. This facility with numbers gave them a powerful tool which formed a base for their calendrical system whose complexity and accuracy surpass those of the Gregorian system used in Europe.

The Maya also invented a writing system based on hieroglyphics and produced many books on a wide variety of topics. These books were written on bark cloth and illustrated with scenes depicting activities in Maya society. They also painted frescoes in their temples and carved scenes on the walls of the buildings. It was common practice to erect a stella near each large building to record who was responsible for its construction and the date. This was calculated from a mythical origin and was displayed in glyph form down the side of the stella.

Maya civilisation began to decline approximately 1200 years ago due to a complex interaction of factors which are not yet fully understood. The first European expeditions into the area, initiated by Cortez in AD 1525, encountered a civilisation which was collapsing. The Spanish hastened this where the Maya class structure was still intact, as in the Peten region of present day Guatemala. Having destroyed the authority and power base of both the priests and aristocracy, the scattered peasantry then came under European domination.

The Spanish pursued their policy of subjugation by force, especially in the Peten and Yucatan, following it up with measures designed to impose social control. The Roman Catholic religion was introduced to the Maya, and their traditional religion was discredited. Maya books were collected and burnt by the Spaniards on account of the religious heresy that they were supposed to contain. As a result of this action the skills needed to write and read the Maya texts were lost. Only three of these books or 'codices' still remain, but most of the text is indecipherable to the modern reader. Similarly many of the glyphs carved into the stone of the ancient Maya buildings are nowadays incomprehensible.

However the Maya system of numeration is fairly well understood as are their time glyphs and calendar, which is still used in a simplified form by some Maya in Guatemala. Temples are even now being discovered in the forests of Central America and the stellae bearing the date glyphs have enabled archaeologists to date the buildings with a fair degree of accuracy.

The Maya numerical system
The Maya represented numbers from 1 to 19 in groups of fives and ones. Zero was portrayed as an empty shell, 1 as one dot, 2 as two dots and so on up to 4, after which 5 was written as a line or bar. Hence 6 was one dot and a line, 7 two dots and a line, up to 10 which was two lines. The system extended logically up to 19 (four dots over three lines).

Maya numerical notation 0–19

0	• — 1	•• — 2	••• — 3	•••• — 4	— 5
	• — — 6	•• — — 7	••• — — 8	•••• — — 9	— — 10
	• — — — 11	•• — — — 12	••• — — — 13	•••• — — — 14	— — — 15
	• — — — — 16	•• — — — — 17	••• — — — — 18	•••• — — — — 19	

After 19, the system changed to a base 20. Hence 20 was represented by one dot in the 20s position and a shell in the units. The Maya had a true place-value system, the columns being of the following values: units, 20s, 400s (20 × 20), 8000s (20 × 20 × 20) and so on.

Maya numerical notation 20–399

20s	•	•	••	••	•••	•••	••••
1s	shell	—	shell	—	shell	—	shell
	20	30	40	50	60	70	80

20s	•••• —	— —	— —	— —	••• — —
1s	—	shell	shell	shell	— —
	90	100	200	300	399

Although their number words below 20 did not reflect the pseudo base 5 system used there, Maya words for multiples of 20 reflect the new base 20. For example the Maya of the Yucatan counted thus:

1 hun	11 buluc
2 ca	12 lah-ca (10 + 2)
3 ox	13 ox-lahun (3 + 10)
4 can	14 can-lahun (4 + 10)
5 ho	15 ho-lahun (5 + 10)
6 uac	16 uac-lahun (6 + 10)
7 uuc	17 uuc-lahun (7 + 10)
8 uaxac	18 uacac-lahun (8 + 10)
9 bolon	19 bolon-lahun (9 + 10)
10 lahun	

Powers of 20 were:

1		hun
20		hun-kal
20^2	(400)	hun-bak
20^3	(8000)	hun-pic
20^4	(160 000)	calab

The system of counting from 20 to 400 shows a subtractive count in base 20 was used in order to achieve numbers such as 30:

30	lahun-cakal	(2 × 20 − 10)
40	ca-ikal	(2 × 20)
50	lahu-y-oxkal	(3 × 20 − 10)
60	oxkal	(3 × 20)
70	lahu-cankal	(4 × 20 − 10)
80	can-kal	(4 × 20)
90	lahu-y-hokal	(5 × 20 − 10)
100	ho-kal	(5 × 20)
120	uac-kal	(6 × 20)
140	uuc-kal	(7 × 20)
200	lahun-kal	(10 × 20)
300	ho-lhu-kal	(15 × 20)

Thus from their numbers both written and in words, it can be seen that the Maya had at one time a complete base 20 number system. This they used in order to help them with their concept of time, for example in constructing their calendar, which was extremely complex. It was composed of two types of year, the sacred year (Tzolkin) of 260 days and the calendar year (Haab) of 365 days. The 260 days of the sacred year were formed by prefixing the numerals 1 to 13 to the 20 Maya day glyphs. This year enmeshed with the calendar year of 365 days, which consisted of 18 months of 20 days each and one month of 5 days. Thus any one day in the year could be referred to by its sacred or everyday calendrical position, the pattern of which being repeated every 18 980 days (52 calendrical years), the former number being the LCM of 260 and 365. The

Maya had a symbol for zero, and made use of it regularly: hence the Maya New Year's Day was written as Zero Pop, Pop being the first month of the year. Days in the month were numbered from zero to 19 as there were 20 days in the month. The final 'filler' month had 5 days numbered from zero to 4.

Base 20 in the Maya time sequence

The Maya used base 20 when counting up their periods of time; however in order to make it more akin to the 365 days of the year, the second column had a value of 18. Hence column values were:

Amount	Name	Value
1	kin	20^0
20 kins	1 uinal = 20 days	20^1
18 uinals	1 tun = 360 days	$18 . 20^1$
20 tuns	1 katun = 7200 days	$18 . 20^2$
20 katuns	1 baktun = 144 000 days	$18 . 20^3$
20 baktuns	1 pictun = 2 800 000 days	$18 . 20^4$
20 pictuns	1 calabtun = 57 600 000 days	$18 . 20^5$
20 calabtuns	1 kinchiltun = 1 152 000 000 days	$18 . 20^6$
20 kinchiltuns	1 alautun = 23 040 000 000 days	$18 . 20^7$

The Maya had glyphs for each of these time periods and hence could depict large chunks of time very efficiently. This helped them to portray dates which were calculated from a mythical origin, about 5000 years ago. Stone stellae were carved with a series of glyphs which represented a date and had the following information:
1. The numbering of days in baktuns, katuns, tuns, uinals, and kins from the starting point of Maya chronology.
2. The Tzolkin designation of the terminal date.
3. The name of the god who was the patron of the nine-day series.
4. Information about the phase of the moon on the date recorded.
5. The length of the lunar month in which the date fell.
6. The number of lunations in the half year series.
7. The date of the civil year calendar.

The Maya recognised that the year is more than 365 days long, and incorporated a calendar correction formula in their inscriptions. By this means the Maya showed that they had measured the length of the solar year very accurately, and a comparison with European measurements is as follows:

length of the year according to modern astronomy	365.2422 days
length of Julian Year	365.25 days
length of Gregorian year	365.2425 days
length of year according to Maya astronomy	365.2420 days

Also the Maya developed a means of recording very accurately the length of the lunar month in their dates, as well as recording other astronomical data, for example the cycle of Venus. All this was done using instruments no more complex than a crossed stick. Unfortunately this knowledge was lost when the Europeans invaded the Maya area, burnt their books and destroyed their social system.

Using the Maya numerical system as a teaching topic

In an attempt to make maths more enjoyable for both pupils and teachers, a unit on the Maya numerical system can be introduced into the syllabus. Since number systems were not usually evolved as abstract mental exercises, but in order to perform definite functions, a study of the social context of the society which developed the system is very relevant. Hence any mathematical unit on Maya maths should be designed to be run in conjunction with units in other subject areas, involving a study of the Maya as a people. These areas could be social studies, geography, RE, history, art and so forth. Thus pupils should be given an insight into all aspects of Maya history and culture, extending to a study of present day Central America emphasising political and social changes in that region. An integrated approach should break down the traditional barriers that exist in the school curriculum between mathematics and some of the non-science subjects. In this way, pupils should be made aware that mathematics has played a great part in the social development of human society and that it is a subject with great relevance to everyday life. Equally, one would hope that by the same process, non-science subjects such as the humanities should not be seen as distinct or even opposed to the sciences but rather that each discipline complements the others.

A study of the Maya is suitable for a wide age range if properly presented, from the junior to upper secondary levels. Young children can easily appreciate the number system from zero to 19 using the pseudo-base 5 while at the other end of the age scale the Maya vigisimal system has been used in Open University units. There is certainly enough content in the entire Maya number system to keep Advanced Level students occupied in investigations.

Teaching techniques

One consequence of choosing material which is rarely, if ever, covered in school textbooks is that teaching materials must be produced with both teacher and pupil in mind. These should be attractive to all participants in the learning process so that there is a favourable environment for the acquisition of knowledge. Visual presentation is a very suitable medium, and the topic may be put over either using slides or else OHP transparencies. I have tended to favour the latter when teaching the topic because they are relatively easy to produce, and may be overwritten or else reveal and/or overlay technique used. This medium is especially appropriate when producing materials about the time-glyphs for example, which are much too complex to draw out by hand and may best be made up as an OHP transparency using the photocopier. An added advantage is that handouts and worksheets can be produced by the same means so that pupils may have in front of them the same information that is displayed on the screen. In addition wallcharts, posters and maps may well prove to be a useful aid to the teaching process.

Detailed teaching strategies
It is important when using any unit on Maya maths to introduce the subject fully by placing the Maya people in a geographical and historical context. Hence some time should be taken to explain the location of the areas inhabited by the Maya in Central America, their relationship with present-day nation states, and also to put the area into the general context of the Caribbean. Mention should be made to the pupils when they study the section on Maya history of their treatment during the conquest by Spain in order to explain our present-day inability to read their books and other works. Pupils should easily become familiar with the symbols for numbers below 20, and will find counting in groups of fives easy. They should be encouraged to perform simple addition and subtraction sums involving numbers in this range. Teachers should discourage translation into Hindu-Arabic notation and/or English number words so that pupils work with the Maya symbols only e.g.

• + •• = •••
—   —   —
            —

The bars and dots are added up separately in this addition. When 5 dots are created in the sum then one bar is written instead:

••• + •• = —
—   —   —
          —

Subtraction becomes even more testing for the pupils as 'borrowing' skills will be needed to be exercised:

••• − • = ••
—   —   —
—   —

But:

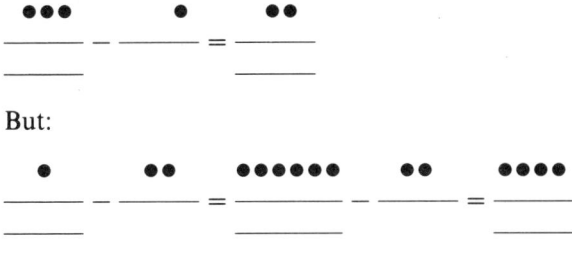

Some time may be needed to reinforce these ideas and if the pupils are experiencing any difficulties the teacher may refer to the analogy of fingers for dots and a fist or closed hand for a line (5).

Progression to base 20

Pupils may readily suggest that 20 is represented by four lines in the Maya counting system. However they should see that a counting system based on 5s would be cumbersome for large numbers. Also, using the analogy of human anatomy, four lines would represent all the digits on one human body and so 20 could be seen as being a new number. At this juncture the teacher needs to put over the concept of place value in a representational number system. I have found that the only really difficult idea for pupils to accept is the fact that the Maya columns run vertically instead of horizontally. Care should be taken to emphasize the difference between numbers less than 20 and those over 20 which have a similar appearance to each other but are not of the same value. Hence for example 6 and 25 may be confused:

```
        1s   •              20s   •
       ─────                 1s   ─────
         6                         25
```

However, if some kind of column labelling is adopted, as in the above example, this confusion should be avoided. Once the concept has been established, addition and subtraction of large numbers may be attempted. As well as adopting a column labelling convention, the teacher should be clear about the representation of the subtraction and equal signs which might be confused with 5 and 10 respectively. I suggest that all the 4 operations signs ($+ - \times \div$) are enclosed in circles and if possible written in a different colour to the number symbols. A word of caution: since it is quite difficult to learn the times tables in a combination of base 5 and base 20, multiplication and division are best avoided.

If pupils become conversant with the numerical notation up to base 20, they might be interested in extending their knowledge of the number system to the number words. This will emphasise the parallels and differences with the European language with which they are most familiar which employs a base 20: i.e. French. 80 in French is 'quatre-vingts', or 4 × 20 and in Maya it is can-kal (4 × 20). 90 in French is 'quatre-vingt-dix', or 4 × 20 + 10, but in Maya it is lahu-y-hokal or 5 × 20 − 10. This emphasises the subtractive system employed in Maya number words. The Maya representation of time using time glyphs is a suitable subject for pupils of all age groups although it will be more comprehensible if they have studied the calendrical system, especially the secular count. Pupils are often fascinated by the ability of the Maya to represent large numbers of days by one glyph. Colouring in copies of stellae is also another popular activity.

Other approaches

I have chosen to make a detailed study of one particular approach to multicultural mathematics as I felt it would be more useful than outlining superficially several different ones. It should be stressed, however, that the Maya material can be taken even farther and that there are a number of quite different approaches that can be taken when teaching mathematics from a multicultural viewpoint.

The study of the Maya system should lead on to an investigation of other languages which use a non-denary base in their counting system. The obvious example to school children is probably French which retains a vestige of a vigisimal count in 80 (quatre vingt = 4×20) and used to count up to at least 300 in twenties (there is a hospital in Paris which is today called Les Quinze-vingts because it was originally founded for 300 patients).

Other languages employ more complete systems in non-denary bases, notably some African languages. The common bases on that continent are denary and vigisimal, and many West African languages use a 20s count. Yoruba and Ibo are among these, and both have a very complex number system. For example, Yoruba has a *subtractive* base system; hence 38 is presented as $(2 \times 20) - 2$. Pupils and teachers may wish to examine this further. One interesting line of investigation is for pupils to bring in to the classroom examples of languages they know in order to examine them for their base-structure.

A completely different approach is to study the way in which different societies use geometrical patterns to cultural and religious ends. One important example is the development by Muslim societies of art forms which are based on the geometry of the circle and which heavily stress tesselation. These designs can be very complex and make a good introduction to the study of regular geometrical shapes as well as circle properties. Classes may try to reproduce these traditional patterns using ruler and compass, or may use computers to simulate them. It is quite easy to reproduce the regular Islamic patterns using a computer language such as Logo which easily produces a graphical output. Many other cultures make use of designs which can be analysed in this way. Such studies can lead to co-operation between departments in schools. Different peoples can be studied – in maths, their use of design and contribution to mathematics – while other aspects are dealt with by the other disciplines.

A third obviously useful approach is to use mathematics to illustrate statistically the multicultural studies being undertaken by other departments. Pie charts, tables, graphs etc. are invaluable in illustrating clearly facts and once again, the maths department can co-operate with others in producing such work.

Chapter 12

PEACE STUDIES: AN ACTIVE APPROACH TO TUTORING

Peter Davies

> Pimlico School is a seven form entry mixed comprehensive with a roll of about 1500. The intake is drawn mainly from the boroughs of Brixton and Lambeth with relatively few students from the immediate neighbourhood. Teaching is organised on a mixed ability basis in the lower school and in many departments thereafter.
>
> Peter Davies, now Head of Icknield Comprehensive School and Community Centre, was formerly Principal Deputy and then Acting Head of Pimlico School. He is a member of the Peace Education Network and serves on the management committee of the Council for Education in World Citizenship (CEWC). He has published articles in the *Times Educational Supplement*, *Forum* and *Peace News* and is preparing a chapter for *The Dove in the Classroom*, to be edited by Richard Keeble for Junction Books.

Good practice in multicultural education has been identified in those schools which have begun to make a critical re-examination of the *whole* curriculum in the context of education for a multi-ethnic society. Such good practice as exists is reflected in the diversification of resources and courses representing a conscious shift from explicit Anglocentricism, and this is to be much applauded.

Unfortunately, the *implicit* chauvinism of the so-called covert curriculum tends all too often to elude such scrutiny. It seems hypocritical for us to think in terms of having made any headway towards multicultural education unless we have begun to attack, in a very practical way, the attitudes which feed prejudice on one hand, and, equally importantly, cultural reticence on the other.

Teachers reading this collection of case studies will not need to be reminded of the diversity of behaviour in school – within the classroom and the playground – which is culture specific. Moreover, even the most casual observation of older school students at work and play reveals this diversity to be a ready source of self-segregation. The problem is not that self-segregation is *ipso facto* a bad thing – indeed most of us would want our children to learn to discriminate *wisely*–but that this form of discrimination and self-segregation is based on ignorance and its constituent anxieties, furthermore, that it results in an unwillingness to communicate with other discrete groups.

Ironically, the withdrawal which this unwillingness to communicate produces is often aided by the basic tools of the modern teacher, the book, the video and worst – the worksheet. Indeed we could do worse than heed Rousseau in respect of this particular problem: 'Distrust those cosmopolitans who search out remote duties in their books and neglect those that lie nearest.'[1] For the child who wants to withdraw into familiar cultural territory (or closer) the worksheet provides the perfect defence by duty. Children clutch at paper, not necessarily to write on or read, but as part of a technique to avoid communication.

The case study which follows is of a programme of tutorial sessions at Pimlico School which rely heavily on the oral conventions, much neglected in British state education. In fact, no books or worksheets are used throughout the eight week period and no one has to write anything at all, though I did ask my group to write an appraisal of the programme at the end.

The activities which constitute the programme aim to explore differences between people in the group and develop mutual trust and respect. The programme relies heavily on co-operative activities which are often centred around some externally imposed problem. In the latter part of the programme, when sufficient group confidence has been developed, the students negotiate with the teacher an important area to investigate in depth. The single criterion was that it had to be about something which affected the lives of all the students in the group in a very personal way. My group chose 'The nuclear debate', though there was considerable interest in 'The politics of unemployment'.

I do not think it necessary to put a name to the programme, but I saw it as Peace Education, not so much because of the final issue, but because of the aims of the initial activities outlined above. I believe the programme made a contribution to multicultural education in a multi-ethnic school; I hope it helped students understand and respect each other in the context of their differences, and I hope it started them thinking about the major threats to global harmony. As I have suggested in the case study, there are, perhaps, more logical directions in which to proceed following the initial activities, and the 'threats to survival' outlined by Ronald Higgins, author of 'The Seventh Enemy',[2] may offer a useful starting point from which to start discussing the second part of the programme. They are: the population explosion; environmental degradation; nuclear abuse; and, science and technology running beyond human control. *Learning for change in World Society*[3] which is referred to again later would offer complementary guidance.

As well as developing a multicultural perspective within the formal curriculum I believe we should scrutinise, as far as we can, the hidden curriculum. We should certainly make a start by spending more time on multicultural tutorial work. To this end I hope these activities are helpful. Unless otherwise stated the accounts refer to one fifty-five minute session once a week. The reader will form her/his own conclusion about the appropriate allocation of time to the pastoral curriculum.

Peace education programme
Session 1
This started with a simple personal encounter activity. The aim was to develop trust by deliberately removing personal defences within the context of a finite group activity. (It is always surprising when using this activity to see how little of each other students know – even though they may have been in the same class for two or three years.)

Resources required
A drum; a large room; stacked chairs sufficient for the group.

The room was first cleared of chairs and the students were told what was going to happen. They were asked to commit themselves to the activity and do everything that the leader (teacher/tutor) asked them to. It was explained to them that the activity would not be as threatening as it might appear. At this stage they were allowed to opt out but none did. They were told that one beat of the drum was to be their signal for random silent movement around the room; two beats meant stop. This sequence was repeated several times and the drum was then beaten twice and the students were asked to relax. They were then asked to make observations about what was happening. After some initial observations that 'it was stupid', that 'nothing was going on', they began to recall that they had been moving without exception in a herd, in a circular fashion and always in the same anti-clockwise direction. They were asked to try again and to be more random in their movement. This time a triple drum beat was introduced to indicate moving at double time. The students were asked at this stage to avoid physical contact. After repeating this sequence several times the students were once again asked to relax. They were told that for the next part of the exercise the double drum beat was a signal to stop and turn immediately to the person closest to them. Each pair should take it in turn to *describe* six simple observable facts about the other. It was explained to them that it was important to be purely descriptive; that personal observations should be positive. This sequence was repeated twice. It was clear that some pairs had stayed together in moving around so as to avoid having to work with a stranger. This was pointed out and the sequence was repeated several times sometimes using the triple beat (double time) variation to encourage mixing.

Various alternatives and developments of this basic procedure can and have been used. An excellent development is to talk about greeting gestures (Desmond Morris – *Manwatching*) and to ask pairs to spend five or ten minutes developing their own better method of formal greeting. Each pair can then demonstrate to the rest of the group. The alternative can be further developed by having the pairs split and return to the original movement sequence, thus taking different partners each of whom has to explain to the other her/his own form of salutation *without using language.*

It may be a good idea to introduce physical contact – a simple hand shake or arm slap. Alternatively, participants can be given a card with a number of introductory questions to be used in the latter stages of the activity.

Two examples of the simple questions which have been used are:

A (1) What is your name? (2) Where do you live? (3) What are your hobbies and sports? (4) What is your favourite food? (5) What are your pet dislikes? (6) What are your ambitions? (7) About what do you hold strong opinions?

B (1) Who are you? Tell me about yourself. (2) What are your shortcomings? (3) What do you think your good points are? (4) What do you like doing with time? (5) What sort of person do you hope to become? (6) Tell me about what you value or believe in.

The discerning teacher will develop many more alternative extensions to this activity which can be returned to at any time during the programme. The programme which forms the basis of this case study was limited in time both by duration and session length. One fifty-five minute session is only long enough for the basic sequences.

Session 2

The aim of this session is to build on the trust developed in the first session.

Resources required

Large room with chairs arranged in a circle. *The New Games Book*.[4]

The students were asked to sit down. The leader (teacher/tutor) took a place in the circle and waited for the group to become silent and relax.

Group relaxation is a complex concept and it will be hard for the group to understand what you want at first. Tell them you want them to *relax completely*. Some members of the group *will* relax very quickly, others will take a long time. It is important that the whole group is quite at rest before proceeding. This requires immense self-discipline on the part of the leader. It is important not to interfere and to be totally non-directive. The very occasional question to persistent fidgeters, whisperers and gigglers may be helpful, but if in doubt, it is better to keep quite silent. Reaching this state of group relaxation can, in any case, take only minutes or up to an hour. It is important that once the session has been embarked upon the state is achieved. It is imperative to this end that no-one enters or leaves the room as this seriously disrupts the process. Students who have to leave during the session should therefore be excused the whole session; tannoy speakers should be turned off as should noisy heating or cooling appliances; measures should be taken to ensure that colleagues do not interrupt. A particularly unrelaxed group may not achieve a state of rest at all. The leader should be neither disheartened nor reproachful. Complete wakeful rest is a difficult state for adolescents to achieve. Tell them that it is important to achieve this stage before going on. Clearly the more this programme is an option chosen by the students the more ready they will be to try again. Teachers familiar with Yoga technique will no doubt have much useful experience to add.

They were then asked to move their chairs back five paces and form two equal groups. (It is sometimes better for the leader to predetermine the groups.) This was the first trust game we played and it worked well. The participants were asked to stand in a circle facing the centre with shoulders touching. They were then asked to put their right arms into the circle and join hands with another member of the group. The same was repeated for the left arms and hands so that a knot was formed. The group was then asked to unravel the knot without any one member issuing instructions and without links being broken.

The experience of the groups which form this case study was, it must be said, a frustrated one. However, they all wanted to try again and I heard subsequently that a group succeeded later, after the class. I have known some groups of ten or more succeed in less than five minutes – an average time would be 15–20 minutes. A particularly successful group can be asked to substitute the leader for one of its members who becomes the leader. The group, instead of working co-operatively, is directed by the new 'leader'. Individuals only move to her/his orders as s/he tries to make sense of the tangle. It appears that it is much more difficult to succeed by this method. Some of the contortions are extraordinary!

We went on to play the ultimate trust game. The group were asked to form a double column in rank order of height and a 'volunteer' was passed along the fingertips from the front of the column (shortest) to the back (tallest). Clearly this exercise only works if a considerable degree of trust has been developed. The leader needs to be ready to assist the volunteer, who will be several metres off the ground, to the floor at the end of the column. The leader can, of course, volunteer, thereby demonstrating her/his complete trust in the group, (this is not recommended for heavy leaders working with less than substantial groups!)

Other games which have proved successful include 'blind leader' and 'self supporting circle', and there is now plenty of published material explaining the aims and methods of trust games. In practice most peace education programmes like that in this case study will, I suspect, not incorporate more than two or three sessions of trust games.

Session 3
This comprised two co-operative learning activities both of which were discussed at some length with the students on completion.

Resources required
Table and chairs in groups of five; 'Getting it Together' envelopes (prepared before the session); 'Co-operative Strip' packs (prepared before the session).

The idea of the 'Getting it Together' exercise is best described by its authors in *Learning for Change in World Society*.

'Co-operative Strip' is best played with three rather than five. Apart from developing the more obvious skills of communication and discussion, the particular purpose of this co-operative game is to get the students to examine the way in which decisions are made in a *small* group and to prompt them to *think* about the development of arms – the subject. 'Co-operative Strip' involves a sheet from the UNESCO Development Education pack on Peace Studies and has been devised by Simon Fisher of The One World Trust. One sheet was obtained for each group. The sheets were cut up into their constituent parts before the session and the parts arranged into packs. Each group was dealt the contents of one pack face down. The individuals in the group were then asked to describe their 'cards' to the other players each taking one card at a time in turn until all the cards had been described. They were then asked to discuss *without looking at the cards* an appropriate order for them to be laid out on the table so as to form a logically coherent cartoon strip. They were told that any player might be asked to redescribe her/his cards – but the cards were not to be laid out until the final decision had been made. The game worked well and formed a useful session with 'Getting it together'. It stimulated less discussion than 'Building a Square' which was, as the authors had suggested, a rich object lesson. For not only did the students discuss how it has been necessary to share resources in order for the group to survive but, those who had started with only two pieces described the frustration they had felt at the beginning of the game. Many students were profoundly reflective in describing feelings of vulnerability which had turned into feelings of hostility and aggression.

Session 4
The remaining sessions of the programme concentrated on the question of the nuclear deterrent. Though to have looked at the arms trade and third world development might have been a much more natural step following this introduction the students felt they wanted to examine more closely the whole debate currently surrounding the NATO alliance and nuclear disarmament. As most sessions speak for themselves it will not be necessary to describe them in the same detail as sessions 1–3. Qualifying notes have been added where they appear to be helpful.

Two films were shown: The British Atlantic Committee propaganda film *A Better Road to Peace*, and *Protest and Survive* made for the *Open Door* BBC programme by Schools Against the Bomb. These two films were chosen in order to represent two opinions as closely conflicting as possible. Whilst the *Protest and Survive* film was an excellent piece of amateur documentary, the BAC production was a collection of stills with 'talk over' and did not work as a film. Nevertheless in this area of education where objectivity is of paramount importance we must be aware of commercially-produced propaganda and at least be certain that it is adequately annotated.

Bradford University have produced a useful booklet to accompany the BAC film called *Which Road to Peace?* which attempts to clarify some of the factual distortions. It is available from the School for Peace Studies there and it does not carry a copyright. In retrospect this booklet would have helped resource a useful discussion following the film and the SAB film might have been shown on another occasion. A *Better Road to Peace* has now been supplemented by *The Peace Game* and it is to be hoped that John Pilger's *The Truth Game* will be made available for educational use. This may well prove to be a suitable film to show in conjunction with the BAC material as a basis for discussion.

Session 5

An appropriate follow-up to the two films seemed to us to be an open discussion involving well-informed representatives with different perspectives on the disarmament issue. We invited the Education Officer of the Peace Pledge Union, a pacifist organisation and one of the Directors of the British Atlantic Committee, the government-sponsored organisation responsible for providing information about NATO and for distributing both *A Better Road to Peace* and *The Peace Game*. Each speaker was asked to state his own position and talk for four minutes about the policies of the organisation he represented. Stimulating discussions followed.

Session 6

During this session most students went out of school to see the American documentary film *The Atomic Cafe*. The film mapped the history of nuclear testing in the United States during the 1950s. Comprised entirely of newsreel and official government film cuts it highlighted the experimental nature of the testing and the ignorance of the general public about the high doses of radioactive fall-out to which they were being subjected. There is no documentary comment, the sound track being that of the original sequences accompanied by original 50s rock. Because the material was tightly presented and the film was historical and about America, it was quite demanding on a young British audience. Current interest in the topic and the revival of rock music helped to make it more accessible to them. *Paul Jacobs and the Nuclear Gang* available from Concord Films, Ipswich, deals with the same topic more effectively in less footage.

Session 7

A senior hospital physician was invited to talk about the medical effects of nuclear war. He gave a dispassionate account of the effects of the various destructive energies associated with a nuclear explosion on the human body. The central theme of his lecture, however, was the inability of the emergency services to cope with the aftermath of such an event. London was taken as an example and the talk was accompanied by well presented slides.

A leading article in the *British Medical Journal*, 10 March 1983 states: 'In realistic terms no rational plans can be made for coping with a nuclear attack'. Help with teaching about this area of the subject can be obtained from the author.

Session 8
In this final session the students were asked to write for the first time about the subject. The title given was 'Nuclear Disarmament – problems and possibilities'.

In addition to these sessions the students became involved in other exciting and educationally stimulating activities related to the subject. Every encouragement was given to students to see the programme not in finite terms but as part of a continuing debate in which they could be involved, hopefully as better informed and more articulate members.

Later in the year one group of students took part in a radio discussion and another organised a visit to the Auschwitz Exhibition. I believe that this self-generated experiential learning was very important.

As a conclusion to this contribution I would like to refer to the nature of the institutional organisation of schooling. Colin Reid has written recently that peace should be taught and not learnt, but there is no doubt that by their very nature schools are unsuitable places for this to happen. We must look at the messages of the hidden curriculum; the institutionalised authoritarianism and regimentation which might well be removed in the interest of peace education. Bells and bleeps, uniforms, prefectorial systems, captains, the kudos of aggressive/competitive games are all dehumanising activities – but they have been in the past, and still are, the stuff that schools are made of, and until we change that schools will remain unsuitable places for people to learn to live well. Comprehensive education has been a major advance but whilst schools continue to accentuate and encourage in young people division rather than pluralism we cannot hope for a better future.

References
1 Rousseau, J. J., *Emile*, Everyman, 1911
2 Higgins, R. in *World Studies Journal*, vol 1, no 1
3 *Learning for Change in World Society* Pub. One World Trust (available from Houseman's Bookshop at £1.75 and published by the One World Trust, 24 Palace Chambers, Bridge Street, SW1A 2JT)
4 Flueglman, A., *The New Games Book*, Sidgwick and Jackson, 1978

Bibliography
The Construction of World Studies, Richard Hatcher in NAME Journal Vol. 2 No. 1.
'Teaching World Studies' Dave Hicks and Simon Fisher in *NUT Primary Education Review* No. 15.
British Medical Journal 10 March 1983
Ideas into Action: Curriculum for a changing World, 1980 – ILEA 1981

Peace Education Newsletter 7. A highly comprehensive guide to resources in this area. Published by Fellowship of Reconciliation, 9 Coombe Road, New Malden, Surrey.

Games and Simulations in Education for Peace, Graham Pike in World Studies Journal Vol. 3, No. 3, available Groby Community College, Leicester.

Trust Games

Orkick, T. *The Co-operation Sports and Games Book, Winners All* published by Pax Christi

Chapter 13

THE ROLE OF THE LANGUAGES DEPARTMENT IN A MULTICULTURAL SCHOOL

Sol Garson

> North Westminster Community School is a mixed comprehensive school on three sites with a roll of 1500. It is the ILEA's only federal school. The intake is drawn from Paddington and the West End, and from farther afield – some pupils travel a considerable distance. It reflects the multicultural character of the area and includes Afro-Caribbean, Bengali and Moroccan students.
>
> Sol Garson is Head of Languages at North Westminster Community School.

The multicultural/multi-ethnic school intake presupposes multilingual pupils. Many school departments regard this phenomenon of bilingualism, or relative bilingualism, as a hindrance to communication. Limited linguistic competence in the vernacular is seen as an over-riding obstacle. Lack of knowledge and mutual understanding can lead to cultural introversion in all pupils. The result is increasing ethnic polarisation.

Instead of seeing cultural diversity as an obstacle to syllabus writing, linguists (especially in monolingual England) should accept that bilingualism is an asset, not an handicap. Modern or foreign languages departments can exploit the linguistic wealth present in most urban secondary schools. At the North Westminster Community School (NWCS) in London, we have implemented a languages programme which utilises this multilingualism to break down the sort of ethnic polarisation described above.

Language policy in North Westminster Community School

At the latest count there were 55 languages represented among our pupils at NWCS. We have sought to develop a language policy appropriate to this culturally diverse intake. The fact that a multi-ethnic, multilingual intake and community is beneficial to a languages department and to all pupils is obvious to most educationalists; yet few linguists have dared to allow this awareness to widen the limited scope that their own language specialism and university and teaching training experience have imposed on them. Our programme avoids such entrenchment by deliberately questioning some traditional educational principles, while at the same time holding to the premise that the role of the language department is to teach foreign languages to the standards required nationally.

Every school is different and may well have different needs. The NWCS programme is not a panacea; it is only a beginning. Errors are being rectified and additions to different areas considered. Variations and improvements in the implementation, and even more radical programmes, may be taken up by schools trying to reflect diverse intakes and exploit their own range of specialisms.

The range of responsibilities

The new scheme was initiated in September 1980 with the approval and support of the ILEA's Languages Inspectorate, and soon afterwards reviewed and encouraged by the Department of Education and Science Languages Inspectorate. The impetus for change came initially from our far-sighted head teacher, Michael Marland who was concerned that foreign language provision was essentially Eurocentric. The languages staff readily accepted his premise that not all the intellectual, cultural, utilitarian and skill supports aims of language learning are met by five years of a single language,

> especially if that language is of the country which is our nearest neighbour and whose history and culture have been intertwined with ours. It is particularly important to consider the relation between the study of languages and the broader multiracial world views which all schools ought to have whatever the pupil body. The relation between language learning and world perspectives has rarely been satisfactorily discussed.[1]

We saw that proper language provision was still elitist in the Upper School, with a markedly small number of boys studying languages. The head teacher's reasoned concern about the Eurocentricity of the existing language provision stimulated us to consider and create a programme which would cater for the needs of all and redress the inadequacies of standard linguistic provisions within schools.

We first created a broader central language provision by instituting a rotation scheme for European languages. Then we moved on to develop non-European language study, including a World Languages Project (WLP – to be discussed later) which with its units on the history of language development and language families provides a language awareness component.

To be able to continue discussion and to monitor and evaluate the programme, we had to create a structure of responsibilities which affected all departments in the school and would require them to work in concert. The departure from a Eurocentric language programme not only needs approval from the headmaster and acceptance by all language teachers and the teacher dedicated to the promotion of mother-tongue learning, but also requires the following:

1 total co-operation from the Director of Curriculum and the timetabler;
2 advice from and exchange of ideas with the ESL department;
3 the injection of non-European literature into the library;
4 the inclusion of clearly stated language objectives in the multi-ethnic policy

of the school;
5 the assistance of non-language specialists in passing information and encouraging pride in and respect for the mother tongue and its continued study;
6 the involvement of representatives from the community;
7 advice and assistance from the school's monitoring and evaluation committee;
8 ratification by the school governing body of the language policy.

It is only if the groups above accept collective responsibility that the Inspectorate can give the go-ahead to a programme as a serious educational proposition and encourage the areas of change.

Areas of change

There were three areas where the school immediately initiated policy adaptations:
1 extra-curricular;
2 the school curriculum;
3 the language department's programme and syllabus.

Extra-curricular

> Racism can be manifested in the school's attitudes to non-standard dialects, accents, and mother tongues of ethnic minorities. It can also be seen in the failure to value bilingualism and to acknowledge the needs of bilingual pupils.[2]

There is increasing evidence that reinforcing competence in the mother tongue assists in the learning of English, the fostering of confident learning in general and in the development of communicative skills. Our policy is therefore to give all our bilingual pupils access to continued study of their mother tongue. The present provision for mother tongue teaching falls under the following three categories.

a) Self-financing outside groups using our premises outside school hours, and their own teachers, making classes accessible to our pupils. The school is used extensively for Spanish and Portuguese run by the Education departments of the respective consulates and Arabic and Bengali run by cultural bodies and parent associations.

b) Direct employment of teachers by North Westminster under the Urban Aid Grant. We have appointed teachers of Cantonese, Bengali and Standard Arabic for Moroccan children. They teach four sessions outside school hours which provide classes from basic literacy to advanced and public examinations.

c) The arrangement of access to mother tongue study for pupils whose needs are not catered for under (a) or (b). The responsibility for giving advice and information to pupils for whom there is no provision in school lies with the language department. We advise on outside classes and individual tuition by liaising with embassies, accepting assistance offered by members of the public and using other staff members who are in a position to help. We give guidance to pupils on mother tongue public examinations, set papers and have them corrected.

All these activities involve only bilingual pupils, mostly working outside school hours. But in order to encourage our pupils to maintain mother tongue learning and respect their cultural identity we include in the WLP a unit on mother tongue maintenance and use the *Languages Minorities Project* questionnaire and video, filmed with our own pupils, as part of the induction programme for the new intake.

We aim to assert that the 'home language' is a positive asset over and above the accepted cultural advantages'.[3]

Mother tongue teachers have to participate in the continuing discussions and interchange of ideas on methodology and the elaboration of schemes and materials for the teaching of languages. It is essential to appoint a member of the language department specifically to carry out such a programme not only because time and expertise are needed if it is to be done properly, but if it is to be credible and to have any status with the local community and other supportive groups it must be granted the highest priority. The link with the community created by such an appointment gave us the opportunity to find out what provision was needed to ensure that all ethnic groups were well represented in our language journeys abroad and any extra-curricular activities. Arrangements were made so that we catered for specific dietary considerations and a financial source was found to provide us with an extra accompanying adult to see that particular cultural or religious needs were met. The school runs annually a Dieppe-Paris journey, one to Normandy and Belgium, one to the 'Arabic' cities of Southern Spain, one to the Rhine, and we are now making arrangements for an annual journey to Egypt.

2 *The school curriculum*

The large language department in NWCS, for all its diversity and expertise, was essentially Eurocentric. Although the language staff can be asked to participate in foundation courses in non-European languages, specialist staff are needed if (as is essential) some of these languages are to be studied to the higher levels, on a par with the traditional European languages. By September 1980, after Arabic and Hindi had been offered as fourth year options, we appointed the first teacher of Arabic in a secondary school in the United Kingdom. Although Hindi was not taken up by the pupils the success of the Arabic proved that there were languages with definite utilitarian value outside the traditional European spectrum, which parents and pupils were eager to pursue. This addition to the curriculum was warmly welcomed in educational circles and by the media and aroused enormous interest and support from many varied quarters.

3 The Language Department and syllabus

It is important to emphasise that both 1 and 2 are extensions of our programme in which pupils participate voluntarily. Without a scheme which involves all pupils in the school at the earliest possible stage both 1 and 2 could be seen merely as token gestures, very soon to go unnoticed by the majority of the pupils and staff. We have therefore devised a languages foundation course for all our first year pupils in which they are taught French, Spanish and German each for one term in the first year. The process is repeated in the same order in the second year. The last six hours of each term are dedicated to one unit of the WLP. This foundation course is divided in such a way as to develop language-learning skills, complexity of grammatical understanding and familiarity with geo-linguistics, other alphabets and graphemes and tonal systems. The three main languages units are written with a progressive linear thread linking their thematic and grammatical content. The WLP units are as diverse as conversational Arabic, (produced by the languages staff together with our Arabic-speaking pupils), transcribing English phonetically into Hebrew script, studying the language patterns of Bahasa Indonesia, language skills in Swedish, the Russian alphabet, the common linguistic foundations of language groups, or an analysis of the reasoning behind the need for Portuguese migrant workers' children to maintain mother tongue learning. We are continually increasing the scope of this bank of units so that our pupils have the ease and confidence to accept that any language is accessible through applying the skills acquired from different areas of previous language study.

> The use of French, Spanish and German as the main languages taught in a foundation languages course is to give a continuous, structured development to pupils' awareness of language. The precision and accuracy (in all four skills) necessary to learning these languages provide a very useful foundation to the learning of any language. Precise listening in languages whose vocabulary is not so remote from English (particularly German) provides a useful step in building up pupils' confidence and ability to listen to languages which are very different. Details of writing peculiar to particular languages (e.g. initial capital letters for all nouns in German, punctuation peculiarities in Spanish, accents in French and Spanish etc.) sensitise pupils to the precision necessary to writing in foreign languages and prepare the way to using different alphabets and scripts.[4]

Each class in the first two years is taught by the same teacher. The school will only employ staff who are willing to participate fully by offering two languages from French, Spanish and German with a readiness to learn and teach two terms of the third language as well as all the units in the WLP. To have the teacher obviously participating as a fellow student, albeit guide, consulting with children on what aspects of their mother tongue are to be taught, is an enormous step towards breaking down the myth among so many pupils that teachers are an infallible source of knowledge and have no need to study to acquire a new language.

By the time our pupils reach the third year where they start to concentrate on the study of one or more languages, we have laid

> the foundations of good habits in the systematic language learning which the more able pupils are going to have to undertake ... they have learnt about the phenomenon of language as it occurs in many parts of the world, putting the languages studied in a wider cultural context ... trying to break down 'anti-foreign' prejudice and assisting in providing motivation for going to the very considerable trouble of learning foreign languages.[5]

The World Languages Project is a scheme which sensitises and exposes to language awareness, to comparative and para-linguistics. It aims to

> steer clear of parading an eye-catching but impractical display of languages by approaching each of these from a different aspect e.g. orally for Arabic, through the written alphabet for Hebrew, through emphasising the 'market language nature' of Bahasa Indonesia or by looking at the grammar of Swedish.[6]

The non-subjective educational approach to the WLP, the contents of which do not represent a numerical reflection of any particular ethnic group, is an honest attempt to broaden linguistic and cultural perceptions rather than a gesture of containment and appeasement of pupil and community aspirations.

> The foundation course is a linguistic exercise attempting to break down reluctance and intolerance, and open the mind to becoming receptive and encouraging the curiosity necessary to conceive ideas, be it on a linguistic, cultural or political basis.[7]

Conclusion

As the head of a committed department who has shared the first two years of the languages programme with hard-working colleagues, who took it upon themselves to do the necessary research through community channels and academic institutions, I have no hesitation in saying that although the monitoring and evaluation must always continue, we have opened new doors which have liberated teachers from entrenched positions and made the study of languages an education for pupils and staff alike. The warmth with which this departure from the norm has been received has only provided further encouragement and I now feel fully justified in advocating that schools do not hesitate to question their possibly restricted language provision and create the right structure and atmosphere in which to innovate, experiment and learn.

References

1 'Non-European Languages and the Curriculum', NWCS Discussion Document, Michael Marland CBE (Symposium December 1980)
2 'Towards a Multi-cultural Philosophy', NWCS Internal Paper, Staff Working Party (June 1982)
3 'Mother Tongue Provision', NWCS Language Policy Document, Anna Valentine (January 1982)
4 Discussion on the World Languages Project, NWCS Internal Paper, Cathy Pomphrey, Language Dept (January 1981)
5 'Non-European Languages', NWCS Internal Paper, Jerry Hicken, Lan-

guages Dept (June 1980)
6 'The European Component in the World Languages Programme', NWCS Internal Paper, Jenny Willis, Languages Dept (January 1981)
7 'Languages at North Westminster', NWCS Newsletter, Barbara Hill, Language Department (June 1982)

Chapter 14

DRAMA FOR A MULTICULTURAL SOCIETY

Elyse Dodgson

> Vauxhall Manor School amalgamated with Beaufoy School to become the Lilian Baylis School in September 1983. Previously it was a girl's comprehensive with about 850 on the roll. The intake, which was drawn from Vauxhall, Kennington and the Oval, Brixton and parts of Clapham and Wandsworth, was predominantly West Indian but many other cultures were represented. The teaching was organised on a mixed ability basis throughout the entire age range.
>
> Elyse Dodgson, now Head of Drama at the Lilian Baylis School, was formerly Head of Drama at Vauxhall Manor School. From 1981 to 1983 she co-ordinated the ILEA School Focused INSET Project which was developing materials through drama in the areas of multicultural and women's studies. She directed *Motherland*, one of the results of the project, as a stage play and an ILEA video. Her book on the project will be published by Heinemann in 1984.

The work of the drama department at Vauxhall Manor described here is based on an approach to drama that has evolved over a number of years.

It is my wish as a teacher to help my pupils achieve a better understanding of the world they live in and to become dynamic, active people. I would like them to appreciate some of the concepts that are going to affect their lives and to have the courage and conviction to deal with the social and political issues they will encounter. Thus, over the past five years I have tried to devise strategies and develop materials that will help us explore social, political and historical issues through drama.

The issues that many of my pupils choose to explore are often directly related to their own experiences of being female and black. Concern with these issues has extended beyond the classroom to intensive production work with pupils of all ages. As the concept of 'community education' has begun to flourish in the school, we have forged strong links with parents and others in the locality. Drama has extended across the curriculum as collaborative work with other subjects has emerged. In my view, drama has a vital role to play in educating pupils, parents and teachers for a multicultural society.

In attempting to define my own approach to drama, I can see that there are three elements present in all the work I have done; whether that be in the context of classroom drama, or working towards production, or of collaboration with other teachers.

First and foremost the teacher and the pupils must be able to operate the drama form. I believe this requires skills that we can all develop – the ability to explore another person's role, context and situation and, through the understanding that this brings, the ability to make decisions within the drama form while at the same time reflecting critically upon that role and situation. This requires the ability to co-operate within the group in the growth of drama work. Each participant must be able to identify actively with the drama situation and to work effectively with the rest of the group. In drama, the part played by language is crucial. Although movement and mime are important, it is largely the pupils' use of language which will determine the depth and intensity of the drama experience.

In my view the skills necessary for classroom drama need to be defined, but I don't believe they should be taught as skills for their own sake. These skills can be learnt from the drama itself. Drama is a unique method of learning. It provides the participants with a first-hand experience of living through, engaging with, and acting upon, a range of subject matter. It also requires constant consideration of the structure of the drama on the part of the teacher; of its conventions and the range of devices and strategies available.

Finally I have become more and more aware of the need to do research in order to introduce background materials into this work. In recent years I have become dissatisfied with many of the lessons I have taught, participated in, or observed, lessons dealing with the whole area of social issues teaching through drama, but particularly those which attempt to explore racism and sexism through drama. Themes surrounding these issues were for me becoming repetitive and superficial when approached primarily at the level of subjective feeling and intuition. It seems to me that an approach such as this which does not introduce an element of fact, personal testimony and political analysis leaves us teaching pupils no more than what they in fact already know. We thus fail to give them the tools with which to gain an altered perspective that would affect their lives and bring about personal and political change.

The criteria for choosing material will vary according to subject and focus. One criterion however, remains constant: the teacher must be able to see dramatic potential in the material. I tend to choose material that falls into at least one of five categories: *factual material* that might help to inform the drama; *dilemmas* that would confront the pupils with the problems that are faced or have been faced by others; *vivid images* that could be used to heighten the drama and sometimes provide a focus for it; *analysis* of a particular issue that would help to place the work in a wider context; and *personal testimony* that records the individual struggles, the triumphs and the frustrations of other people's lives. It is the introduction of authentic personal accounts into the lesson that engages my pupils most profoundly on an emotional level with the knowledge that the work they are doing is based on real situations and the experience of real people.

Drama in the classroom

A fourth year group wanting to explore the theme of racism and racial discrimination finally decided after a lengthy discussion to explore through drama the notion of apartheid in South Africa. One of the girls mentioned the word 'apartheid' and it became clear that some of the others had never heard of it. They didn't realise that Julie, who is white, would not be going to the same school as Alison, who is black and is sitting next to her in class. This produced shock and a lot of incentive to find out more.

Before their next lesson I collected books, articles and pamphlets for us to read. The fourth year social studies course covers this topic so there were materials available for both the girls and me to look at. I wanted the pupils to understand something about a person's own individual struggle against apartheid whether they be black or white. I finally decided to concentrate on a series of incidents described in a book by Hilda Bernstein, *For Their Triumphs and For Their Tears*,[1] a moving document about women's experiences in apartheid South Africa.

The incidents had to do with the pass laws and the decision of the South African government to issue pass books to women in the 1950s, a condition that was up until then only imposed upon African men. The description of these events contained a great deal of factual material about the system of apartheid. It presented us with some powerful dilemmas that would affect both black and white people living under this system, and offered us the opportunity of imagining the lives of individual women in this situation through the personal testimony given in this book. I planned to use the pass books as a symbol of apartheid. In order to do this I needed to develop a structure that would enable us to maximise the potential of the material.

Teacher in role
The device of teacher in role is one I most often employ in order to feed information into the drama. To employ this effectively I sometimes have to memorise information beforehand. In the first lesson I decided to adopt the role of a protest organiser in the 'pass book compaign.' I would address a secret meeting of black and white women to inform them of the kinds of demonstrations that were beginning all over the nation in response to the pass books being issued to women for the first time. In role, I could explain, from a position within the drama, the significance of the pass books and how they would affect people's lives. I could give the pupils information about how the passbooks restricted freedom of movement and choice of occupation and, in role, they could respond to this information.

I told them of some of the protests that had previously taken place: silent marches, the burning of the pass books, making banners, and composing songs and slogans. This was all based on the factual information in Bernstein's book, from which I prepared and rehearsed my speech as if working from a script. Then I asked them what this particular group of women could do that would serve as their own individual protest. The passbooks were to be introduced in their areas the following week. They must prepare their own act of defiance.

Making theatrical statements
By asking the girls to create and execute their own particular protest in some formal way I was really asking them to prepare and rehearse a piece of theatre. I find asking pupils to make theatrical statements of this kind a useful means of giving focus to the work. It provides a powerful stimulus for moving the drama on and illustrates the very thin line I believe to exist between drama and theatre.

The girls designed and rehearsed the following protest. According to their plan, the pass books would be coming to the town by train, and they, black and white women together, would sit in a tight circle, lock hands on the train rails and try to stop the train. At the same time they would shout and chant the slogan they had composed:
'Remember all us women,
Remember what we mean,
If you will not hear us,
We will still be seen,
We won't have these pass books,
We just want to be free!'
There was great involvement in the preparation of the protest. The pupils decided to wear black arm bands as a further act of defiance. I was designated the official who was to disembark from the train when, and if, the women succeeded in stopping it. They rehearsed their demonstration over again until they were confident that it would have an impact on the officials.

Spontaneous improvisation
I asked them, before they actually took their places on the tracks, to look in the direction of the train and state how they felt about what they were going to do:
'I'm scared, but I have nothing to lose.'
'I'm scared, but we must all be equal in this country.'
'They have no right to stop me on the street; they will split up all the families.'
I noticed that already the girls were beginning to use information they have received in previous lessons. The material was beginning to give them something to think about and to provide a basis for their drama work. It was also beginning to extend their use of language. When they all took their places the planned protest began and I stepped out of the train, acting the part of a bemused and disbelieving government official. They continued with their chanting as I laughed at their protest and raged at the fact that black and white women were joining hands.[2]

Several days after the lesson one of the girls explained what the work had meant to her.
'I think what we found out in the drama surprised most of us ... Sometimes when you thought of it you just wished it was made up. It was like a shock; you never thought it could be that bad ... Afterwards when we weren't in

lessons we got together and talked about it and we said if we would we'd like to do something about it.'

Towards production

For many drama specialists there is a distinction between drama as a process of learning and theatre as an end product. In recent years these two approaches have been brought closer together with the recognition that many drama teachers use theatrical elements in their work even if this is not directed towards polished performance. An exclusive regard for drama as a 'final text' can of course be damaging to the process of exploration which constitutes the stuff of drama. For me, however, working towards theatrical production has been a most useful and rewarding part of my approach to drama. I see it as a chance to extend the work that takes place in the classroom. It affords us the opportunity of intensifying and developing materials and strategies that are used in the drama lesson. Working after school without a rigid time limit there is more incentive for experiment, reflection and follow-up work. It also enables pupils across the whole secondary age range to work together.

Throughout the past five years working towards production has given us the opportunity to develop specific ideas that pupils have had and to turn these ideas into long term projects. For example, one project, *Slave Girl*, was about the female experience of slavery in nineteenth century America. Another project, which we called *Wicked Women*, looked at the persecution of women as witches in medieval Europe. *Motherland*,[3] our most recent venture, was about women's experiences of migration from the West Indies to Britain in the 1950s. Marcia Smith, who as a pupil had been involved in the previous projects, interviewed twenty-three women in the local community; the testimony gathered from the interviews was used as the basis of the play. A brief attempt to describe the 'rehearsal' process in relation to *Motherland* may give some understanding of the potential and problems of this kind of work. The phases are not discrete; each new phase encompasses the previous one. What we are concerned with here is a process of building, not simply a linear progression. We worked on each of the plays for nearly a year – having enough time is crucial.

Phase One – absorbing

It is essential that the pupils spend a considerable amount of time familiarising themselves with the available materials.[4] In this initial phase, therefore, the emphasis is on becoming familiar with the topic and introducing background materials – primary sources and other documents containing the social history of the period – to all those who are going to take part in the project.

We began during the autumn term to publicise the formation of the *Motherland* Company. This was open to all pupils from the first to sixth form. At the same time, Marcia Smith began interviewing the women, starting with her own mother and other female members of her family. At first the interviews were tentative and rather general, as was much of the early work in drama. With time, however, they became more sharply focused.

At our first meeting we introduced some of the materials to the group. I worked in role as a recruitment officer from Britain who had been sent to the West Indies to conduct a series of meetings about migration. I spoke to family groups about the opportunities they would have in Britain. Having worked in small groups on the economic situation in the West Indies after the Second World War, the girls, working in role, arrived at the meeting expressing hope but also a great deal of fear and doubt. In my role I could allay some of those doubts while at the same time giving more information about the conditions in the West Indies at the time.

Phase Two – experimenting
In this kind of work it is important that the notion of a final polished text is deferred as long as possible. This then is not only the longest but to me the most important phase. The principle of experimentation underlies all of the work, stressing the contribution of each 'rehearsal' to the final production. This phase incorporates all the exploration we do on the theme through drama.

By January 1982, we were meeting for three two-hour sessions per week. We worked thematically, choosing a particular aspect of the women's experiences to focus on; such as first impressions, housing, earning a living, bringing up children and relationships with men. The transcribed interviews fed directly into the rehearsals. We worked in many different ways: as a whole group with the teacher in role; in smaller groups developing improvised work; and individually trying to recreate personal experiences and then writing about them. We worked through mime and movement, wrote verse and told stories. It was at this stage that the element of song became so important. Excited by a particular aspect of the drama work, girls would come back with new ideas; lyrics sometimes scribbled on crumpled pieces of paper and melodies recorded on tapes. The songs recorded the girls' own attempts to come to terms with the significance of the materials and became part of *Motherland*.

Phase Three – forming
A willingness to think creatively about the drama form lies at the heart of the work that we have undertaken over the last five years. At a certain stage we begin to think more deliberately about shaping the play. Throughout this period experimenting is more vital than ever. Some things will work immediately and the group feels certain that they will want to incorporate them into the final product. We have been less sure about other ideas we tried.

At the heart of the *Motherland* project were the twenty-three women who had each by the end of spring term been interviewed four or five times. Over half of them were mothers of the girls in the play. We felt we needed to meet them as often as possible. Through a series of open rehearsals we shared with them our interpretation of their life stories. At the first open rehearsal we decided to select several aspects of our 'work in progress' to show them. The women were visibly moved by what they saw, made suggestions, shared anecdotes and songs, and pointed out anything anachronistic. The girls seemed eager to learn and continued to seek assurances from the women that they had 'got it right'. The open rehearsals reassured us that we were heading in the right direction.

Phase Four – polishing
In working towards a finished product, it becomes necessary to gain a clear sense of audience. We begin to visualise the play with its technical effects, design, lighting, costume and musical accompaniment. We become increasingly concerned with projection, movement and stage groupings as we begin to see the drama more from an audience's point of view.

It is significant that throughout this phase in *Motherland* we were still absorbing new information – the interviews were still taking place. We were still experimenting – scenes were being cut and new scenes developed. We were still forming. We had our last rehearsal with the interviewees present just before we moved into the Oval House Theatre for our run of nine performances. *Motherland* was finally a polished product, but the elements that contributed to its process were an integral part of every performance.

I believe the contribution that drama has made to those involved in the project can best be summed up by the following statement made by one of the company and a daughter of one of the twenty-three women:

'When you have to say the testimony that the women have said, when you have to sit there, when you think about it especially when you have to learn it, you're understanding it. You begin to understand what your parents always told you.'

Drama across the curriculum

Theatrical presentation is but one possible outcome of this basic approach to drama. As I tried to emphasise earlier, drama doesn't have to lead to production or even to a polished presentation. There may be many different outcomes to work in drama. Pupils can be stimulated to find out more about a particular historical period; they can be prompted to practise a range of different kinds of writing; they can learn the value of explorative talk and discussion. All these are valuable outcomes of the drama process.

In the documentation which follows I shall show drama being used as a way of exploring social and political issues in the context of humanities teaching. The range of drama in fact goes beyond this area of the curriculum. Since most of my own work has been carried out in collaboration with history and social studies teachers, I shall limit myself, however, to discussing the application of drama to this particular field of enquiry.

The following is an account of the work done with two history teachers at Vauxhall Manor – Jane Woodall and Terri Carey – on the third year history course. The course, 'People on the Move To Britain', is structured around a series of in-depth case studies about migration to Britain.[5] The first case study focuses on the Roman occupation; the second on the growth of the black community in Britain, with particular reference to migration from the West Indies after the Second World War.

I worked alongside both teachers in the classroom throughout the year, using drama where and when it was appropriate. It was not our concern to make the teaching of history more dramatic, but rather to use drama to enable all pupils to gain a better understanding of historical events, personalities, concepts and ideas – in short to become better historians. The lesson documented here is an example of how the history teachers and I combined our subject specialisms to show that there were black people living in Britain long before the 1950s, and to give our pupils some insight into the experiences of the black community in the past.[6]

The 'black poor', London, 1786

By the eighteenth century, most black people living in Britain were free but the majority faced terrible hardships and poverty. In the spring of 1786, after one of the worst winters on record, the Committee for the Relief of the Black Poor was set up by a group of wealthy philanthropists. The plan adopted by the committee involved the 'repatriation' of black people in Britain to Sierra Leone.[7]

The pupils, having been informed of the conditions prevailing in the winter of 1786, were asked to take on the roles of the poor while contemporary newspaper accounts describing their plight were read to them. They were then asked to speak aloud a word or phrase which expressed their feelings. Some of their responses were as follows:

'I need warmth and heat.'
'I'm perishing.'
'I'm starving.'
'Sleep.'
'I cannot bear it.'
'Why am I alive?'

The pupils, still in role, were then told that they had survived the winter and that, at last, there was a ray of hope as the Committee for the Relief of the Black Poor had called a meeting of the black community to be held in Lisson Grove, Paddington. In the improvised version of this meeting that ensued Jane Woodall took on the role of Jonas Hanway, chairman of the committee, and read out a speech based on primary sources which outlined the benefits of the 'repatriation' scheme. The pupils were encouraged to sign a document (a simplified version of the 1786 original)[8] thereby pledging their commitment to the scheme whereby they would migrate to Sierra Leone.

There was much discussion in role about the advantages and disadvantages of signing the document and a number of questions addressed to Jonas Hanway concerning the implication of his committee's plan of action. Following this large-group discussion the pupils were divided into groups of between three and five (kinship groups of families or friends) and asked to work out in role whether they would accept 'repatriation' or remain to face continuing hardships in Britain. This raised the question of historical accuracy. For most of the girls in role initially decided to sign the memorandum whereas, in fact, the majority of the black community in the eighteenth century had resisted.

In this case the problem of inaccuracy was resolved within the structure of the drama. Anticipating this situation, I had researched for the role of Ottobah Cugoano, a leader of the black community initially employed by the Committee to recruit volunteers for repatriation. He quickly realised the problems inherent in the scheme and began to warn the black community. Just as the pupils had completed the signing of the memorandum, I adopted the role of Cugoano and put forward the arguments against Jonas Hanway's scheme.

The lesson ended with a brief discussion during which both teachers clarified the relationship between what had just happened in the lesson and what took place in 1786.

Mary Seacole

The question of historical accuracy was raised again in our lesson about Mary Seacole. This example shows how drama can be used to enable pupils to understand the role played by an individual in history. Mary Seacole was a little-known black nurse, a contemporary of Florence Nightingale who, despite establishment opposition, went to the Crimea to nurse the wounded soldiers of the British Army in the mid-nineteenth century. Terri Carey took on the role of Mary Seacole and the class was given a problem to solve. As government officials, employed by the War Office, the girls were given the responsibility of finding out about Mary Seacole's experience of nursing and of deciding whether or not to send her to the Crimea to nurse.

We had already done a lot of work about nineteenth century attitudes to women with the class and had discussed the kinds of questions an interviewing body of men might ask a black woman wanting to nurse British Troops. The pupils were asked to prepare the room for the interview. In role, as representatives of the War Office, they asked:

'How did you manage to get to Britain?'

'What references and qualifications do you have?'

'What is your experience of nursing?'

The teacher, also in role, managed not only to convey biographical information about Mary Seacole's life,[9] but also to give some indication of the personality of this determined and courageous woman.

When asked to give their verdict on whether or not to send her, the class decided in Mary Seacole's favour. The problem was that in 1854 the War Office had come to precisely the opposite conclusion. Clearly, our pupils had empathised with Mary Seacole more than the War Office representatives had done. However, this historical inaccuracy was resolved in the follow-up discussion. In this case the girls were forced to face the reality of the nineteenth century attitudes by contrasting them with their own decision within the drama. The impact of this discussion was heightened as the 'co-teacher', still in role as Mary Seacole, read extracts from her autobiography, showing her feelings of anger, frustration and grief at being turned down; and her ultimate determination to continue the work by financing herself as a nurse in the Crimea.

Some indication of the contribution that drama can make to the teaching of history is given by the girls' own comments on these lessons:

'You enjoy it more when you're doing drama.'
'You can experience what it was like in those days.'
'It makes it more interesting, it gives you more experience.'
'When you put drama and history together we know what we're doing. We're not making up silly things – we're doing actual things.'

In this piece I have tried to outline my basic approach to drama as a subject, as an art form and as a method of learning. In offering brief illustrations of the use of drama in a variety of situations I have necessarily simplified a highly complex development. Nevertheless, each of these snapshots illustrates an important dimension of the drama work at Vauxhall Manor: its basis in collaborative learning, between both pupils and pupils and teachers; its links with the local community; and its stress on the need for an informed approach to multicultural education. In my opinion, neither racial prejudice nor racial discrimination will come to an end if conceived in purely ahistorical terms. In order to contribute to social change, work in schools should be informed by an understanding of the historical roots of racism and sexism that reach into the very structure of society.

Clearly drama has a vital role to play in any such attempt. It can only fulfill its potential in this area, however, if it is seen not only as a teaching tool, but as a highly sophisticated way of thinking about historical and social issues. This means that all those with responsibility for drama both at the classroom and the administrative levels need to develop it as a vital cross-curricular force capable of confronting two major concerns within contemporary schooling: education for a multicultural society and equality of opportunity for girls.

References
1 Bernstein, H., *For Their Triumphs and For Their Tears: Women in Apartheid South Africa,* (revised edition), International Defense and Aid Fund, 1978
2 For a more detailed account of this series of lessons see: Dodgson, E.

'Exploring Social Issues' in Nixon, J. (ed.) *Drama and the Whole Curriculum*, Hutchinson, 1982
3 See: *Motherland Video*, ILEA Learning Materials Service, Thackeray Road, London, S.W.8., 1983
For a more detailed account of the process involved in *Motherland* see: Dodgson, E. 'The Making of *Motherland*,' in *London Drama Magazine*, Vol. 6 No. 7, winter, 1982, reprinted in *Multi-ethnic Education Review*, Vol. 2, No. 2 ILEA, summer, 1983
4 These materials are included in a resource pack for pupils and teachers: Dodgson, E. *Motherland*, Heinemann, 1984
5 For a further account of this course see: Woodall, Carey, Dodgson, 'Teaching History Through Drama' in *CLIO: History and Social Sciences Teachers' Centre Review*, Vol 3, No. 3, ILEA, summer, 1983
6 Videos of both these lessons are available: *Drama Across the Curriculum, Part 1: Mary Seacole, Part 2: The Black Poor London, 1786*, ILEA Learning Materials Service, 1983
7 For further details of this episode see: Shyllon, F. O. *Black People in Britain, 1555–1833*, Oxford University Press, 1977
8 A copy of the original memorandum and other documents relating to the events of 1786 can be found in: File, N. & Power, C. *Black Settlers in Britain 1555–1958*, Heinemann, 1981
9 For more on Mary Seacole see: Alexander, Z. and Dewjee A. *Mary Seacole*, Brent Library Service, 1982

Resources and teacher training

Introduction
David Buckingham

The evaluation of resources is often regarded as one of the central issues in multi-ethnic/anti-racist education. Yet, as the contributions in this section repeatedly illustrate, resources are only one aspect of a broader problem. In certain cases, the activity of assessing resources for 'bias' can permit an evasion of the more painful, and more urgent, task of self-examination. Directing criticisms outwards at others can allow us (as white people) to feel safe, even self-satisfied, and to postpone the fundamental recognition that, as Tuku Mukherjee clearly states, we are part of the problem.

David James' and Garner Griffiths' contribution points to the dangers of superficial change. As they suggest, much thinking about resources remains at the level of a bland 'multiculturalism' which fails to acknowledge or analyse racism. Although such an approach may be a start on a process of change, it clearly has significant problems. The dominant focus on superficial forms of 'inter-racial harmony' tends to validate instances of assimilation and to undervalue the unique characteristics of non-white cultures, and thus to disguise continuing inequality and injustice.

As Tuku Mukherjee indicates, society has established 'whiteness' as a norm, to the extent that white people do not think of themselves in terms of colour. In this context, a concentration on black 'ethnicity' allows white people to avoid confronting their own identity and attitudes and hence their own political standpoint.

Ultimately, as David James and Garner Griffiths imply, the only changes which are likely to be effective are those which are deeply embedded in the system, and which transform established subject divisions and administrative practices. This inevitably involves confronting personal and institutional racism, and directly challenging established white power and privilege: in this respect, the ILEA's 'Anti-Racist Statement' is quite unambiguous.

The contributions in this section emphasise the importance of the critical assessment not only of resources themselves, but also of the ways in which resources are *used*. As well as attempting to provide 'unbiased' resources (an activity which, as Helene Fawcett suggests, has diminishing returns), we should be encouraging pupils themselves to be aware of bias, both by means of direct teaching and also by developing critical ways of *using* recourses. My contribution on educational television suggests that even overtly anti-racist resources may engender racist responses, and need careful handling in the classroom. As Helene Fawcett's contribution indicates, we cannot look at resources in isolation – students' experience in school needs to be seen in the context of their experience of racism in society as a whole, and attempting artificially to 'shelter' them from dominant forms of racist bias is, at the very least, misguided. In this sense, assisting students in confronting racism is part of the broader aim of developing their independence as learners and their critical awareness of all forms of prejudice.

Michael Simons' contribution on literature further emphasises the importance of providing a critical context for the use of resources. While teachers may choose to reject certain books on the grounds of racist bias, they may need to contextualise others in order to encourage students to see them in their social and historical context. Even with very 'well-intentioned' texts, which explicitly focus on racism, there may be a complex range of responses which need to be discussed in an informed and sensitive way.

The contribution on mother tongue teaching argues for the central importance of such work, the need for it to be supported both on an LEA and a classroom level, and to be integrated with mainstream subject teaching. As John Wright indicates, the materials used have to be judged by the same standards as are applied to English Language materials – both in terms of presentation and, crucially, of content. Yet here again, the issue of classroom use is central if mother-tongue teaching is not to be relegated to a ghetto, or to be merely tokenism: pupils have to be given freedom of choice, and bilingual language teaching offered as an option to *all*, both English speaking pupils *and* those from minority language groups. Much of the success of such an approach lies, as John Wright's contribution suggests, not merely in the provision of materials, but in the way such materials are made available in the classroom situation, and the kind of status they are given by the teacher.

The contributions in this section all underline the fact that resources cannot be seen as a 'safe area': it is clearly inadequate to view resources in isolation from the way in which they are used, or to assume that we shall ever find 'unbiased' resources which will somehow do the job for us.

While applying checklists of criteria may be of some limited value for those faced with the daunting task of selecting resources, it is no substitute for developing awareness in ourselves and, most crucially, in the students with whom we work. As Tuku Mukherjee states, that awareness can only come, for white people, as a result of confronting one's own racism, and recognising one's own place within white institutions and the white power structure. This is inevitably a process of political conflict which is the very opposite of safe.

Chapter 15

THE WHITES OF THEIR EYES: A CASE STUDY IN RESPONSES TO EDUCATIONAL TELEVISION

David Buckingham

> David Buckingham is Media Resources Officer at Acland Burghley School. He is currently doing part-time research at the Institute of Education, London University.

Television is a medium which commands acceptance. Its claim to objectivity and impartiality is not merely in response to a legal obligation; it is embodied in its whole way of representing the world. By suppressing any evidence of selectivity, of its own construction, television claims to act as a 'window on the world', an unmediated reflection of reality. Television addresses us in ways which assert its authority. The assured tones of presenters and narrators (often male, always middle-class) are seen to represent a natural order, a reasoned, common-sense view of the world. Words on television serve to restrict and define the meaning of its images. Images act as evidence to prove the truth of words. Words, sounds and images are combined in ways which simulate the directness of 'real', lived experience, from which it is difficult to distance ourselves. Even non-fictional television constructs narratives, 'little stories', which direct our interpretations.

For many teachers, even teachers who are otherwise critical of what they regard as the enormous influence of the medium, it is precisely this apparent power of television which makes it such a valuable teaching resource. Television allows us to experience other people's lives directly, and hence all the more forcefully; and, if we choose the 'right' programmes, it can act as a powerful form of propaganda for the 'right' causes. Television appears to be able to call forth the 'correct' response with a regularity which even the most charismatic of teachers could not hope to guarantee.

Yet some teachers' experience in using multi-ethnic and anti-racist materials would tend to suggest that it is not quite so straightforward as that. Anti-racist films or programmes may call forth extremely racist responses, which might not otherwise have been voiced, and which become very difficult to handle. My own impressions of pupils' responses to programmes like *Somebody's Daughter, I'm here* and *The Whites of their Eyes* (the programme discussed in this article) indicate that the impeccably anti-racist intentions of the films' producers are often far from being fulfilled.

I would like to suggest here that if such programmes do encourage the expression of a 'latent' racism, this is not simply a function of their subject matter. It is also a function of the ways in which such programmes address their audience – the kind of assumptions they make about what the viewers bring with them, in terms of prior attitudes, skills, patterns of attention, likes and dislikes, and so on. In other words, such programmes may not 'work' because of a mismatch between the 'ideal' audience addressed in the programme and the real audience in the classroom.

Recent research on audience responses to television confirms this impression that 'correct' responses can not be guaranteed. The work of David Morley and others indicates that a number of social factors are likely to influence the way in which a programme is 'decoded' – in particular social class, sub-cultural grouping, ethnicity and gender. In studying responses to *Nationwide*, Morley found that while certain groups tended to accept the way in which the programme formulated issues, and the programme's own position on those issues, other groups rejected it outright – groups of black further education students, in particular, were totally alienated by the programme's attempts to make them identify with its values, largely because of the fact that they saw it as addressing a white, middle-class audience.

While there has been very little adequate research on educational television, such work as has been undertaken tends to confirm the impression that pupils do not always respond in the desired or expected manner. Graeme Kemelfield's ten-year-old study on the Granada programme *Our Neighbours from Pakistan* showed that although students from schools with few immigrant children tended to have a more favourable opinion of Pakistanis after seeing the programme, those from schools with a higher proportion of immigrants tended to be *less* favourably disposed towards them and less tolerant of cultural differences as a result of seeing the programme. He suggests that for the latter group, who were initially more accepting of Pakistanis, 'the programme had developed an awareness of differences, and perhaps a self-consciousness about them, which had not entered into their previous thinking to the same extent.' As Kemelfield concludes, 'in such circumstances the classroom teacher is likely to be faced with a complex set of reactions, which will make demands on his or her skill, sensitivity and prior preparedness, if creative use is to be made of them.'

Case study

As part of my own research on educational TV, I have studied the responses of a number of groups of London school pupils to the programme *The Whites of their Eyes* in the Thames TV series 'Viewpoint 2'. The programme looks at the way in which black people are presented and represented in the media, and incorporates a number of extracts from TV comedy shows, feature films about the British Empire, and TV news and current affairs programmes. These are linked together by a voice-over commentary read by Stuart Hall, Professor of Sociology at the Open University. In addition, there are a few brief 'vox pop' sequences in which (unidentified) black people give their own criticisms of the way they are represented in the media.

The programme specifies a number of ways in which the media may be seen to be racist. It suggests that racist jokes and comedy programmes show black people as primitive and inferior; that media images of the British Empire reinforce notions of 'natural' white superiority; that the representation of Third World Countries shows them as helpless and disorganised; and that black people in Britain are often depicted as criminals or troublemakers. In the words of the teachers' notes, 'though not all media images follow the pattern, the bulk of them still portray stereotypes that have helped to build prejudices in the older generation.'

For my research, I gathered responses by means of relatively open-ended questionnaires, and also by group discussions. Two major points emerged from my analysis of these responses. Firstly, that although the anti-racist intention of the programme was clearly perceived by all groups, a number of the more complex points made in the programme were either ignored or misinterpreted: and secondly that there was a quite spectacular diversity in responses between different groups – while some groups were more disposed to accept the programme, others perceived it as a direct attack on quite deeply-held prejudices, and 'refused' it for that reason. What is particularly important is the *connection* between these two points – it was precisely the pupils' failure to understand crucial parts of the programme's arguments which made it possible for them to interpret it as a *personal* attack.

In general, for instance, pupils failed to perceive that the programme was concerned with racism *in the media*, and this led many to assume that the programme was suggesting that *all* white people are racist.

Likewise few pupils picked up on the programme's arguments about the causes of racism, and fewer still seem to have noticed its implicit suggestions about how racism might be eradicated. While the programme provides a fairly clear historical context for the discussion of racism, pupils generally failed to make connections between this and the examples of racism in the media today.

A number of reasons may be suggested for this. Part of the difficulty may lie in the complexity of the programme's language: the section on the British Empire, for instance, includes words like 'colonisation', 'inferiority', 'regimented', 'paternal' and so on, which were not generally understood by the fifteen-year-olds who viewed the programme. In addition, pupils tended to pay more attention to the visual elements in the programme than to the commentary; although, here again, the significance of the programme's ironic use of montage (for instance in juxtaposing fictional and non-fictional material) tended to be lost. Some pupils also found difficulty in distinguishing between the commentary of *Viewpoint* (i.e. Stuart Hall) and the commentary of the programmes 'quoted'.

This may point to a flaw in the programme's strategy of attempting to 'demystify' or even to subvert 'commonsense ideology' by working from the familiar and the popular to the unfamiliar and less popular. As my pre-viewing questionnaires demonstrated, many of the prime targets of the programme, and particularly the TV situation comedies, were very popular with their audience, and proved extremely difficult to dislodge in their affections. The familiar, well-liked images clearly carried more weight than, and therefore distracted from, the less familiar arguments.

(Interestingly, these programmes were liked equally by black *and* white pupils, although (one would surmise) for different reasons. The sequence from *Love Thy Neighbour* which is included in the programme shows a white racist being 'cooked' in a cauldron by his black fellow-workers, who have 'returned to the jungle'. While a racist white audience might find the scene amusing because it 'confirms' (in a comic and exaggerated form) their notions about the underlying savagery of black people, a black audience might enjoy it because it parodies those notions, and shows the well-deserved come-uppance of those who believe in them. This clearly gives the lie to the implicit assumption of *The Whites of their Eyes* that programmes and films can be divided into 'racist' and 'non-racist' – as this whole study demonstrates, 'racism' is a function of the interaction between audience and text, not an *inherent* property which texts either do or do not possess.)

Although these basic misunderstandings were slightly less noticeable in groups which had indicated anti-racist attitudes in pre-viewing questionnaires, they were fairly standard across all groups – indicating that the programme was possibly making unrealistic demands of the average pupil's viewing competence. However, in a couple of almost exclusively white groups, these crucial misunderstandings reinforced the tendency to reject the programme outright.

Thus, a number of pupils in these groups said that they didn't like the programme at all, and a few even refused to complete the questionnaire. Others tended to give priority to elements which featured the humiliation of black people (admittedly there are many), or which tended to confirm their notions of black people as violent or anti-social – particularly the film of riots. These groups also gave priority to the sequence on the British Empire, and at least half of the pupils were under the impression that the programme was glorifying it. The programme's remarks on racist humour were particularly controversial for these groups: although a minority appeared to believe that the programme was actively celebrating it(!), the majority understood that it was opposing it – although a high proportion were concerned to reject this argument when given the opportunity to write about it or discuss it. These groups also tended to ignore, or play down, the programme's few 'positive images' of blacks, such as the sequence on Mugabe, and they tended to caricature the programme's arguments – it was saying 'that blacks weren't bad, that the police caused riots, not the blacks', or that 'white people have got all the riches, and people that haven't are black, they're slaves.'

In a minority of cases, the questionnaires provided an opportunity for the expression of quite disturbing race hatred. A significant number of pupils in one school (a boys' public school) consistently referred to 'niggers', 'pakis', 'wogs' and so on: and when given the space to express their own views brought forth a stream of abuse:

> 'Blacks can't do anything right. Rule the corner shops. Riotous people, smell the country out. What the hell did they let them in for?'

> '... blacks are generally nasty characters and deserve to be prejudiced against. They are, after all, inferior and less intelligent and so deserve it. The blacks should stay in their own country and not interfere with other people's lives. They should be destroyed.'

As indicated above, a number of pupils reacted strongly against the programme's remarks on racist humour –

> 'The way blacks and pakis take it proves how animalistic they are, 'cos they can't take it. They get too stroppy too quickly. If everyone did this there would be no law or order. COONS OUT.'

A group of girls in another school were also provoked by the programme into an extended harangue against 'pakis'; although in fact the 'vox pops' in the programme feature only one Asian speaker, and the issue of the media treatment of Asian cultures is not covered at all. This group felt themselves to be surrounded by 'pakis'; they were taking over all the shops in the area, charging exorbitant prices, and would only employ other 'pakis'; and so on. Yet with no sense of contradiction, they were able to assert that they had 'nothing against blacks' themselves.

Although it is quite possible that any programme on this theme would have generated such a response, I would suggest that there are certain specific aspects of *The Whites of their Eyes* which made this more likely. As indicated above, the group's confusion about the programme's 'target' (i.e. the media rather than all white people) and about its historical explanation of the causes of racism were likely to lead them to feel that they were being blamed directly, which was seen as unfair. More crucially, both groups were very aware that there were no white people giving their opinions in the programme, and that the only white people present were being condemned – this would have contributed to a feeling that, in the words of one girl, 'they can say things to us but we can't say things back.' The girls in one school accused the programme makers, and the blacks themselves, of being racist and of 'just showing one point of view'; and in another school one of the boys described the programme as 'propaganda'. This produced a feeling of powerlessness, which in turn led to angry retaliation:

> 'the programme was saying that it's all right for them to slag us down, but not for us to slag them down ... It was saying that we thought we was better than them, which we don't; it's just that ... they seem to cause more trouble ... They think they can over-rule us 'cos they're black but they can't. All blacks that just say whites are against them, it's just so bloody stupid ... if blacks want to say things against the whites then it's up to them, but they've got to learn that we're going to say it back.'

Interestingly, these points were echoed in the discussion in one school where the group were generally sympathetic to the programme's aims. One black girl pointed out the absence of white people's opinions, and the group as a whole felt the programme should have been more 'balanced', in terms of including whites, as well as blacks. However, it was also suggested that programmes like *Panorama* were themselves not balanced, and tended to give 'the white point of view'. Either way, the group seemed to be aware of potential problems which could (and in the examples quoted above, clearly did) arise when conventional notions of balance are rejected.

Although this group were very sympathetic to the aims of the programme, and already fairly critical of the media, they suggested that the programme as a whole was both confused and confusing. One boy suggested 'maybe if at the end they had the bloke who made it going over the points we might have missed, or we *did* miss, going over them clearly...'

Furthermore, in another school, a fairly vociferous group of black girls almost resented the programme: I initially interpreted their complaint that there were 'too many Africans' in the programme as evidence of West Indian anti-African prejudice (not an uncommon phenomenon), but it later emerged that they felt that this might encourage white people to see all black people as 'primitive'. These fears were precisely confirmed by the responses of the boys quoted above.

Conclusions
This study could well be seen as leading towards the conclusion that programmes like *The Whites of their Eyes* should be avoided as potentially or actually 'racist'.

But in favour of what? The controversies surrounding other recent offerings from schools television suggest that there are few adequate alternatives. The BBC's *One World* series on the Caribbean, for instance, has been criticised for presenting a touristic, uncritical view of the 'interdependence' between North and South – a view which fails to mention the economic exploitation of the Caribbean by British and American companies. The BBC's response to these criticisms fell back lamely on claims to objectivity, which are, to say the least, spurious.

The recent Yorkshire TV series *Tomorrow's People* exemplifies a number of current orthodoxies in thinking about multicultural resources, and a number of typical problems. In particular, it attempts to avoid a number of the common 'negative' stereotypes of Asian and Caribbean people, and to replace these with 'positive images' of these cultures, and of inter-racial harmony. As such, like *One World*, it is obviously well-intentioned, and clearly preferable to programmes which uncritically reproduce racist stereotypes. Nevertheless, its images are ultimately only 'positive' from a white viewpoint. Its representation of non-white cultures, while 'sympathetic', implicitly reinforces Anglocentric norms and values: Caribbean, and particularly Asian, cultures are presented in terms of implicit criticism and even mockery which are not applied to white culture, and there is a strong and approving emphasis on the assimilation of these 'deviations' into the norm. In this context, the teacher's notes are wrong to suggest that the series acknowledges racism: it acknowledges racial prejudice, certainly, but not racism, which, as the notes themselves define it is fundamentally concerned with power relations. Without such a perspective, the 'positive images' promoted by the series can be seen as not merely glossy and vaguely patronising, but as potentially quite dangerous. Furthermore, the manner and context in which such prejudice is voiced have disturbing implications for audience responses.

Programmes such as these clearly generate similar if perhaps less acute, problems in classroom use than *The Whites of their Eyes*. Ultimately, I would argue that the search for the pure 'non-racist' text is futile, and even dangerous – it is akin to the notion, condemned in the programme, that if you ignore racism, it will go away. What is crucial, and what teachers can control, is the context within which such programmes are 'decoded'.

This is not simply a question of prior attitudes, or even of what one will or will not allow pupils to say in the classroom. The response to the programme was clearly 'better' (more in line with the producer's intentions, or simply easier to handle) in groups which already held anti-racist attitudes; yet after all, preaching to the converted is easy. The crucial fact is that *most* pupils were ill-equipped to understand, let alone evaluate, the programme's arguments: and it was this failure to understand which contributed to the violence of the reactions quoted above.

Rather than pursuing the chimera of the 'non-racist text', we should be concentrating on finding new and critical ways of *using* texts. It will never be possible to *eradicate* bias or stereotyping. All texts (all people) are 'biased' and none is *more* biased than any other; all texts (all people) use 'stereotypes' as a means of classifying and making sense of the world. The myth which *does* need to be exploded is the one which suggests that it is ever possible to see the world in ways which are *not* partial. Rather than attempting to protect pupils from these 'evils', we should be teaching them to detect and analyse them.

The Whites of their Eyes has the positive value of being concerned with precisely these issues; however, as I have suggested, the form in which it raises them may generate more problems than it solves. It can precipitate the teacher into a meaningless confrontation, and one which could be positively harmful in the context of a multiracial classroom.

Certain stereotypes are clearly more pernicious than others: and *The Whites of their Eyes* definitely provides a substantial collection. What the programme ultimately prevents, and what on the contrary I feel should be encouraged, is the *analysis* of these sterotypes in their diversity and complexity.

Chapter 16

LIBRARY RESOURCES

Helene Fawcett

> Acland Burghley School is a mixed comprehensive with a roll of approximately 1000. The intake is mainly white working class from Kentish Town and Holloway. There are also some Afro-Caribbean pupils. The teaching is organised on a mixed ability basis.
>
> Helene Fawcett, formerly Librarian at Acland Burghley, is now Librarian at North Westminster Community School. She worked in Australian universities for ten years before coming to Britain. She is a member of NAME and was involved in the Afro-Caribbean Research Project.

The Rampton Committee made eighty-one recommendations in its interim report, one of which related to books and teaching materials. It stated that teachers should examine critically textbooks and materials for their suitability for a multicultural society, local education authorities should be prepared to replace those resources with 'a negative cultural bias', and school and public libraries should stock a balanced range of books reflecting our society. The Schools Council pamphlet 18, *Multi-ethnic education: the way forward*, in its recommendations for action by schools listed 'consideration of the appropriateness for a multi-ethnic society of the materials used in the school'. Teachers' unions have made similar recommendations, as has the Commission for Racial Equality, and other concerned professional and non-professional associations. So the Rampton recommendations are neither new nor surprising. We have been hearing and reading the like for more than a decade. In 1971 Alison Day commented that 'to retain a library that is almost exclusively devoted to the works of white authors is to encourage the belief in all our pupils that "white" means "superior"'.

In the time between that concise statement and Rampton there has developed a tradition of talking about resources for multicultural education which embraces terms such as stereotyping, tokenism, positive/negative images, racist/non-racist, Eurocentric, ethnocentric, cultural pluralism and diversity. To examine critically teaching resources is an arduous task and a subjective one. Who does it? Who in the school is to take the responsibility for seeing that these recommendations are put into practice? Who will throw out the books? Who will light the fires? There is plenty of fuel.

Using guidelines

There are several sets of guidelines for assessing bias in resources. Examples are: *Assessing children's books for a multi-ethnic society* from ILEA Centre for Urban Educational Studies, *In black and white* from the National Union of Teachers, *10 quick ways to analyse children's books for racism and sexism* from the Council on Inter-racial books for children, *Criteria for assessing bias in resources* from the Multicultural resource unit of Birmingham Education Authority, and 'Images in textbooks', p. 69 of *Learning for changing in world society*, from the World Studies Project of One World Trust.

There are also many lists of materials recommended for use in the multicultural school. Some of these lists have been produced by experienced teachers, librarians, and professional groups. For example Bedfordshire Education Resource unit's *Multi-ethnic education resources list for teachers*; the Library Association Youth Libraries group's *Multiracial books for the classroom* compiled by J. Elkin and the Commission for racial equality; *Education for a multicultural society*: a bibliography for teachers. They aim to assist in the selection of suitable resources for multicultural classrooms and libraries. They give some clues as to ways of measuring stereotyping, tokenism, sexism, racism, etc. through characterisation, value-laden language, illustration and misrepresentation of fact.

In recent years, some publishers have started to list books which fall into the multicultural category. Penguin provide *A multi-ethnic booklist for children of all ages* compiled by Rosemary Stones; Books for Students provide Multi-ethnic books; A. and C. Black have a multicultural section in their catalogue; Evans have a multi-ethnic subsection in the English section of their catalogue. The Evans selection is of folklore from India, Africa and Morocco as well as a series about a small African boy and his family and village, while A. and C. Black's includes the Strands series which 'aims to encourage an understanding of people from different cultural backgrounds, with the stress on people rather than cultures.' These are all set in Britain. Photographs provide images of, among others, Cypriot, Sikh, Gypsy, Chinese, Welsh families. But one would miss some other titles which could be labelled 'multicultural' if one only looked at publishers' multicultural sections.

Making Simple Clothes[1] and *The Singing Bird*[2] could also be called 'multicultural'. The Hamish Hamilton catalogue does not have a separate section for multicultural titles: the Joan Solomon books are listed after the series which has a 'closer look' at bears and ants, Bedouin and Aborigines. Heinemann and Oxford do not identify multicultural texts as such – librarians do well not to identify them either.

It is necessary to ask how many of the 'recommended' resources would survive rigorous application of the criteria for selection included in the guidelines. One could end up with as few as six books! In the search for material which is 'ideologically' pure, in the sifting, selecting, censoring process there is an inherent danger of being left with a glossy image of reality. If the materials available in school are only those which are 'approved' then they will contradict what pupils experience outside school. Are we going to invent a method by which pupils will understand how to measure the distance between positive image and negative experience? Pupils' experiences do not begin and end with school. Outside the schoolrooms they continue to encounter a range of media full of stereotyping, misrepresentation, ethnocentric perspectives and negative images. To suppose that they will not notice is to underestimate their abilities and sensitivities. There is a daily encounter with racist graffiti for each person who travels by London underground. Is it surprising that pupils sometimes react in a racist way to non-racist materials? How many teachers, attempting to introduce the single African, Caribbean or Asian novelist out of context can cope with the remark, 'Oh, we are always reading about black people!' or 'Must we read this book, Miss?'

Soon after acquiring *Pavan is a Sikh*[3] I found that 'He's got something wrong with his head' had been inscribed on the cover. More recently I noticed that there are comments in Arabic on the reproduction of Blake's painting 'The Ancient of Days' in a copy of Gombrich's *The Story of Art*.

The combined effect of guidelines and recommended or labelled resources could be the falsely secure belief that there are 'safe' resources, and that by their very presence, equality, harmony, understanding, respect and truth will permeate the consciousness of pupils.

Having on the shelves or in the cupboard *East End at Your Feet*,[4] *City Summer*,[5] *Old Mali and the Boy*,[6] Heinemann's African Writers series, and *Everyday Life in Early India*[7] is not going to make pupils forget what they already know and accept.

A fairly straightforward exercise is to take the Macdonald series on countries, direct pupils to the section on 'national characteristics' and ask them to discuss whether this kind of description is of any value. It may be that people in India have an amazing ability to live on top of each other, but so do people in most densely-populated cities of the world. After looking at several of the books in this series, pupils are not that keen to identify with any of the nationalities as they are described.

The guidelines are a helpful exercise in developing critical abilities such as detecting and coping with prejudice, recognising and counteracting the language of bias and dealing with trivialisation and tokenism. Consciousness raising is another essential function of guidelines so that those who are responsible for providing and dealing with the learning resources may be aware of the need to diversify the sources of the 'facts' which are available to our pupils. Though it could be argued that the selection process tends to be reduced by an undue reliance on recommended texts, one could do worse than spend the dwindling budget on the publishers' multicultural products, but there are few, if any, 'safe' teaching materials. 'Few books are forgivable' said R. D. Laing when he began to write on *The Politics of Experience*.[8] It is possible to built up a range of resources which reflect our society, but how will it reflect the imbalance of society?

The school library

What stock is selected for the school library? How is it done, and by whom? Ten years ago, when I began to work as a librarian in a school, I asked all heads of departments and teachers in charge of subjects to make recommendations for additions to the library collection. I received few replies: the sole item on one list was *Cliff Tragedy* by Eileen Dover. It took a couple of years of dialogue with pupils and teachers, displays and discussion of particular topics and individual titles for the appropriate response to result in an increase in requests and to make an impact on the library budget. In 1975, the climate was more congenial for a librarian who expected interest to be shown in library resources, with recommendation 250 from the Bullock Report. Meanwhile the only black teacher in the school introduced me to John LaRose of New Beacon books, and there I found a comprehensive supply of books which were tremendously popular with pupils. Among those that had the most appeal were: James Baldwin – *The Fire Next Time*,[9] Richard Wright – *Black Boy*[10] and *Native Son*,[11] Eldridge Cleaver – *Soul on Ice*,[12] C. L. R. James – *Black Jacobins*,[13] Peter Abrahams – *Mine Boy*,[14] *The Diary of Anne Frank*,[15] S. Davis – *Reggae Bloodlines*,[16] etc.

There were no 'multicultural' sections in the publishers' catalogues then, and ordering titles from smaller publishing houses through the cumbersome centralised supply system which at times seemed deliberately obstructive, was often unsuccessful. As the library collection became more relevant to pupils' interests and enthusiasms, it was no longer necessary for the lunchtime session to include board games so that they were keen to come in. They came in to read and look through books, periodicals and newspapers.

The only way to measure the effectiveness of the library is to observe its use, that is to see who uses it and for what purposes. The librarian may be seen as leader through the conflicting maze of knowledge represented in the library stock. There is no certainty that the appropriate source may appear. Yes, look at the published text on immigrants but look also at CRE fact sheets – and keep asking the questions and enquiring further.

The aim is to lead users towards authoritative knowledge and to teach the skills of identifying such. It is important to lead them to materials which provide another viewpoint, to the newspaper article, to the article in the weekly or monthly periodicals. One might take the subject specialist around the shelves to show her/him the various places where information may be found and stress the interconnectedness of information sources and the inadequacy of library classification schemes. The picture for the pupil in the Art Department may not be among the art books, but may well be in a book in the history, geography or sociology section.

Initially, the groups of users were identifiable by their specific interests or by their cultural attachment. For example groups of pupils, attracted by a wide range of books and magazines on sports and sports people increased the numbers of children who found their way into the library at morning break, during the lunch hour and after school. Eventually they came to use books on a number of other topics.

Black girls and boys soon discovered that they could find information on the issues of black identify, racism and on the experience, history and literature of black people which were of increasing interest among London's black communities. As the titles on the black experience in Britain, America, Africa and the Caribbean increased, so did their use of the library. Their white friends gradually diversified their own browsing and reading to include these books among those that they borrowed.

By responding to the demands of particular groups the library was providing a wider range of reading material and a broader base of information for all pupils and staff. I remember the delight on the face of a small Nepalese boy who told me that 'this is *my* god' when he noticed the cover of the Thames and Hudson paperback *Indian Art*. Caribbean history books like S. Duncker's *A Visual History of the West Indies*[17] and *The People Who Came*[18] were welcome additions to stock as well as *Ebony*[19] and *Staunch*.[20] Mike Rosen's *John Bull, a poem on British racism,*[21] Carol Adam's *Women and the Nazis*[22], J. Shelland's *The Old Nazis, the New Nazis*[23] ... stimulated much argument and discussion among older pupils, and the Poster Collective's first set of posters were displayed around the walls. I put the one 'we are here because you were there' above the photocopier, and yes, staff did comment. Books on Cyprus came into stock after much difficulty and went very quickly – the only title which was regularly returned was a turgid tome on Makarios.

There was a general tendency on the part of staff and the pupils themselves to think that those books that were regarded as suitable for pupils in the remedial department were appropriate for all pupils learning English as a Second Language. It became clear to me that this was not the case. The only way to find out what they found attractive was for me to make time to talk to them and to the staff in the ESL department. The ensuing contact and dialogue with the pupils and their teachers led at first to an increase in the number of books on a range of topics relating to the culture, literature, religion and language of the different linguistic groups in the school as well as stories from many lands.

A group of Chinese boys organised a mini-library of their own books and comics in one of the library workroom cupboards. A fourth-year pupil took on the arduous task of sorting through a substantial collection of photographs and memorabilia of the old school. Perhaps some of the most rewarding purchases were a globe and lots of maps of the local area and countries other than the UK.

Catalogues, bookshops, exhibitions, the ILEA Centre for Learning Resources and the Centre for Urban Educational Studies – all these were useful in the gradual improvement of the library section were by section. First there were the attractive well-illustrated and up-to-date books on different countries, India, Pakistan, Spain, Portugal, Greece, Cyprus, Turkey, the USA, Canada, Nigeria, Ghana, Jamaica, Trinidad, St Lucia, Chile, Bangladesh, Argentina,

Australia, New Zealand, Japan, Korea, France, Germany, the USSR and a host of other countries. Then there was a multicultural collection of attractive paperbacks, fiction and non-fiction, not labelled as 'multi-cultural' but kept on constant display through an ever-changing selection of topics and categories.

An important aim, because of the popularity of these genres among all first and second year pupils, was to provide the most complete collection of legends, myths and folk tales of the world that the budget would allow, given all the other pressing demands of a library which was rapidly becoming (as a library and resources area should be) the most central and important area of learning in the school. Now and again a teacher might come in to read during a lunchtime session, and it was possible to imagine that the library was on the way to becoming the 'heart of the school's resources for learning'.

All teachers need to be aware of the way books and pictures shape children's attitudes to one another and to society, and of the ethnocentric bias of many books in use in schools. When selecting books for schools, teachers and librarians should include books that reflect the experience of children from families of overseas origin and material about their homelands and cultures. There is a general shortage of such books, and publishers could make a valuable contribution by fulfilling this need.

However, teacher expectations and attitudes often affect directly the choice, provision and display of resources not only in the classroom but in the resources area as well. When I first began to paper the walls of the library and the hallway and staircase outside with attractive thought-provoking posters, the Head of Science warned me that pupils would tear them down, or damage them by graffiti, and that I was wasting my time. The posters were never damaged by pupils. The only one which was torn from the wall came from the National Council for Civil Liberties, and the teacher's face reddened with effort as she did it, lecturing me at the same time about how I was 'filling the children's heads with nonsense'. (Her subject was British constitution.)

The role of the librarian

Librarians in schools have a major responsibility for resources provision and use in schools. Their overall responsibilities are variously described as organisation, management, development, co-ordination, exploitation, promotion and evaluation so that the library service is effective. Their role is a long way from the dictionary definition 'keeper of the library'. But since they are librarians working in educational institutions, their work is in the tradition of other academic institutions. They have to support the work of all readers and users and maintain the underlying philosophy of their school. Their main focus is academic rather than recreational. Yet in the view of many, librarians are 'non-teaching staff'. They are contracted to non-teach for a specified number of hours a week. They have no clear duty statement, the role they take in the school is the one they make, and is directly related to the kinds of relationships they form, the demands they meet, the collection they develop, and the way in which they manage its use.

In reality, the librarian is the head of a department and, in consultation with other heads of department, must formulate policy for resources selection and provision with the school. The librarian has a central role to play, with all subject departments or faculties, with each teacher, with the head teacher and deputies, non-teaching staff, the pupils and their families. It is important that the librarian is aware of the impact of her/his service on all groups within the school, the local community, the educational community, and the profession of librarianship. The librarian must be fully informed about all aspects of the curriculum and all activities of the school. All who work in or attend the school should want to know about the policy, functions and contents of the library. Compared to most teachers, librarians have a tremendous advantage in the space at their disposal: a fixed space, with workroom, telephone, water and power supply. The outcome of the service is that the needs of staff and pupils are to be met. How are those *needs* identified and defined? Finding a place to start is easy if the syllabus of each department is written down, and available. Better still if it includes a list of the teaching materials used. This is where the curriculum dialogue can begin. Some useful texts are Norman Beswick's *Resource-based Learning*[24], *Changing the Curriculum*[25] by Barry Macdonald and Rob Walker, *Culture and the Classroom*[26] by J. Reynolds and M. Skilbeck and *Authority, Emancipation and Education*[27] by Lawrence Stenhouse.

The librarian is an information merchant. Through that function s/he establishes relationships with teachers, by relating to areas of knowledge, by providing sources of information additional to those they already have. Librarians are not experts in all areas of knowledge, but they should be expert at evaluation, assessment, selection and rejection. Through familiarity and experience with books, librarians become skilled at recognising the ways in which writers of texts organise, classify, select and analyse information and knowledge, and the ways in which those texts are produced and packaged. Librarians have a responsibility to share this expertise, to encourage the development of rigorously critical approaches to texts. It is easier to enter into a dialogue about the appropriateness of teaching materials in, say, geography or history, than in maths or science. There has been considerable examination of textbooks and teaching materials by David Hicks and Dawn Gill, for example. But it can be difficult to persuade the busy head of department to take a look at such publications; they may gather dust in the teacher education section of the collection. When the librarian is regularly examining the library stock, s/he must call on the assistance of teachers to share their subject expertise with her/him. Texts which may have ended up on the fire may be found useful for teaching and discussion.

Obviously, guidelines are very useful – when they are worked on with teachers and pupils – to diagnose the strengths and weaknesses of resources and to establish a continuing dialogue about their contents and format. Whose knowledge has been produced and packaged? Why? There are far more questions to consider that those in any set of guidelines. Raising those questions means challenging the authority of writers of texts, the authority of teachers, the authority of institutions, the authority of librarians.

My experience has been that these waters are murky, that some teachers do not welcome the idea that sacred texts are to be questioned or discarded, or that carefully designed teaching materials are open to criticism. I have been lucky, I have worked with people who supported my approach. It was by chance that I had constant access to persons whose responsibilities covered the whole curriculum, there being no other space than the library workroom for them to leave the mess that curriculum co-ordination created. But I have not been successful in attempts to establish regular systematic examinations of texts – it has been more a case of grabbing teachers on their way to the photocopier or the MRO (Media Resources Office). Librarians should work through a resources committee, or set up such a committee if one does not exist. Resources committees I have known have concentrated on use of rooms, blackout, videos and reprographics – discussion of textbooks or library stock was not a welcome item on the agenda. This fragmented approach to textbooks and materials will not satisfy the need for critical examination and evaluation of them. It takes a fair amount of time to develop the kinds of relationships with colleagues which allow for open discussion on teaching methods and materials.

Developing library resources
The role of the school librarian is usually discussed in terms of reading encouragement of one form or another. Libraries are good things. Books are good for you. If you are a consumer of books you will improve yourself. Libraries are prestige-winners – always on the guided tour of the school building for prospective parents, pupils and visitors. Traditionally they are quiet places, lack of noise is also a good thing. The silent interaction of pupil and printed word is admired. It may be evidence that learning is taking place.

At Acland Burghley School I took advantage of the fact that the English oral exams were held in the library each year and made this the time when I 'nobbled' teaching staff to look more closely at library stock. Texts which we decided to dispose of were then stacked on tables and during lunchtime sessions I would talk to pupils about why they were rejected, and encourage them to look for more. One pupil told me that nearly all the science books had to go because they were racist – a few history of science books would remain if she had had her way. And, as for the handicrafts books...!

Soon major initiatives began to come from a number of library user departments in the school. The outstanding example was the Social Education Department. Their requests highlighted the number of books on the major concerns of our society – age concern, the disabled, housing, employment, adolescence, child development, racism, sexism, conflict, peace, the third world, etc. Such periodicals as *New Society, New Statesman, Spare Rib, West Africa,*

The Listener, West Indian Digest, UNESCO Courier, New Internationalist, New Equals were in constant use in lessons and in the individual pupil assignments. A and O level students were led to these materials and gradually teachers and other students began to find them useful.

As the demand for relevant ephemeral material grew, so we began an ever-expanding collection of cuttings on contemporary issues, from the dailies, including the ethnic minority press and local newspapers. Pupils, teachers and friends began to add to these, using and thus identifying for us, new sources for relevant materials. A range of attractive multicultural posters lined the walls of the library and the walls on either side of the wide staircase leading up to the library. Some were in Bengali, Chinese, Greek and other mother tongues of the bilingual pupils in the school. Many of the posters had to be changed frequently as they were about exhibitions in museums, art galleries, parks, or about plays, concerts and other events among the various communities of London. Thus it was clear to all the pupils and staff that their reference and information sources reached out beyond the classrooms and the library into the wider world of our great metropolis and beyond. It was not without conflict that that was achieved.

In an organic way 'resource consciousness' developed in the school. It became clear, however, that structural changes were necessary to consolidate the significant innovations and to provide a framework of support for pupils and staff.

A closer merging of the Media Resources and library was essential. As there had always been co-operation with the MRO, this was easy to achieve. The staff and pupils, however, had to be made aware of this so that it would influence the pattern of their work and of their studies. There was an essential role here for the head, curriculum co-ordinator, the librarian, the MRO and the subject departments. Already a clear pattern had been emerging. Sources of the curriculum content both for the formal and informal curriculum had become more diverse and multicultural. The problem was how to make all these resources accessible to all departments at the points where they would directly affect the pupils' learning. Some co-operation and even generosity was essential but a plan soon began to take shape.

Clerical and secretarial support for the school curriculum was provided through the judicious use of the Alternative Use of Resources Allowance. The library workroom provided space for two typists, the MRO provided the space for the graphic designer, and the departments, including the library, pooled their resources to provide the necessary range of reprographic and audio-visual equipment for the use of the whole school. All departments derived some benefit from this arrangement, particularly those that most needed and were keen to produce good quality, well illustrated and printed materials of their own – the ESL, Sociology, Integrated Studies, Home Economics and Art Departments.

This at Acland Burghley School was achieved through a combination of formal and informal contacts and horse-dealing with the rest of the school, parents and Camden Committee for Community Relations.

The process of growth outlined in this account may appear to have been accomplished easily and overnight. But the growth was attended by considerable pain over a period of several years. Librarians are more effective when spared the pain which arises from the attitudes and unenlightened practices deprecated in the first part of this article.

At North Westminster Community School, there is an increasing consciousness of the role of the library in learning throughout the school. The senior librarian is a member of the Curriculum Directorate, and has a place on Curriculum, General Purposes and Pastoral sub-committees, as well as Review and planning, the senior staff sub-committee. Many team leaders see it as an essential part of their job to maximise library resources and services.

Pupil and the library

While working as a librarian in schools, I have watched 'library lessons' which consisted of a class being brought in, instructed that in five minutes they were to find a book to read, sit down and read it in silence until the end of the lesson. I'm not against reading in silence, I question the limit of five minutes to choose. Try it on a student at the tertiary level! It implies that anything you can find in that amount of time will do you good. It often takes me much longer. Pupils show good sense when they come into secondary school with the idea that all books are stories, and we do them no favours when we try to teach them the difference between fiction and non-fiction unless we are very careful about the way we do it. In answer to a quiz about the meanings of these terms, pupils will readily acknowledge that fiction means made-up stories, but it then follows that all the rest is non-fiction, a term which covers a multitude of possibilities. It is a good starting-point for a discussion about information and factual truth, about who has organised what knowledge and for whom. Pupils are ready to dismiss information that they know from their experience to be wrong, will be readily critical of texts which leave out what they know.

What kinds of access do pupils have to library stock? Librarians do them no favours when they construct barriers between the pupils and the books, when they insist that in order to find a book it is necessary to jump the impossible hurdle of a catalogue which may or may not relate to current stock, that they have to follow an unclear system of shelf-guiding, or look in several different format-related sequences, and then wait in a queue while the librarian controls the issue system. There is an advantage in librarians not identifying themselves with teachers, in their involving themselves in the learning process – but not to the extent of setting exercises, homework, reading resumes, writing. There is a disadvantage in the library being another classroom, where the activities which take place are similar to classroom experience, or where the production of a piece of work is expected at the end of the session. Most of us learn about libraries by being in them, about books by becoming familiar with a wide range of them. The organisational arrangements of most schools do not allow for the kind of access pupils need to become familiar with libraries and their peculiarities until the sixth form, so that they become yet another prize for only a few.

It is important that the atmosphere in the library be one in which it is possible for pupils to, as Archbishop Temple once said: 'learn how to feel together and think alone rather than how to think together and feel alone'. It cannot happen unless there is respect for the privacy and priorities of users, unless they feel easy about being in the library, unless they are allowed to explore its stock. The library can be a place of refuge from the 'heady' space of the classroom, where pupils can learn for themselves, where they can reclaim the initiative for learning. The librarian is there to lead users through the conflicting maze of intellectual and cultural resources. There has been a shift away from the one lesson a week with the English teacher and pupils don't often sit in the comfortable chairs listening to stories of the decimal classification system while gazing out of the windows thinking of other more adventurous inventions. They are more likely to be doing the 'information skills curriculum', learning how to produce their own 'books' by researching the information sources available.

The library skills sessions, information skills sessions, study skills sessions needed to include all the techniques used to produce, systematise, classify, reject, extract, synthesise, select, organise what constitutes knowledge, and it must not leave out *who is doing it and why and for what purpose*. What purports to be truth may be racist or sexist, and 'until the lions have their historians, tales of hunting will always glorify the hunter' (African proverb). Librarians have to be judgemental about texts, to teach others how to be so, to be seen to hurl inappropriate items into the bin, and to continue to have discussions about the power of images and the printed word.

> To be imprisoned inside the misinterpretation and misunderstanding of others can be a withering form of incarceration. It is a fate which can afflict whole nations and cultures as painfully as individuals.[28]

Libraries are not safe.

Postscript for pupils

> You are in the process of being indoctrinated. We have not yet evolved a system of education that is not a system of indoctrination. We are sorry, but it is the best we can do. What you are being taught here is an amalgam of current prejudice and the choices of this particular culture. The slightest look at history will show how impermanent these must be. You are being taught by people who have been able to accommodate themselves to a regime of thought laid down by their predecessors. It is a self-perpetuating system. Those of you who are more robust and individual than others will be encouraged to leave and find ways of educating yourself – educating your own judgement. Those that stay must remember always

and all the time, that they are being moulded and patterned to fit into the narrow and particular needs of this society.[29]

References
1. Hamre, I. and Meedom, H., *Making Simple Clothes*, A. and C. Black, 1980
2. Resch, B., *The Singing Bird*, A. and C. Black, 1977
3. Lyle, S., *Pavan is a Sikh*, A. and C. Black, 1977
4. Dhondy, F., *East End at Your Feet*, Macmillan, 1976
5. Jackson, R. and Johnson, P., *City Summer*, A. and C. Black
6. Sherman, D. L., *Old Mali and the Boy*, Penguin, 1973
7. Edwardes, M., *Everyday Life in Early India*, Batsford, 1969
8. Laing, R. D., *The Politics of Experience* and *The Bird of Paradise*, Penguin, 1970
9. Baldwin, J., *The Fire Next Time*, Penguin, 1964
10. Wright, R., *Black Boy*, Longman, 1970
11. Wright, R., *Native Son*, Pan, 1972
12. Cleaver, E., *Soul on Ice*, Hodder and Stoughton, 1979
13. James, C. L. R., *Black Jacobins*, Allison and Busby, 1980
14. Abrahams, P., *Mine Boy*, Heinemann, 1963
15. *The Diary of Anne Frank*, Pan, 1954
16. Davis, S., *Reggae Bloodlines*, Heinemann Educational, 1977
17. Duncker, S., *A Visual History of the West Indies*, Evans, 1965
18. Edwardes, M., *The People Who Came*, Longman, 1970
19. *Ebony* (journal)
20. *Staunch* Black family magazine, available from 180B Holland Road, London W14
21. Rosen, M., *John Bull, a poem on British racism*
22. Adams, C., *Women and the Nazis*
23. Shelland, J., *The Old Nazis, the New Nazis*
24. Beswick, N. W., *Resource-based Learning*, Heinemann Educational, 1977
25. Macdonald, B. and Walker, R., *Changing the Curriculum*, Open Books, 1976
26. Reynolds, J. and Skilbech, M., *Culture and the Classroom*, Open Books 1976
27. Stenhouse, L., *Authority, Emancipation and Education*
28. Smith, A., *The Geopolitics of Information: How Western culture dominates the world*, Faber and Faber, 1980
29. Lessing, D., *The Golden Notebook*, Panther, 1973

Bibliography
A Language for Life: report of the Committee of Inquiry appointed by the Secretary of State for Education and Science under the chairmanship of Sir Alan Bullock

Day, A., 'The library in the multiracial secondary school: a Caribbean booklist', *School Librarian,* vol 19 no 3, September 1971

Gill, D., *Geography for the Young School Leaver: a critique* and *Secondary School geography in London: an assessment of its contribution to multicultural education,* London, Centre for Multicultural Education, University of London, Institute of Education, Working Paper no 2

Hicks, D., *Images of the World,* University of London, Centre for Multicultural Education, Occasional Paper no 2, 1980

Hicks, D., *Minorities: a teacher's resource book for the multi-ethnic curriculum,* Heinemann Educational, 1981

Learning for Change in World Society: Reflections, Activities, Resources (revised edition), World Studies Project, One World Trust 1979

Little, A., and Wiley, R., *Multi-ethnic education: the way forward,* Schools Council, 1981 Schools Council pamphlet 18

West Indian children in our schools: interim report of the Committee of Inquiry into children from ethnic minority groups, Chairman Anthony Rampton, HMSO, 1981

Chapter 17

TEACHING RESOURCES

David James and Garner Griffiths

> Lambeth Teachers' Centre is an ILEA Divisional Centre in Brixton. It serves 2000 teachers in 150 schools and educational establishments in Lambeth – a borough with a considerable social and cultural mix.
>
> David James is Warden of Lambeth Teachers' Centre and has taught in both primary and secondary schools.
>
> Garner Griffiths is Deputy Warden of the Centre and has taught in both primary and secondary schools.

The area of multi-ethnic and anti-racist education is a semantic minefield. Our excuse for not venturing into the danger area is that other chapters in this book have already covered the ground and shown how difficult it is to trace safe routes through such terrain. David Milner in the final chapter of his latest book *Children and Race Ten Years On* uses the phrase 'education for equality' and goes on to define two objectives of multicultural education.[1] For us the emphasis should be on resources for anti-racist education in Britain now and not on more vague notions concerning cultural backgrounds, no matter how justified the special needs of some pupils for language, religion, dress and diet may be.

Definitions of resources are difficult to frame and we will begin with one so wide that it is almost useless. Anything or anyone that can be used by teachers and pupils to promote education for equality should be sought out by teachers and be used in schools. There are no quick and easy answers to the problem of resources for equality. It is certainly not a case of searching out the materials for schools to do the job. The whole process is a subtle and complex one of 'the operation' of racism. The resources aspect is only one small part of the overall issue and must be seen in context. It is perfectly possible for individual teachers or small groups of teachers to spend hours sifting through existing learning material, to reject racist items, to buy in, or produce new 'approved' resources; but unless the context of the school as an institution is also reviewed and the way in which racism is operating is investigated all this resource-gathering will generate only minor changes. Resources, and learning materials particularly, are often chosen as the safe starting point in the process of trying to make changes and teaching for equality. Black British children do consistently underachieve in our schools and it is very difficult to accept this is the fault of the system, the schools and the teachers. All too often the pupils themselves have been blamed for their underachievement. When uncomfortable notions of guilt and blame begin to come home to roost one relatively straightforward way of beginning to tackle the problem while keeping it at a safe distance is to review learning resources for racial bias. This is essentially a critical and destructive process.

An impressive list of obvious resources can be quickly produced. All schools have stocks of books, maps, charts, posters, slides, filmstrips; and many more are easily available along with videos, films and photographs. Of course, these materials should be of the highest quality and be racially unbiased. There are a wide range of immediate practical objections centring around time and money to such reviews of traditional teaching materials and their replacement. The Rampton Report recommended that teachers should critically examine the text books and teaching materials they use and take account of their appropriateness to today's multicultural society. The recommendations also advocated replacement of those materials having a negative bias as financial resources permitted.[2] There are less conventional resources available to schools which can also be used – visits, visitors, parents, pupils and teachers themselves. Community groups, pupils' experiences recorded as their own work can also be seen as resources for teaching for equality. Access to these resources is vitally important to schools. However, they are only likely to be used regularly and extensively as a means of teaching for equality when they are placed in a wider school context of anti-racist policy and practices.[3]

At a general level, resources are not the critical factor in teaching for equality. Inevitably more time and more money are always demanded and all schools should have large, sophisticated and well documented sets of physical resources that are updated regularly. Attitude and awareness are the critical factors as they determine approaches and sensitivity to teaching for equality and where this appears on any list of priorities.

> What learning material to use is a matter of professional judgement which will take account of the age and ability of the pupils and the objectives of the lesson. Clearly it is preferable to have an unbiased teacher using biased material than vice versa. Nevertheless, it is important to assess the racial bias and positive/negative images in material as an element in that professional judgement.[4]

We have already made several references to the need to see resources for teaching for equality in context. Some education authorities and many schools have policy statements on teaching for equality. Resources are an aid to the implementation of policy but will rarely lead the way. Policy statements often show a 'top-down' approach which is a danger in a field that requires individual involvement. However, clear policy statements from LEAs and schools do legitimise the activities of individuals and small groups of teachers, and offer help and support. If change towards teaching for equality is to come about in educational institutions there must be people on whom such changes can be based. Policies are developed through consultation but must be clear and contain provision for action and review if they are to influence practice and effect change.[5] Once this process has begun then resources become important. In this wider context resources will include the LEA's own policy, Inspectors and Advisers, Teachers' Centres, central collections and production of teaching materials, co-ordinated information and in-service education courses and projects. However, such provision will only be of real help to schools if it is related to mainstream LEA policy and structures and not seen as some separate appendage.[6] Within a framework of such support individual schools and teachers could find change a slightly easier task.

The enormity of the task of change involved in teaching for equality can often involve the response 'I am only one teacher, what can I do?' This reaction recognises the extent and complexity of racism in society and education. The individual teacher in the classroom can begin on the process of change in her/his teaching especially if the LEA provides support in terms of policy and resources and teaching colleagues and other partners in education (pupils and parents have a stake too) give their help. Decisions as to curriculum content, the choice of a topic and its content can often be made or influenced by individual teachers as can decisions about the learning materials to be used and the way in which the topic is taught. At a structural level such change is relatively easy to introduce but external support is likely to be needed for it to be sustained. Changes at school level are more complex, more difficult to begin, and take longer. Given the background of LEA support and the active participation of a number of teachers then schools can quickly create a policy. Co-ordination and implementation of that policy and review of effectiveness will inevitably take time. Here decisions about priorities and allocation of resources are crucial for the policy on teaching for equality to become embedded in the structure and normal running of the school. A whole-school approach will be a less complicated task in primary schools. At an LEA level policy formulation is a relatively quick process but review of the policy and allocation of resources related to policy is far more difficult and time-consuming. The effect of these different time scales is that many of the resources for teaching for equality are based around individuals, a few for small numbers of particular schools and seldom for all schools in an LEA. We are still at an early stage in this process of change.

> 'It is upon consideration and discussion by individual teachers and by the staffs of schools and departments that the development of educational practice appropriate to multicultural Britain depends.'[7]

Educational institutions and all those concerned with them are at different levels and stages of development with regard to education for equality. There is a growing awareness of overt racism and some recognition of hidden and institutionalised racism but the relationship at a personal level between these two is not usually explored. There are a few committed anti-racist individuals and groups with an even smaller number of people giving examples of positive teaching for equality. It is a crude match but there are also a wide range and different levels of resources available which are appropriate to the different groups. At a general level there are general, bland, safe resources on cultural background, religions, customs, arts and crafts and historical backgrounds. At the level of background information and knowledge for a large number of people these resources are appropriate but it must be recognised that this multicultural approach is only a beginning. The approach has been used for some years and is probably where the majority of people start the process of change and is where the majority still are in terms of the level of resources used and approach to teaching for equality. Within the field of multi-ethnic education this cultural approach has long since been abandoned in favour of a more radical approach based upon recognition of racism and attempts to understand how it operates.

The general cultural approach can open the way for progress to another stage. Facts and information can be sought out and whilst *they* do not change; attitudes, perceptions and interpretations towards the information can alter. There are many examples of this process, many of them to do with colonial history. For example the fact that there is an African history and civilisation that predates the arrival of Europeans may enable the discoverer to challenge the traditional ways in which Africa has been and is presented in learning materials used in school.

The vast majority of people in education are not overtly racist but will probably not realise they are racist by default. Resources and learning materials that help to uncover racism and the way in which it operates are important. This process can begin with the relatively bland multicultural approach. The next stage must involve the study of British Black experience as racism will inevitably become an issue through such study. Here factual information can provide a starting point. The Runnymede Trust and the Commission for Racial Equality produce a wealth of detailed factual information. There are a number of television programmes that have dealt with this theme and government statistics, reports and legislation are available. Again factual information is needed alongside discussion of attitude and belief. Case studies of successful British Blacks are a good resource as long as they are not confined to the fields of sport and entertainment. Eventually anti-racist materials will be needed and a number of packs and workshops are becoming available. One good general introductory discussion pack has been produced by the Open University.[8] Another racism awareness pack worth looking at has been produced as a tape-slide presentation with notes by the City of Birmingham Education Department.[9]

The decision as to the appropriate level of resources for particular stages of development is a crucial one. The business of becoming aware of individual racism and the way one relates to institutional racism is a difficult and painful process. The minority of those involved in education who are at this stage must be supported and be encouraged to produce materials for equality for education. However, the majority have not yet been through such a process and suddenly to present people with anti-racist courses and materials without allowing time for preparation and discussion could well be counter-productive. At best the relevance of anti-racist materials will not be seen and at worst attitudes will become entrenched or even regress. Teachers must reach a level of awareness of their own racism to be able to handle the contentious issues which will be raised in class discussion. In-service education must be appropriate to particular groups and take account of stages of development and appropriate levels of resources.

The educational materials on racism need to include specific examples of racism showing how it operates in areas such as housing and employment as well as in education. There also needs to be discussion of the effects of racism on both the indigenous population and minority groups; highly specific teaching materials for equality will have to be developed. *Race in the Classroom* is a book produced by ALTARF which explains ways of teaching against racism in the primary school. ALTARF have also produced a television programme in the BBC Open Door series.[10] Education for equality is not a subject in its own right, but a field of knowledge that needs to permeate all subject areas. This presents a structural problem, as education at LEA level, at secondary school level and to a large extent at primary school level, is organised upon a subject basis. The power structure and resources are also organised along subject lines. As a result it is very difficult to work across subject boundaries and the temptation is to work narrowly within subjects to produce materials suitable for them. This incremental approach is very difficult and time-consuming and runs the risk of the total effect being far less than the sum of the individual subject parts. It is far easier to work within subjects such as the humanities than in others like mathematics and the sciences. Power in education lies largely within the subject areas and education for equality must develop resources and find ways of working within and more importantly, across the subject disciplines.

Anecdotes do not always help general arguments. However, one short story will show that the authors of this section are far from perfect and will also demonstrate how careful we all need to be. Exhibitions are a good resource for teachers. At the Teachers' Centre we have a strong commitment to education for equality and have regularly run a large number of courses and exhibitions for teachers for many years. Recently we ran a two-week exhibition from a major publisher of popular children's books. Included within the general exhibition was a special collection of multicultural materials and matching catalogue for teachers to take away. This was a popular exhibition. It was quite correctly pointed out to us that there were at least four racist books on display. An interesting set of excuses and justifications almost began to trip off the tongue. The books were all put out in a hurry at the end of a hectic week, the free multicultural catalogues were popular as were the books on display, especially those in the multicultural collection. On balance the exhibition was a good one and beneficial to the cause of teaching for equality. The four books certainly should not have been included in the exhibition and were removed as soon as we were told of their presence. However, the books were on display because we did not make time to ensure they were not.

A practical example will show the difficulties of collecting resources for teaching for equality. At the Centre we have built up a collection of materials for teaching for equality over a number of years and have also developed a lot of useful contacts and information about resources in this field. Regular requests for information are made by teachers about resources for equality in education. The number of these requests is steadily increasing and we decided upon an attempt to set up a system to deal with these requests and collate information. The pilot project used the ILEA's suite of computer programs called LEEP run on a Research Machine 380Z microcomputer.[11]

We began by writing down a number of typical enquiries made by teachers about resources for teaching for equality. Next we wrote down the sort of replies and references the Centre would give to such enquiries and discussed how they might be classified. This was a fascinating process and we spent many hours arguing and discussing how best to set out the information we have. The system chosen forced us to condense information, take arbitrary decisions about categories and keep things brief. The first decision taken was to limit the details to organisations and general information and not to quote specific resource items. The coding sheet for information reproduced in the Appendix shows the nature of the compromise reached. Name, address and telephone number are obviously necessary. Field 4 – Culture/Geography shows the first compromise. As mentioned earlier many people require information on cultural backgrounds of settlers in this country and up-to-date information about countries of origin of settlers and their families. The categories chosen are almost ridiculously wide yet still have important gaps. We were attempting to deal practically with enquiries made, not to erect a comprehensive system. African is a vast category and overlaps with Caribbean for much information yet we felt it practical to separate the two. Indian sub-continent is an equally broad category but the distinction was made to separate enquiries about the Indian sub-Continent as many queries initially used 'Asian' when really meaning within the Indian sub-continent. Geographic categories as a cultural classification was far too difficult, complex and impractical for the system we adopted.

Field 5 – Subjects also shows a compromise and begins to reflect the different levels of resources and stages we feel are present in the field of education for equality. Subject areas dominate education and school organisation but we deliberately made our categories broad. Religion and customs, history and geography, arts and crafts, language and maths and science are self-explanatory. The first and third certainly reflect a general multicultural style, whilst the second overlaps this approach with some emphasis upon factual information and interpretation. British Black experience was included as representing a move away from the safe multicultural method towards a study of our own society and in particular of the experience of black people in Britain now; a multi-ethnic approach. The final category, race relations is specifically meant to include information on racism and, the way it operates. Perhaps a further category entitled 'Equality' will be added in this section when the project proper is undertaken. The reason for a section on equality is to distinguish between the essentially negative emphasis upon the operation of racism, and a more positive and optimistic emphasis upon equality. However, if we are to maintain our pragmatic approach of reflecting enquiries made and resources available we may well have to defer such a section until a future update of the system. Field 6 contains a set of obvious categories, the final one in this section, school experience, was included so that those with practical teaching experience of developing and using resources for equality could be included. Field 7 needs no explanation; fields 8 and 9 were included as we felt was essential so that the date and source of the information entered was known and therefore could be challenged as could the comments made under field 10. The system we are developing is only a rough and ready one, open to numerous criticisms. However, it does seem to work and reflect the type of enquiries regularly made.

Two examples of the type of enquiry the system can cope with, and that are made, are briefly set out below:
1 An enquiry about a particular festival of a faith from the Indian sub-Continent with a request for speakers with school experience to help with a project being run in a primary school would result in a search being made and the name, address and telephone number of organisations who have knowledge of such festivals from that particular culture/geographic area being printed out. The search would reveal those organisations coded as having information relevant to the Indian sub-Continent (Field 4). Religions and Customs (Field 5), Speakers (Field 6), Primary (Field 7) and would automatically cross reference data on the file to print out that coded information. In addition to the obvious details required as to name, address and telephone number of the organisation the enquirer could also request the source together with date of entry and any comments.
2 An enquiry about books on racism in Britain relevant to secondary schools would result in a search being made of the data to extract information from British Black Experience and Race Relations (Field 5) and Publications (Field 6) and Secondary (Field 7). This would print out a list of organisations with publications suitable for secondary age pupils on the topic of Race Relations in Britain. The enquirer could also ask for information about the organisation, normally name, address and telephone number together with details of the source of the entry.

It is unlikely that everyone will have read and agreed with all that has just been written with regard to the meaning and uses of resources in education for equality. This fact however underlines the point which has repeatedly been made in this chapter that everyone is at different stages of development – including the writers of this section. The meaning and uses to which resources are put will thus vary from situation to situation and person to person.

References

1. Milner, D., *Children and Race, Ten Years On*, Ward Lock Educational 1983
2. *West Indian Children in Our Schools*, HMSO 1981
3. Unpublished Report of ILEA, Lambeth Whole School Project, ILEA 1982
4. Issues and Resources, AFFOR, Birmingham 1983
5. *Anti-Racist School Policies*, ILEA Multi-Ethnic Education Inspectorate, June 1982
6. ILEA Anti-Racist Statement, Guidelines and Delivery 1983
7. Willey, R., *Teaching in Multi-cultural Britain*, Schools Council 1982
8. *Racism in the Workplace and Community*, Open University Press, Milton Keynes 1983
9. *Recognising Racism*, City of Birmingham Education Department 1982. Available from the Multicultural Support Services Unit, Bordesley Centre, Stratford Road, Birmingham B11 1AR
10. *Race in the Classroom – Teaching Against Racism in the Primary School*, published by All London Teachers Against Racism and Facism, c/o Lambeth Teachers' Centre, Santley Street, Brixton, London, SW4 7QD
11. LEEP is the Luton Education Enquiry Package, a suite of programs for data, storage and retrieval available from the Inner London Education Computing Centre, Bethwin Road, London. It is about to be replaced by a better suite of programs entitled SCAN from the same source and the project proper will use this more convenient suite of programs.

Chapter 18

RACISM AND LITERATURE

Michael Simons and Paul Ashton

> Michael Simons is Director of the ILEA English Centre which provides support and publishes materials for teachers in the Authority. He is a founder member of ALTARF.
>
> Paul Ashton was an Advisory Teacher based at the English Centre and is now an Education Officer at the BBC.

Some observers have accused English teachers of focusing their energies on images and representations rather than on the real issues of racism as a social practice. They have a point; the social and political dimensions of racial oppression and resistance defy easy analysis and resolution whereas representations seem to hold out the promise of tangible action. Arguments about positive and negative stereotypes and about censorship give the impression of energy and intense commitment. Controversy about the definitions of what constitutes a racist, a non-racist or an anti-racist book are good grist for an article and can be guaranteed to provoke a healthy string of rejoinders and letters.

We have certainly taken our turn at trying to disentangle the various currents in the debate over the representation of black and ethnic minorities in fiction for young people. In the first part of an article on literature and racism in the *English Magazine No 3*, we argue that *critical reading* is a far more constructive strategy than *censorship*. We feel that guidelines have a valuable role to play, not only in providing a basis for discussion about what kinds of text should be put before pupils, but also in helping teachers to organise class and group discussions about the ideological sub-text of any work of fiction. We come out in favour of *continual dialogue* in the classroom about the nature of racism and how it consciously or unconsciously affects the writer's values and attitudes. This is as true for the 'classics' as for popular fiction; it is at its most subtle in the case of non-racist books written by well-intentioned white writers. Our only grounds for censorship are in cases where books contain negative or insulting references which are uncontested by the author either in the narrative or through the mouths of any of the characters.

On the whole we feel that fiction has the potential for mediating to pupils the central themes of a racist society and that stereotype spotting is a less important activity than taking on the social and political forces which produce the stereotypes in the first place.

One possibility that we suggest as a means of raising the issue of racism in the classroom is to use stories with an explicit focus on racism. The nature and extent of the pupils' response is illustrated by the following case study.

We decided to take a short story, 'KBW'[1] by Farrukh Dhondy, in order to observe the ways in which children in different kinds of groupings responded to the story. (The two collections *East End at Your Feet* and *Come to Mecca*[2] are without any doubt the finest stories dealing with racial topics available to teachers at the moment. The insights into the Asian community in London, and the opportunity to see how things look from their position are made all the more valuable by the author's refusal to dodge painful or controversial questions that arise from within the Asian community itself.) We worked with a number of teachers and a variety of different kinds of class. As we expected, the response varied enormously according to the cultural mix of the class and the way in which the teacher organised the follow-up discussions.

A summary of research on how attitudes to ethnic minorities are affected by reading in Sara Goodman Zimet's book, *Print and Prejudice*,[3] brings out two points relevant to teachers of English; one, that a coherent series of lessons has more impact on attitudes than one-off lessons; and two, that discussion of reading material increases the likelihood of attitude-change. We are looking here, however, not at a series of lessons but at a single lesson; in fact, for the majority of pupils involved, it was their first experience of explicit classroom discussion on race.

Several points began to emerge from our unsystematic study. For instance, it gradually became clear to us that large groups were not conducive to the open exploration of racial issues. Some children opted out, others felt the need to 'stand by' provocative or racist statements, attitudes were easily polarised and it was extremely difficult to sustain one line of enquiry. In smaller groups, pupils could move with considerable fluency between the story, the issues it raised and their own personal experiences. However, where racism is concerned, only the most 'liberal' of teachers would feel entirely comfortable in allowing pupils to have a 'good discussion', regardless of the viewpoints eventually arrived at. So we compared unmonitored, free, small group discussions with groups where a structure had been offered by the teacher, either with or without the teacher's presence.

KBW synopsis

'KBW' is narrated by a young white boy who lives with his mother and father next door to a Bangladeshi family, the Habibs, in an East End block of flats. The narrator's father is a communist well-known for his anti-racist views, and he encourages his son to make a relationship with Tahir, Mr Habib's son. The two boys play chess with each other and Tahir is introduced to the local cricket team where he is especially valued for his skills as a bowler. The first crisis in the story comes when the boys in the cricket team refuse to share from Tahir's cup because they have heard a story, originating in the *Sun*, that a local girl is dying of typhoid. (The disease was in fact contracted in Spain). Tahir's friend regrets his lack of courage in not drinking from the cup. Tension begins to mount as the girl's condition worsens. A Mrs Biggles visits the narrator's mother and relates all the usual racist mythology. The mother is not prejudiced but on the other hand she does not argue against Mrs Biggles. The climax of the story is a full-scale attack on the Habibs' flat after the girl has died. When the attack comes, despite his wife's urgings, the narrator's father does not intervene because the odds are too great. At the end of the story the Habibs leave the estate, Tahir leaves the cricket team, and the friendship between the two boys is broken. (Reading time – 20 minutes).

Whole class discussion
The following account of a class discussion is based on a transcript with the observing teacher's comments, and comes from a school where black children constitute about 20 per cent of the total population.

The teacher explains the presence of a stranger with a tape-recorder, and while copies of the story are being passed round she explains that the story is from *East End at Your Feet*, which they've already read two stories from. Audible whisper: 'What does KBW mean?' No answer.

Teacher starts to read. Three boys at the back have decided not to follow the text, but just listen. When the phrase 'Niggers Out' comes up, the W.I. boy at the back throws a piece of paper up against the window. All very quiet. No reaction at all to the 'Pakis and coons' reference in the story.

Laughter over 'David Essex or Slade'. Someone says, 'You didn't tell us this was a nineteenth-century story!'

Uneasy reaction when Mrs Biggles says, 'It's the blacks bring these things here...' (The teacher had already decided to read the story straight through without stopping for discussion on the way.) All following hard.

End of story, 20 minutes after start. 'Is it finished?' 'Is that it?' W.I. boy calls out good-humouredly to Asian girl, 'Did they kick you out too, Manji?' Other girls immediately tell him to leave her alone. Teacher gets attention, and asks why they think she picked that story.

Boy: 'Cos the tape-recorder's here!
Boy: It's happening now, innit?
Girl: A lot of people are prejudiced against other people...
Teacher: Do you all know what *prejudiced* means?
Girl: You don't like 'em ... It's colour.
Teacher: Is there anyone in the story you really sympathise with?
(Silence)
Girl: What's that boy's name ... the white boy? I sympathise with his dad, 'cos he's got to live there still, with all the other tenants. He could walk out and they'd all start on him.
(General agreement)
Boy: But if you believe in something, you should have the guts to stand up and say what you believe in.
Boy: I sympathise with Mr Habib – he's the one actually getting attacked.

Teacher: Yes, he's only been in England for eight months, and ... why did he leave Bangladesh?
Boy: There was fighting over there ...
Boy: ... and he come over and got more!
(Laughter)
Teacher: Why do you laugh?
Boy: It's funny ... he come over for a bit of peace, and ...
Teacher: *Is* it funny?
Boy (committed to this line): Yeah!

Up to this point the discussion has been conducted entirely among whites. There's a tense, excited feeling in the room, as if some taboo subject has been raised, and anyone who speaks is listened to intently. The teacher turns to a W.I. girl, and the girl says how she saw her cousin being chased along the street by a gang of white boys. This contribution brings a slight pause: it ties in with the story, and raises the same difficult, and as yet unspoken, issues. Whatever sympathy the class feels is abruptly challenged with a non sequitur:

Boy (who rarely contributes in discussion normally): All these pakis and coons on the estate ...
(Uproar, with almost everyone speaking at once, except the Chinese boys, one of whom writes a note in Chinese and hands it to the other.)
Everyone: Don't use that stupid word!
They're the same as everyone else, ain't they?
You don't have to call them coons!
This isn't right!
Boy (on the defensive, but apparently rather pleased to be the focus): That's what it says in the book, right? So there you are then.
Boy: We emigrate to other countries, so maybe the people there feel the same as we do about them ...
Teacher: Who are the ones who get picked on?
Girl: Mostly pakis ... er, Pakistanis.
Boy: They never do nothing; they don't fight.
Teacher: Why doesn't Mr Habib fight? He's strong ...
Boy: Yeah, karate!
(Silence; perhaps the futility of one man fighting against twenty is too obvious to need saying.)
Boy (the same one who introduced the 'pakis and coons' comment): The flats were all dirty, and all that ... it could have been the flats ...
Boy: But it's happening round here, and the flats are all right and no-one's got fever. They still beat 'em up.
Boy (his only contribution): They've got sod all else to do.
(Three or four separate dicussions arise for about three minutes. Then one boy raises his voice and the class listens.)
Boy: They've got shops over here and everything. There's a shop down

Colville Street. I don't know how many years I been going down there ... it's always been a shop ... I mean, now it's a paki shop.

Teacher: Do you object to Pakistanis having shops?

Several voices: Not really ... some of them are really nice ... there's rice all over the floor ... they've got a lovely little girl ... don't be so *stupid*! (Laughter)

Boy: This is all getting a bit out of hand.

(Silence)

Teacher: You weren't laughing just now ...

Same boy: I just don't find the things people have been saying very funny.

Girl: Some Pakistanis are unsociable, and that's ...

Girl: They've got their own, you know, and they just want to know their own ...

Boy: That's how they get the shops. They work all hours and send the money back.

Boy: You think people shouldn't work ...

Boy: Miss! Miss! What about these people on the boats, coming here ... we've been waiting for a house, right? – somewhere round here, for ages, and they just come in and take their pick, get a nice house ...

Boy: You were waiting long before they came. How can it be their fault?

The lesson ended after about 25 minutes discussion with the whole class. Several points emerge:

1. The size of the group meant that any issue was liable to be interrupted by a comment on a different tack, and several pupils (notably the W.I. ones) opted out because a sizeable group within the class had made the discussion their own.
2. The story, which is very simple, triggered off many different responses which are anything but simple, and constantly drew the class's attention away from the story to real experiences and issues; i.e., the structure of the story did not structure the discussion, and the pupils, given almost complete freedom, did not explore the issues in anything like a systematic way. The teacher could have either directed attention back to the story, and insisted on it as the subject, or, predicting which way the discussion would go, have prepared material of a factual kind to steady the discussion, and give it more depth.
3. In a free large-group discussion, retailing of slogans or unconsidered racist myths is liable either to be not countered at all, as here, because the black pupils feel at a disadvantage, or to raise the temperature so quickly that no real interaction takes place. Perhaps this is a symptom of an early stage in the discussion of racial issues, and in a series of lessons it would die away because the pupils involved would have got it off their chest. In this discussion, to have challenged every single racist comment would have meant the teacher assuming a more and more didactic role, and yet the very low profile she chose to adopt meant that Dhondy's intentions, and the feelings of the black pupils, had got very short shrift.

Small group discussion (A)
The following group's discussion comes from the same class as the above extract. The small size of the group enabled the same pupils to respond more openly to those issues; they felt they had the space to conjecture, tell stories, ask questions, and clarify their positions. The only 'structure', however, was the presence of the teacher and the same tendencies emerged as in the previous transcript, of assertion and counter-assertion round racial issues. Nevertheless, the level of argument is far sharper and higher and the atmosphere much calmer.

One group discussed Asian doctors, immigration controls, standing up for other people, National Front marches and counter-demonstrations, influences on public opinion, freedom of speech and its relationship with violence. In another group one of the W.I. girls was able to say things she had wanted to say that morning.

W.I. girl: I'm proud to be British.
White boy: Were you born in England?
Girl: Where do you expect me to be born?
Boy: You might have been born in Jamaica, or somewhere.
Girl: You think we're born in the trees, and climb down?
Boy: I didn't say that...
Asian-looking boy (in fact from S. America): All English people think that.
Teacher: No, they don't. I don't.
White boy: There's a good and a bad side to everybody.
W.I. girl: That's not what we're talking about!
S.A. boy: When I was in Primary School, there was this book about a black kid in Africa, and they dug up roots and ate them... now what black kid does that? You never read a white kid doing that!
W.I. girl: I hate it when they call Manji a Paki.
White boy: What else can you call 'em?
Girl: A girl.
Teacher: Where do these words come from?
S.A. boy: English people invented words like that so they can think they're better than everyone else. Look at America. There were thousands of Red Indians, right, now there's only a few. Just like the buffalo. The English said, you're savage, you can't live here, we want to live here. Do you know what? All those thousands of Europeans pouring into South America, right, and then when a few Pakistanis arrive there, they start groaning and mumbling...
White boy: Don't you like England, then?
(Later)
Boy: Why do some coloured people talk common, like I talk, and then, when they want, they say 'Raasclaat' and things like that?
W.I. girl: It's how your parents talk, and school... they're different.
Boy: Putting things on telly (like *Roots*) has made the white people look really bad, you know.

W.I. girl: But some of them *were* bad, and *are* bad.
Boy: But I didn't do it ... I weren't there, was I?
(Later)
Boy: Why is it so rare you see a black person owning a shop?

The children all felt afterwards that the discussions had been valuable, but were sceptical about the possibility of a story on its own influencing their own, or anybody's opinions. All agreed that it would be good to have such lessons regularly, bearing out Zimet's observation, perhaps, that to have any real impact such reading must not be a one-off experience.

Small group discussion (B)
In the next group four West Indian boys discussed the story on their own. The absence of the teacher meant that the thread of the discussion is exploratory, and the group's homogenity makes the discussion free of seriously conflicting views. It is worth noting that there is none of the supposed hostility towards the Asian community sometimes attributed to West Indian boys.

The boys spend some time discussing typhoid and immigration control.

– I think they only liked that boy because he was a good bowler. Mostly they were prejudiced against him.
– I don't blame the boy for leaving the school. If that had been me I wouldn't have stayed around.
– Especially as the people in C Block were causing a lot of trouble.
– I think they were given the worst flat, don't you?
– They always get the worst conditions.
– If the family was to tell the council about what happened, they wouldn't do anything, would they?
– What do you think?
– There's one of them NF marches next week ...
– That's got nothing to do with the story!
– It's got a lot to do ...
– Sorry ...
– The thing is, they give them bad housing and then people think they're dirty people.
– What are you laughing for? It's not true. They're very clean – as clean as all the rest of the people ...
– I think the newspapers were very wrong in writing that story about the family. They didn't investigate, or give any details about how it came about.
– About when they were having coffee. I think that Tahir's friend should have drunk the coffee. Tahir wouldn't have been playing cricket if he'd had it (the disease). He would've been in fever.
– I think Tahir's friend's dad was wrong to take Tahir's dad to the pub, because he didn't drink; it was against his religion. He was just causing trouble.
– He didn't want to cause trouble.
– He's a dummy.

— He thought he was helping him, and showing him around the place. But it all came back on him ...

It's clear how thoughtful these boys have been in relating the incidents of the story outwards to their own experiences; of the NF, of the media, and 'them' (the council). It's also more than likely that, given more time, issues would have become better organised and further developed. However, the absence of any monitoring from a teacher has perhaps allowed more issues to be raised than would otherwise be the case. One important point is that there is an appeal to down-to-earth common sense in these comments; Tahir's friend should have known that Tahir was not ill, and so he could safely drink from Tahir's cup without having to make a gesture out of it, and the father should not have forced Tahir's dad into the pub just to make a gesture of solidarity. This is all very sensible, but the pupils are not touching on one of the central issues of the story (which the pupils in the next discussion take up fully), which is the area between overt anti-racist activities on the one hand, and no response at all to racism on the grounds of avoiding trouble, on the other. The set-up of the story, which has only one man on the Asian family's side, against a whole estate block of racists, is pessimistic at this level, and is probably influencing the discussable options for positive action.

Small group discussion (C)
In order to see whether it was possible to focus group discussions more effectively we decided to formulate a checklist of assertions about the story to see whether this would act as a catalyst for directing the talk to specific issues raised by the story. The groups had to agree among themselves which three statements were most important to them after reading the story. We feel that this checklist could be criticised on many grounds, not least that it appears to predetermine or channel responses. In fact, quite the opposite seems to have occurred. The statements provoke the pupils into re-entering and re-constructing the story. While questions seem to presuppose specific answers, the statements do not lead to the usual guess-what's-in-my-head routine.

In addition to this, some teachers also decided to try out some prediction exercises as a framework for discussion. This simply involved stopping the story at two key points and giving the class five minutes in pairs or groups to work out what might happen next. This proved another very useful strategy for getting the pupils to concentrate on the story. The precise period of time allowed, and the fact that the interest in the outcome of the story is quickened, seem to maximise the chance of successful collaborative talk.

KBW checklist
Tick the three statements which seem most important to you after reading the story.
1 The narrator's father was a communist.
2 Tahir was a good cricketer.
3 Bad housing can create bad feelings between races.

4 The narrator's father should have helped Tahir's father when they were attacked.
5 People were wrong to blame Tahir's family.
6 The way newspapers report things can cause trouble.
7 The narrator should have drunk from the cup Tahir used.
8 The author wrote this story to show what racial prejudice is like.
9 Tahir should have carried on playing cricket.

Here two black and two white girls were discussing the story, using the checklist. They were working their way through the points, beginning with Statements 1 and 4.

– He should have helped.
– No, I don't think he should have.
– It would only have made matters worse.
– Two people would have got beaten up then. It's a matter for the police to sort out.
– If he's a communist, why does he say to the mother to get back into the kitchen and sit down? When he comes up against racial prejudice, he backs down.
– He was very strong in his communism.
– But why speak out, and then when it comes to the real thing...
– Yes, but if he'd gone out he'd have been acting on impulse because of his communism.
– I don't think his communism was so strong. I don't think you can truly say he was against racial prejudice, except to a certain extent, because he was a communist. When Mr Habib was being hounded by those hooligans, he just helps orally, with his mouth.
– What kind of help is that, just pushing his wife back into the kitchen?
– They don't like getting the police involved.
– He was only against racial prejudice because of his communism.
– But communism is total equality for everyone.
– I can't understand that. I'm sorry.
– Can't you see – there was so many against one...
– Too many, right, But to succeed, you've got to fight. I don't mean you've got to smash people, but if he'd just stood in the doorway it would have showed he was against them, just by standing there. He said he wouldn't be seen dead at the girl's funeral, but that was after it was all over.
– But he'd have put his family in a position where they would have been in danger.
– But he does that from the beginning, by asking his son to look after Tahir.
– But they weren't actually physical then, were they?

Two strands run through this rather hectic exchange. One is that there is a difference between a moral objection to racism and a political one, and the other is that both forms of objection imply some kind of behaviour that goes beyond just speaking your mind. The first strand falls away when it is crudely linked with theory ('I can't understand that'), but the second generates some nice discriminations between different implications of action. Perhaps a whole series of discussions might start from situations rather than propositions?

(Statement 6)
– The media is so corrupted that we don't need to argue that one out. OK, the girl died right, but they make a great big thing more than what it was.
– You can't really say more than what it was because somebody's dead.
– No but they always stir things.
– They moved it, they shift the blame.
– The *Sun* is a conservative newspaper. The *Sun* is more likely to go down in the East End.
– The *Sun* does really slanderous stories – you get the feeling that they're boosting the working class but they're really putting down the working class, right?
(Girl discussing racist grandfather, later)
I said, 'You make me sick.'
'You can't speak to me like that! I'm your grandfather!'
I said, 'I can speak to you any way I like. You might be my grandfather, you might be older than me, but you have to earn respect before you get it. You don't go out into the street and see how white people treat black people. You're only making things up in your head from what you hear in the newspapers and news is oriented by white people for white people against black people. Don't give me all that crap, right?'

(Statement 8)
– I think the mother's ignorant. I would say about 80 per cent of the working-class around the East End bring up their children to be like that – ignorant and one-track-minded.
– You know, when the other woman comes in – Mrs Biggles – she's stirring it, and the mother's slowly but surely going to her way of thinking.
– She doesn't want to open her eyes to what's going on around her.
– The mother has all these feelings inside her head. She hasn't been educated, she doesn't know how to express herself. And another thing – she's scared as well.
– There's nothing she can do to change it, and she doesn't want to get involved like her husband does. Her husband is really outspoken.
– But this world needs more like her than Mrs Biggles.
– Yes, this story is real, though. We see it happen all the time. There's always a Mrs Biggles round the corner.
– Notice the mother came out good in the end. Although she's a bit prejudiced, she's the sort of person who tries to stop herself from being that way, and tries to keep justice...
– I would have liked it more if the father wasn't a communist.

– Yes, definitely.
– Because what I get from the story is that he only thinks racialism is wrong because he's a communist. I think if he wasn't a communist, but just had strong outspoken views against racism it would have been better.

These pupils have identified three varieties of stance within the white community, and a fourth, the overtly racist, is too obvious to need comment here. The construction of the story has helped this breakdown of monolithic perceptions of racism; it would be interesting to hear these pupils discuss varieties of stance within the black community.

The final point made is interesting because it's relatively rare to find remarks directed at the author's intentions. The girl is aware that the writer has a range of choices when constructing a story and from her point of view she feels it was a mistake for Dhondy to make the father a communist in so far as it affects the likely responses of potentially racist readers. We feel that there may be some truth in this and there is some evidence that Dhondy deliberately portrays the communist father in an unflattering light in order to make a particular point.

General issues
In any discussion involving racism two difficulties may arise that other kinds of discussion in English are free from. The first is that consciously racist views may be expressed, and may even be directed against other pupils. It goes against the grain to stifle any pupil's views, but should an exception be made where those views will have the effect of, and may have been intended as a way of, stirring up trouble? The teacher may hope that such views will be adequately dealt with by the class, but they may not, and there is a responsibility to protect the pupils under such attack. The teacher who takes an uncompromisingly anti-racist stance does have the backing of the ILEA's guidelines on multiracial teaching; there is no such thing as neutrality in the presence of racist insults. Perhaps the best approach is to make it clear to the class beforehand just what kinds of comments will be tolerated and what will not.

The second difficulty arises from the possibility that, in the process of listening to and expressing fears, prejudices, conjectures and experiences, some pupils will get angry. There may be a temptation for teachers, and for some pupils, to avoid the whole issue rather than risk this. Our experience is that strong feelings in this context need not be disruptive, and that the teacher is neither 'stirring up' nor 'defusing' genuine feeling by having such discussions. In fact, this may be the calmest forum pupils will experience. The result is nearly always to help the pupils make their expressions of feeling more considered, more articulate and, hopefully, more optimistic.

Although these extracts from group discussions have been necessarily brief, they do show that young people have an enormous breadth of experience and understanding which they can bring to bear on the topic of racism. However, it would confirm the worst aspects of the English teacher's dilettante reputation if the issue were left here. Too often English teachers allow themselves the luxury of leapfrogging from topic to topic according to the perceived level of emotional involvement displayed by the pupils. As the transcripts show, pupils' contributions reveal an unformulated understanding that racism is bound up with wider political and social forces; it ought to be part of an English teacher's responsibility to ensure that her/his pupils are offered some evidence and information that helps to clarify the relationship between personal prejudice and institutionalised racism. We include here a short list of resources which teachers might find useful in this area.

What we have said about the raising of the issue of race will not be new to the English teacher who consistently brings major social issues into the classroom; what we have said about the importance of attention to the way discussion is organised will not be new to the English teacher who gives this sort of attention to all classroom learning. In this article we have tried to show that these two teachers can be one and the same.

References
1 From Dhondy, F., *East End at Your Feet*, Macmillan (Topliner), 1976
2 Dhondy, F., *Come to Mecca*, Fontana Lions, 1978
3 Zimet, S. G., *Print and Prejudice*, Hodder and Stoughton, 1976

Bibliography

Fiction: prejudice and racism

Novels
(The first six titles here could be used with younger pupils.)
Stuart, M., *Marassa amd Midnight*, (HEB New Windmill 0434965006). Twin brothers, slaves; one in Paris during the French revolution, the other in slave revolt in Haiti; their adventures and eventual meeting.
Leeson, R., *The Third Class Genie*, (Armada Lions 006709303). Racial issues introduced delicately into lively urban story of schoolboy who discovers a genie in a tin can.
Drake, T., *Playing It Right*, (Puffin 0140312986). *Playing It Right* is set in and around a school in an anonymous racially mixed urban area. The central characters are 13-year-old boys: two West Indian and one Indian. A worthy though rather clumsy book: clearly anti-racist and pro-ordinary kids, but rather laboured in construction and limited in vision. Nevertheless, this book offers a short, easy read after which it would be possible to discuss questions of racist attitudes and abuse, behaviour in school and teachers' expectations of pupils.
Reid, V. S., *The Young Warriors*, (Longman Caribbean Horizons 0582765692).

The Young Warriors is set in Jamaica at the time of the Maroon's guerilla campaign against their English colonial masters and the Redcoats. It tells the story of how five 14-year-old boys pass their initiation test to become young warriors and play a vital part in protecting their village against Redcoat attack.
Dickinson, P., *The Devil's Children*, (Puffin 0140305467). *The Devil's Children* is set in England sometime in the future after a nationwide rebellion against all types of machinery. The story centres round a girl called Nicky Gore. Separated from her family during the riots in London, Nicky attaches herself to a band of Sikhs, the only people unaffected by 'the madness'. At first their relationship is guarded, but gradually the Sikhs come to value Nicky's judgement and Nicky comes to recognise them as dignified and brave people.
Needle, J., *My Mate Shofiq*, (Fontana Lions 0006715184). *My Mate Shofiq* is set in a Lancashire industrial town and is narrated by Bernard, who seems to be about twelve years old. The story concerns Bernard's growing friendship with Shofiq, a Pakistani Lancashire native. Bernard gets interested in the tough, taciturn, self-contained Shofiq; their friendship develops unsteadily, with Bernard eventually visiting Shofiq's home and then getting involved with Shofiq and his father's attempts to protect the family from the predatory advances of a Mr. Burke of 'the Social Services'.
Richter, H. P., *Friedrich*, (HEB New Windmill 0435122266). The Nazi persecution of the Jews in Germany – the story of Friedrich, a Jewish boy, told by his gentile neighbour and friend. 1925-1942.
Brown, D., *Wounded Knee*, (Fontana Lions 0006713416). An adaptation for younger readers of Dee Brown's gripping and appalling study of the destruction of the Indian people by white Americans.
Mehdevi, A., *Parveen*, (Peacock 0140471111). With an Iranian father and American mother, an American girl confronts sexual and racial problems while living in Iran.
Carter, P., *Under Goliath*, (Puffin 0140311327). *Under Goliath* is set in Belfast in 1969. It is the story of a developing friendship between two boys, one Catholic and the other Protestant who live among the tensions and confusions of sectarian conflict.
Lester, J., *The Basketball Game*, (Peacock 0140471065). Black family moves into white area of Nashville in '50's. Racial adjustments and relationship between Allen, teenage son, and white girl next door. Understanding of segregation in USA useful before reading.
Taylor, M. D., *Roll of Thunder, Hear My Cry*, (Puffin 0140311297). *Roll of Thunder, Hear My Cry* is set in Mississippi during the 1930s Depression and is based on the experiences of the author's own family. Told in the first person by 10-year-old Cassie Logan (who seems somewhat older), the story describes the struggle of a black family to hang on to their bit of land. The family's warmth, solidarity and determination is set against the economic and cultural oppression of the black community.
Needle, J., *Piggy In The Middle*, (Fontana Lions 0006721397). Sandra joins the

police force and finds herself working on a case involving a former shool mate, Mohammed Mansoor, who is accused of murdering his father. As events unfold her loyalties become increasingly divided between the values of the police and those of her journalist boyfriend. In the end, finding she can no longer tolerate the racism and cynicism of the police force, she resigns.

Wright, R., *Black Boy*, (Longman Imprint 0582233801). A powerful autobiographical account of a black child growing up in the racist society of the pre-war American South and gradually becoming aware of how it works.

Smith, R., *Sumitra's Story*, (The Bodley Head 0370304667). A novel set in Uganda and England which describes how Sumitra experiences first the Ugandan Asian lifestyle, then the harrowing flight from Amin's regime and the traumas of early days in England, and, finally, the cultural and racial tensions of life for herself and her family in London. The book's uncertainties about what to make of these tensions are themselves thought-provoking.

Emecheta, B., *Second-Class Citizen*, (Fontana 0006145175). A largely autobiographical account of a Nigerian woman's struggle to overcome discrimination. The discrimination she experiences in Nigeria is against women; coming to London with her husband she faces racial discrimination as well – and the struggle to survive when she is left with sole responsibility for raising her children.

Ngugi wa Thiong'o, *Weep Not Child*, (Heinemann African Writers 0435900072). The story of a family in Kenya in the post-war colonial period, told through the voice of Njoroge, one of the boys in the family. The novel explores the relationship between the villagers and the white settlers in the context of the growing anti-colonial movement.

Abrahams, P., *Tell Freedom*, (Allen & Unwin Windsor Selections 049230018). An autobiographical account of life in pre-Second World War South Africa which describes the author's efforts to survive and make a life for himself in the context of apartheid. The direct and vivid narrative of the early parts of the book is particularly powerful.

Ellison, R., *The Invisible Man*, (Penguin 0140023356). Southern States black boy comes to New York and meets black people representing different experiences of living in the ghetto. A difficult but rewarding book suitable for older pupils.

Short stories

Lester, J., *Long Journey Home*, (Longman Knockout 0582160383 or Peacock 0140309039). Vivid stories about slaves in the southern U.S.

Lester, J., *To Be A Slave*, (Puffin 014030620X). American slaves talk about their experiences, interspersed with author's comments. (Excerpts on double Caedmon TC 2066).

Jackson, D., 'Flame on the Frontier' and 'A Man Called Horse,' in *Ten Western Stories*, ed. C. E. J. Smith (Longman Imprint 058223333X). In the first story two white sisters are captured and brought up by Indians; in the second a white man is captured and used as a slave. Appealing and powerful stories.

Dhondy, F., *East End at Your Feet*, (Topliner 0333199626). Young Asians in the East End find their adolescent problems complicated by the experience of discrimination and the clash of cultures. 'KBW' and 'The China Tea Service' particularly relevant.

Dhondy, F., *Come to Mecca*, (Fontana Lions 0006715192). Strong collection of stories involving Asians and West Indian kids in London. Life-styles and attitudes conveyed in lively narratives.

Lessing, D., *Nine African Stories*, (Longman Imprint 058223378X). 'No Witchcraft for Sale' and 'The Antheap', in particular, deal with relations between white Rhodesian farmers and black workers.

Selvon, S., 'When Greek Meets Greek', in *Stories from the Caribbean*, ed. A Salkey (Elek 0236177974). Wryly funny story about a Trinidadian looking for accommodation in Westbourne Grove and meeting discrimination and stereotyping.

Parker, D., 'Arrangement in Black and White', in *The Best of Dorothy Parker*, (Penguin). A monologue in which a woman from the Southern States of America gushingly asks to be introduced to a famous black singer, revealing her prejudices with every word that she utters.

Gordimer, N., *Six Feet of the Country*, (Penguin 0410065598). A collection of six short stories which explore the brutal and inhuman consequences of apartheid in South Africa. 'A Chip of Glass Ruby' is especially interesting: it is about a Muslim woman who is arrested for engaging in political activity against the pass laws affecting the country's seven million black people. A film of this story, which was originally transmitted on Channel 4, will shortly be available to ILEA teachers through the ILEA Film Library.

Ajegbo, K., *Black Lives, White Worlds*, (Cambridge Educational 0521284635). An anthology of stories and extracts by black American writers including Toni Morrison, George Jackson, Mildred Taylor and Richard Wright.

Needle, J., *A Sense of Shame*, (Fontana Lions 0006719015). An uneven collection of stories dealing with different aspects of prejudice, of which the title story is the most sensitive and the least formulaic.

Chapter 19

COMBATING INSTITUTIONAL RACISM – A TRAINING COURSE FOR EXPERIENCED TEACHERS

Tuku Mukherjee

> Tuku Mukherjee is Senior Lecturer at Roehampton Institute of Higher Education. He is Course Tutor on several courses – Advanced Diploma in Education for a Multicultural Society (for experienced teachers on full time secondment for a year); Race, Class and Schooling (B.Ed honours); Education for Democracy (in service course for teachers).

In my experience the vast majority of teachers through early socialisation and confined life experiences often emerge from training uncritical of their role as teachers or the institution to which they belong. After a soft, safe and protected journey they disembark not only on the battlefield of life but of teaching with a non-conflictual view of life and a liberal, apolitical conscience. They are unaware that the process by which they select and interpret knowledge is a definite political act and that the very act of teaching transforms them from being an ordinary individual into the most powerful political agent of the state in the classroom, able to shape and influence the life styles and chances of their pupils.

The only model the teaching profession has ever learned to operate is a consensus or assimilationist model. The criteria by which teachers work are influenced by attempts to 'uplift' the life chances of their white working class pupils by moulding and shaping them in their own image. To be processed through such a construct inevitably involves a massive denial of self, self-identity and one's roots. The implications are twofold. Those who succeed are more or less forced to forget the experience of such a painful 'slavish' liberal passage – by the time they eventually 'arrive' they have internalised the neutrality of the middle class and a view of life in which conflictual issues which affect life and society are beyond their control and can only be dealt by the state and political parties.

> This has gone on for so long in the British system that thousands of white families seem to have adjusted to the idea that school is merely a fact of life like traffic or low pay, not something that can be expected to deliver goods of any value.[1]

In my view, for most working class children school is but a trip, you get on and you get off as soon as possible. For a vast majority it has no sense of the person and is therefore meaningless. It is a constant denial of the child to conform to middle class values, which are foreign to her/him. The present political climate is fostering a return to 'My Victorian Values'.² Frozen institutions can only produce frozen pupils. Some, attempting to burst out of their deep freeze are causing havoc in schools. 'We are obsessed with developing disciplinary control in our school and teaching has gone out of the window' commented an ILEA school teacher very recently. The profession is under attack not only intellectually, but in schools, where teachers have become symbols of oppression and may be the object of physical attack. Even the physical structure of the school has become a symbol of oppression and attack.

> Last March an arson attack on a history and economics room destroyed vital examination papers by pupils and caused damage estimated at £20,000 (Villies High School).³

The other ideological force operating in the entire education system as well as in society is the ideology of 'race' based on the 'binary' theory of white superiority and black inferiority underpinned by white perspectives, white values and white language. In spite of vast changes in the composition of society, the deep structure and the ideology of the model remains constant – assimilation. I would argue that for education to be creative it must be critical and reflect the changing composition of a society where unity does not mean uniformity. Furthermore, political and cultural continuity, stability and the creativity of a society depend on change, exchange and movement, without which major institutions of the state will inevitably become dysfunctional and those who run the institutions will gradually become deprofessionalised. The ideology of 'race' over these 400 years of history has become an integral part of the class construct, permeating through language and above all through the legacy of 'inheritance' every institution of the state: church, politics, social services, housing, employment and the media. All are infested with the corrosive effect of institutional racism.

The response of the education system has been twofold. On the one hand are the élite, such as Lord Boyle with his policy of dispersal. He responded to the black presence by declaring 'I must regretfully tell the House that one (Southall) school must be regarded now as irretrievably an immigrant school. The important thing to do is to prevent this happening elsewhere.' His analysis defined black pupils as 'problems', solutions for whom were to be provided by the teaching profession. There is no doubt that Boyle responded in all good faith but his response was based on inherited attitudes and part of that legacy is the culture of racial prejudice; not only did he activate the racial dimension of the culture for educationalists and sociologists but black people emerged as a field of anthropological study, constantly and continuously contrasted against white norms. Inevitably black pupils not only emerged as different but deficit – to be studied, to be civilised, disciplined and corrected. What is baffling is the total silence of the academic world on a political analysis of the black presence in British schools. Consciously or unconsciously, either due to lack of awareness or lack of intellectual rigour, they have failed to comprehend what was really happening. Whichever way one looks at the issue it seems to be that institutions of higher education who set the agenda of training have abdicated their responsibility; they remained silent; and to me their inaction has amounted to racism of silent collusion.

To respond differently would mean facing up to the ideology of 'race', whereby black people are separately categorised within British society, and a deep structural division both in the public and private sector is based on the culture of colour. There is either total silence on the issue of 'race', or deflection of the issue, as if it is the prerogative of the National Front and the British Movement to be racists. The silence could be collusion or fear, or both. In my experience the word 'race' has been stereotyped to mean black people and therefore any discussion or debate is far too fearful, emotional, controversial and is a taboo like 'death' and 'sex'. 'I must admit I was not looking forward to attending the course' is a normal response when 'race' is high on the agenda in any course that I have so far seen. My experience informs me that fear is implicit in the ideology of race and must not be discussed at a feeling level, as it is far too conflictual and cannot be accommodated within the 'consensus' and 'assimilative' model that we operate. The structure of meaning inhibits us from questioning the status quo so our institutions remain frozen and become mass objects. In my view, as a teacher, it is demeaning both to myself and those I teach (and an abdication of responsibility) if we do not face up to the issue of 'white racism'. If racism has a colour it is not 'black' but 'white'. But the race relations debate has developed, the concept of multicultural education has been constructed in such a way that the issue is pursued as having nothing to do with white teachers, white institutions and white power structure. Education is in a crisis for complex reasons, but at the core lies the issue of 'race' and racism and the political battle on the streets of 30 cities is the cumulative effect of a 'massive investment' of racism. It has produced a 'culture of revolt' and black alienation is the only force which is beginning to challenge the ethnocentric and racist education system. It is no wonder that

> teachers are somewhat shell-shocked and demoralised. They are no longer sure that anyone believes in education anymore: they are increasingly unsure themselves what it is all supposed to be about.[4]

The process of alienation, frustration and anger is beginning to hit the teaching profession. We need to realise that the political battle is being shifted from the street into schools, and as a consequence for institutions where racism has never been confronted, both oppressed and the oppressor are beginning to emerge as mirror image of each other.

Every training course is based on a theoretical framework, defined and redefined as I go along, an essential exercise for any tutor. I will now try and give a brief account of a short issue-oriented course for teachers.

Multicultural education – with an anti-racist perspective

The most positive approach in my view is:

1 to confront the issue of 'race' head on, examine its effects on teachers, semi-professionalism, alienation and personal growth;
2 to disabuse people of the notion that multicultural education is for 'black people';
3 to argue with clarity and show clearly why white teachers need to be anti-racist, not because of black alienation, but because an ethnocentric racist approach and structure is a denial to all pupils; a distortion of teachers' own integrity.

The content of the course was negotiated with the teachers. It was agreed that we need to examine the following in depth.
1 Our fears and expectations of the course.
2 Critical analysis of multicultural studies and racism – the black perspective.
3 Definitions: racial prejudice, racism, ethnicity and institutional racism.

It wasn't an easy course. For most, it was a painful process of self-location and examination at a personal and institutional level in the 'race' continuum. For the first time participants were faced with the proposition that we were part of the problem and not the solution. We, not just our pupils, were underachieving.

The initial thrust of the course was white racism, white power structure, power relationship across the 'colour line' and gradual erosion of our teachers' professionalism when faced with black affirmation, challenge and the tension of alienation.

Fear and expectations
The session on fears and expectations clearly indicated that:
1 they were frightened to be exposed as racists;
2 they might go away feeling more helpless than before;
3 the course would undermine their confidence;
4 they were afraid of being 'brainwashed';
5 the course would challenge their 'cherished ideals';
6 extra work would be involved since it would mean adding areas of knowledge to their existing curriculum;
7 they found isolation on return to their school.

On the other hand, their expectations clearly showed up the following.
1 That they desperately hoped to develop strategies for change at both a personal and institutional level.
2 The course would bring 'clarity to their thinking about multicultural education and racism, and give a way out from over compensating black pupils'.
3 Since racism is so high on the agenda, it might be counter-productive and reinforce attitudes against multicultural education.

The discussion which followed was highly illuminating. It revealed clearly that they thought that multicultural education was a 'third-rate concept, and any initiative would mean lowering of standards' and would bring 'pressure for extra resources – almost impossible at a time of educational cuts'. The session was crucial for it meant that the organic connection ... between multicultural education and the problematic 'black presence' had to be severed. In my view this connection is the main reason why the concept of multicultural education is considered third rate and has very little relevance to 'white schools'.

In response to feedback from the group I consistently argued that for nearly two decades, teachers have seen the existence of black pupils in our schools merely as a mass problematic, racialised phenomenon and that the ethnocentric selection of knowledge and its transmission adds up to racism by omission for it refuses to acknowledge the reality of black experience. I maintained further that unless the content, the structure, and even the methodology begins to reflect the black reality and the changing composition of our society, we would remain trapped in our cells of racist ethnocentricism and collude with the process of continued deschooling and conflict across the colour line. Schools cannot compensate for society but neither can schools survive insulated and isolated from society.

'The teachers are obsessed with our life style and therefore it's meaningless for us as black people. Our ethnicity has been used as a euphemism for race and your concentration on our ethnicity allows you to deflect from your own racist attitudes. It gives you a let out from addressing yourself to the ideology of race, your own identity as white people and what you stand for politically.' Balrag Purewall (Leader of Southall Youth Movement).

Critical analysis of multicultural studies and racism – the black perspective
This session was a traumatic experience for all, including two black members of the course. 'I hate the phrase multicultural education' was a response of a white head of a primary school. 'I expected to be faced with acknowledging how I personally, have been affected by my cultural heritage – that by being white, I am by definition racist. Also that by being Head of an institution in British society (i.e., a school) I am part of institutional racism. What I had not expected was to be shaken to my roots about my personal weaknesses and forced to face up to them i.e., cowardice, collusion and a term someone else used – chameleon. I feel having been brought to this point, I have reached a turning point in my own personal development and that is something which rarely occurs in the context of a course. Any course which brings people face to face with themselves in this way must I feel, be both invaluable and far-reaching.' (Head teacher.)

An analysis clearly indicates that courses, whether initial or in-service are not about issues, and usually every attempt is made to avoid self-examination, for that involves self-conflict and conflict is not admissable in the non-conflictual world of middle class liberalism. In my view, Institutes of Higher Educations operate from 'green sanctuaries' abdicating their responsibilities by failing to initiate any sense of critical awareness among the students, on the false demeaning assumption that they cannot face themselves or their relationship with the reality. This becomes abundantly clear from the statement made by a student on a diploma course – 'I'm studying at a ... College of Higher Education in "Aspects of language in the multiracial community", leading to a post-graduate diploma. This is one evening a week for two years; I'm in my third term. I still don't know all the names of the people on the course. I have written an essay, read some books and listened to some lectures. I think it'll look good on my curriculum vitae. It has done nothing either to raise my consciousness or to give me fresh courage to fight racism. This course through its intensity and unflinching honesty has done this for me.' I have ghastly feelings that most courses are run as mass clinical operations and course members remain objects without a 'name' and their feelings are never allowed to surface. The objective seems to be, to provide a 'better curriculum vitae' and avoid imperative issues.

'I didn't look at myself as black during my training, neither was I allowed to. I did what everybody did – just fitted in. No one could pronounce my name. People asked me: "How can you tell you are ill? Your colour doesn't show up." I felt threatened and an alien. My only concern was survival.' (A black teacher.)

At a feeling level, what consistently emerged was a floodgate of self-destructive negative attitudes about black people embedded deep down the white psyche. 'I didn't think of black people except as savages, indecent – not like us at all.'

'Happy, dangerous and threatening – couldn't possibly manage on their own.'

'Sunny natured boy – we had to pay a penny in the box, so that a black boy/girl could go to heaven.'

'Objects of pity and sexually dangerous.' They were all teachers, each with a minimum of 7–10 years teaching experience, shaping lives and views of children – black and white – carrying essential components of transforming themselves into conscious or unconscious racists. Their view of life and reality of Britain was so deformed that they were quite incapable of making any sense out of studying black life style, except to offer a distorted sense of compassion, 'help', and 'patronage', let alone address themselves to the issue of black life chances. It threw up clearly and sharply the contradiction between their belief in democratic ideals of fairness and justice and their ability to teach with attitudes which totally contradict their ideals. In my view, it is this contradiction, which has brought Britain face to face with dysfunctionalism and the prospect of continuous ethnic conflict.

The central grid of all training courses is not only to provide a framework of trust and confidence to enable the course members to face the process of self-confrontation, so that they are able to unfold layers of attitudes based on the ideology of 'race', but also to show clearly that racism is a common disaster across the colour line.

> If white people have suffered less obviously from racism than black people, they have nevertheless suffered greatly; the cost has been greater perhaps than we yet know. If the white man has inflicted the wound of racism upon black men [and women – my addition], the cost is that s/he would receive the mirror image of that wound into himself/herself.[5]

The rebellion in 30 cities is a testimony to the conflict and the 'wound'. The personal dehumanising analysis of the effects of white racism on white people as individuals is just one part of the effect of white racism on Britain today. Institutional racism has even greater effects. It is the most difficult concept to get across because it is so invisible, nebulous and indiscernible.

Definitions: racial prejudice, racism, ethnicity and institutional racism
To grasp the definition of the concept of institutional racism theoretically and intellectually does not present problems, but the most critical task was to enable the participants to understand and locate themselves and their participation and collusion in perpetuating the subtle mechanics of structural oppression. All had genuinely accepted that they were carriers of racial prejudice: 'My personal development is at risk, and it's my racial prejudice and the guilt attached to it that makes me fall backwards to accommodate black pupils – but I can't see the connection between myself and the role I have to play in my school.' This was more or less an unanimous response of most teachers – the separation of personal self and their institutional roles. The only way to let them make the connection for themselves was to divide them in groups, and ask them to construct a *Subtly Racist School*. The following construct emerged:

The construct
1 *School policy* Long termly consultation between staff and the head; finally head in consultation with senior staff – but really the head's decision since s/he has the final responsibility. Decisions, mostly formal, coming from the top of the structure, to provide security to staff, parents and children.
2 *Curriculum* Mainly decided by the head in consultation with senior staff or relevant department. Staff have autonomy in what they do in the classroom. Very traditional curriculum – emphasis on 3Rs, presentation, traditional approach to teaching of sciences, history, geography as they have been always taught; school assemblies as they have always been, irrespective of race, colour and creed. *Progressive RE Department* – world religions, moral education but Diwali and Id:. (Diwali: Hindu Festival of Light beginning in the New Year; Id: Muslim festival) do have a place.
3 *Staff and promotion* By head in consultation with the deputy. A 'coloured' teacher on scale 1 for multicultural education. 'Coloured' and black staff as dinner ladies and kitchen staff.
4 *Financial resources* Head in consultation with senior staff.
5 *Discipline* Strict, formal, ignore 'racist' remarks/insults. Policy of no confrontation. It will go away.

6 *Image* A good relationship with parents – encouraged – seen by appointment only to avoid disappointment.

The mere act of constructing, and the ease with which it was constructed had the most powerful and emotional impact on the participants. During the process of debriefing, the extent to which all had internalised subconsciously the ideology of race, the dynamics of power relationship, the concept of tokenism and the insidious, pervasive and subtle form of institutional racism became painfully clear. They all identified with the structure, which is not an exception but a rule – nationally, a structure and a weapon of oppression based originally on the ideology of class which affirms ethnocentric middle class criteria. To succeed through such a construct is virtually impossible for white working class pupils and to 'make it' through such an assimilative structure is at a massive cost of self-denial. For blacks, it is a structure of imprisonment. It shook the course participants to realise their own participation, their non-intervention, their racism of silence, and omission of black presence in the content and the structure:

'That I'm subtly racist and I thought I cared. I'm grateful for a day that has allowed me to stand back and see the methodology of subtle racism in me and the system of which I am a part.'

'Whilst undertaken with some sense of humour, I find the analysis of a subtly racist school disturbing. I had not previously considered just how many of our everyday practices could so easily be identified as slightly racist – which means they could easily veer from slightly into really racist practices.'

Following from above, I realise, more so now than before, that challenging assumptions in our practices is as important as challenging attitudes. Our instruments and articles of government give rise to many of our practices. In my judgement institutional racism is not just a denial of pupils but also the teachers. It would inevitably lead to deprofessionalisation of professionals. Professionalism, the last outpost of white identity, is being affected by the culture of racism, which is having its corrosive effects on the white psyche and white institutions – frozen and unable to function.

Probed in depth, it emerged that not one of the course participants had ever located themselves as 'whites'.

'I have never thought of myself racially.'

'I had taken myself for granted.'

'It is normal to be white.'

'The reason, I guess, I had never thought of myself as white is because it is the norm.'

It is imperative that we critically examine the implications. The white ideology of race has created 'whiteness' as the 'only norm' and it follows that any other criteria without a 'white orientation' and middle class orientation, at that, are bound to be abnormal and deficient. Hence, the assimilationist model, at its worse, is meant to 'absorb' black pupils, at its questionable best to study 'black life style'. Implicit in both the models is the contradiction and conflict between blackness and whiteness. The ideology of 'race' is under attack both nationally and globally, and if our education system wants to emerge from its orthodoxy, dysfunctionalism and historical freeze and 'catch up' with contemporary reality then there is no alternative but to embark on a political initiative to develop an anti-racist perspective. Without this the 'cultural diversity model will remain as static as ever and the 'culture of revolt' will continue to break away from the 'imprisonment of race and colour'. In the final analysis, it is an anti-racist model which could give us a commonality of experience and purpose and unity of action.

References
1 Row, A., 'The Outsider', *Times Educational Supplement*, 20 November 1980
2 'My Victorian Values', *Standard*, 15 April 1983
3 *The Leader*, 25 March 1983
4 The *Guardian*, 23 March 1983
5 Berry, W., *The Hidden Wound*, Houghton-Miffin, Boston 1970

Bibliography
Fromkin, Howard L. and Sherwood, John J. (Eds), *Intergroup and Minority Relations: An Experimental Handbook*, University Associates Inc 1976
Katz, Judy, *White Awareness – Handbook for Anti-racist Training*, University of Oklahoma Press, 1977
Sivanandan, A., *A Different Hunger*, Pluto 1982
Wiener, Martin J., *English Culture and the Decline of the Industrial Spirit: 1850–1980*, Cambridge University Press, 1981

Chapter 20

BILINGUAL RESOURCES IN SECONDARY SCHOOLS

John Wright

> John Wright taught English and ESL in secondary schools for nine years. He now works for the Advisory Centre for Education – an independent charity which gives free advice to parents of children in state schools. He is a member of the *ISSUES* collective.

There are two facts which have to be accepted at the outset. The first is that Britain is, and always has been, a multilingual society. This is a characteristic which we share with a great many other nation states. The second is that there are people being born into our society who will grow up and live their lives through as bilinguals, able to understand and use more than one language. It is all too easy to slip into believing that it is our school policy which determines whether or not society is multilingual; our individual classroom practice which decides whether or not individual pupils shall, or shall not, grow up bilingual.

So what does society, do schools, do teachers make of and choose to do with the issue of bilingualism? Anachronistic questions in so many parts of the world, we have just begun to ask them.

The world in a city

The ILEA Bilingual Education project[1] was set up in 1977 at the ILEA Centre for Urban Educational Studies. It ran for five years and involved working closely with editorial and design staff at ILEA's publishing house: Learning Materials Service. The aim of the project was to produce learning materials in a number of different languages for use in secondary school classrooms by students who were newly arrived in Britain and who were receiving special English Language help for a large part of the school week.

In common with many other LEAs, it is ILEA's policy to admit newly arrived students directly to their nearest school. If second language lessons are felt to be necessary, arrangements are made for students to be withdrawn from the normal timetable for approximately half of the school week to attend special classes in schools or in the Authority's English Language Centres. For the other half of the school week, students attend whatever lessons are timetabled for the groups they have been assigned to.

However, there will inevitably be times when the learning materials being used in mainstream classrooms make too great a demand on students' knowledge of English. The job of the Bilingual Education project was to produce materials which would help students in this situation. The materials would provide a chance to continue (albeit in a limited fashion) their general education during that difficult and frustrating initial period in this country when up to half of the school week is devoted to learning English. In addition, it was hoped that first language materials would allow them a chance to show their ability to achieve on a par with other students in the class in the subject areas.

Over the first year or so of the project a number of tentative dos and don'ts began to emerge. On the basis of these, guidelines for preparing the final materials were drawn up. The issues themselves may have implications for other ways in which mother tongue work is introduced into schools, and therefore may be of interest to teachers other than those using ILEA's bilingual materials.

1 *Materials in other languages must not be brought into the classroom as if they were poor relations. They must be presented in a manner which makes it clear that they have equal status with English materials.*

I made a start on the project by asking teachers I was working with to let me have copies of texts they planned using. I would get these translated into the relevant languages for the students, and duplicated. During the lessons, copies of first language versions were offered to bilingual students who could use them instead of or as well as the books containing the original text in English.

Over a short period of time it emerged that a number of students were either refusing to use their first language versions or using them in a desultory way (scribbling on the sheet, screwing them up, etc.). I realised that English texts were always being presented in a professionally produced form – with photographs, some in colour, and on glossy paper. Next to these were the other languages, presented on flimsy sheets of Roneo duplicating paper. The message 'first world technology for English, third world technology for any other language' was coming over loud and clear to the students. If the bilingual materials were to be used alongside professionally produced materials, they would need to resemble such materials: to be durable, clearly printed and generously illustrated. In short, to be themselves produced professionally.

The implication here is not that mother-tongue material must never be cheaply produced or home made, often that is the only choice teachers have. But it is important to avoid a situation where there is *always* a contrast between the standard of production of English materials and other language materials. It is overall parity of status over a period of time which is likely to be crucial.

2 *Presenting a boring text in a student's first language does not make it any more interesting.*

This seems obvious enough now, but when teachers first began reporting back on their students' responses to trial materials, and included comments like. 'Is able to do the work but says it isn't very interesting', I was shocked ... and a little hurt. After all, this must have been the only time they had been given anything in their own languages to read in schools, and all they could say was that it was 'not very interesting'. Some people have no gratitude!

On reflection I realised that I had been spending all my time ensuring that the right text was getting translated into the right language, being printed in time and delivered to the right classroom for the right lesson. I'd spent very little time thinking critically about the original texts. I'd been assuming that the language medium was the message. From this point, the question of content demanded more and more attention. Writing original texts and getting teachers to comment on them and suggest improvements and follow-up activities became important. In the final materials we consciously aimed at providing a wide variety of topics. We hope that most students find something which they enjoy reading and learning about. But we do not expect all students to be interested in, to use or to learn from all of the materials.

As a general point, I think that we may all be guilty at times of arguing the case for mother-tongue maintenance and mother-tongue teaching without reference to what a student's real communication interests might be, and without reference to content. Apart from professional linguists and language teachers, very few people are interested in studying a language for its own sake. When we argue that provision should be made for mother tongue work in schools, and that LEAs should support voluntary provision in the local community, we need to be quite specific about the content and context of such language work. Otherwise we may sound academic, or even esoteric, and fail to be convincing. And, of course, in order to understand needs and interests of students living in Britain, we need to allow their voices to be heard – especially at the public conferences and meetings which we organise on the issue.

3 *First language materials produced for use within the mainstream secondary classroom must not appear to bilingual students as devices for segregating them, or giving them different treatment.*

Some students were suspicious of the trial materials. One group refused to work on the materials in school. They said that they would do the work in the Language Centre, but not in the class at school. Another student, a Punjabi-speaking boy, refused point blank to use a Punjabi translation of the text being used: 'I don't need that. I can read English!' – as if I had deliberately tried to insult him. We need to be sensitive about these kinds of responses, and to try to understand them. Perhaps they are not so surprising, given that the languages (together with the religious and cultural backgrounds) of Britain's minority groups are ignored and therefore by implication disparaged, in many of our schools. It is understandable, if tragic, that some students should feel defensive about their first languages when they are first introduced into the classroom.

In a sensitive situation like this, the only solution is to allow the students themselves to choose whether or not to use materials in their first languages. The original plan for the project materials was to produce a separate pack in each of the languages being used, together with an English version. However, I realised that this would risk the languages being separated from each other.

The teacher might say something like: 'There you are, Mary, you take the English cards, and Ashraf, these Bengali ones are for you,' thus eliminating the choice which needs to be preserved for the individual students.

We decided, therefore, to produce eight packs each containing 40 cards, each card carrying both a student's first language and English. There are Punjabi-English, Urdu-English, Gujerati-English, Bengali-English, Greek-English, Turkish-English, Spanish-English and Chinese-English versions of the cards. The English and the first language in each case are physically inseparable. Students are always free to choose whether to use one language to the exclusion of the other or, if using both, which one to look at first, or to rely on most.

As well as arranging the languages in a way which avoids being divisive, it seemed important to avoid the risk of the content itself being separatist. It was true that the materials were for a very specific group of students: newly-arrived immigrants, in the literal sense of that often misused word. Yet in order for them to be acceptable to these students, it was necessary that they win a place within the mainstream classroom in the eyes of all the other students, and of the teachers. Therefore they would have to deal with topics which are regarded as legitimate school subjects. The final selection which was made for the project includes social studies, local geography and themes which are popular within Integrated Studies and Humanities departments. There is also work involving citizens' rights (consumer information, education rights, equal opportunities legislation, etc.). Particular skills are emphasised: map reading, timetable reading, understanding job advertisements, filling in forms, letter writing, etc.

Although the materials invite students to reflect on their recent experiences in migrating to Britain, they are not 'multicultural' in the traditional sense. This has caused surprise. One teacher asked 'What use is it for a newly arrived student to learn about a subject like "pollution"; how is that relevant to a student's cultural background?' The answer is that the topic is included because it is popular with teachers in secondary schools and is regarded by all students as a legitimate area of study. There is no good reason why bilingual materials must necessarily be 'multicultural', or culture-reinforcing in content. Indeed, if they are designed for use within the mainstream classroom, there may be good reasons for their not serving such a function. Again, as a general point, perhaps we need to question the link which the EEC automatically makes between the teaching of mother-tongue and teaching about the culture of the country of origin.

4 *It is important to treat a student, even in the early stages of acquiring second language skills, as a bilingual person and not as two monolingual people living in one body.*

What commonly happened in classrooms where early trial material was produced was that students would place both language texts side by side on the desk in front of them and use them, more or less, simultaneously. Very rarely did students read all the way through one version before turning to the other. More usually, they switched texts as they progressed to the end of both. It was impossible to tell from observation what prompted the switching. At times it seemed that the motive was to try to catch the translator out. The trial materials commonly provoked debate over the quality of the translations. The subject matter of the lessons, as far as the bilingual students were concerned, would switch from geography (or history or whatever) to comparative linguistics and back several times over the course of a lesson. And who can claim that the one pursuit is less intellectually challenging or valuable than the other?

In order to help students switch texts rapidly – for whatever reason – we decided that the translation of a text would always be printed on the same side of the card. From a design point of view it would have been easier and neater to print in English on one side of the card and in the other language on the other. But this would have forced students to turn over constantly, and would have slowed up the process of finding the relevant place in the text. We have also tried, wherever possible, to use clear paragraph spacing and bold shoulder headings to assist rapid sign-posting to the equivalent section of the text.

The discussion outlined so far relates to the use of bilingual materials with newly-arrived students. There is a need to define a much broader set of principles, however. These concern the bilingual education policies or programmes which we should be adopting in the interests of *all* students – not just the newly arrived, not just the already bilingual.

Bilingual education: what kind of programme should we be working towards?

We should work out a programme which is based on offering a choice:
1 to minority language/culture group pupils and students to maintain and develop their group languages and to learn and maintain their primary cultural traditions. But also the choice to become fluent in the language and culture of the majority group. The balance between these two is a matter which pupils and students should decide for themselves.
2 to *majority* group pupils and students the opportunity of learning something of the language and background of the minority groups in the school and neighbourhood.

The extent to which individual students are allowed to choose is an important criterion for judging the value of any bilingual education programme (indeed, any education programme). But it is not the sole criterion. Others must be kept in mind by schools:

1 *Bring minority language into the learning situation for utilitarian, not tokenist reasons.*

If children come to the classroom with a skill in a language other than English, then that skill should be utilised for the benefit of the child's overall education development. Utility is a key concept. Attempts to use languages in a non-utilitarian way, e.g., displaying different scripts on noticeboards, having posters headed 'This is the way we say Hello in all of our different languages' are of real but limited use. The danger is that they can too easily be a form of tokenism. Minority language children, once they realise that they are not actually required to *use* their own language, will quickly lose interest in its being displayed. And the majority language group will, after the initial novelty, simply assume that other people's languages are there for trivial purposes and are not real and valuable tools. Utilising the first languages of pupils rather than just displaying them is an important principle. Secondary students using trial material produced as part of the ILEA's Bilingual Education Project soon got over the novelty of being able to opt for materials and texts in their own languages: the medium was not the message for *very* long. First languages materials in the classroom have to compete with all of the other materials available, and if the content of the first language materials is either boring or trivial, their being in minority languages rather than English will not ensure their being used.

So, the languages, when used, should be used as the medium through which information of various kinds is made available and accessible: taped folk tales from different cultures in the listening corner of the infant classroom; books on countries of origin in the languages of those countries in the junior school library; works of reference on subjects such as chemistry, biology, mathematics, etc., in the departments in secondary schools, and in the libraries, a selection of literature in the languages of the minority group students.

2 *Integrate the work stimulated by minority language books/tapes/workcards etc. with the mainstream of class activity.*

If the work which is stimulated by the use of minority languages takes place in the classroom then not only will minority group students see their languages accepted within the classroom – the centre-court of learning in the school – but the majority group students will have the opportunity of seeing that the languages are not just strange mutterings and squiggles, that they have a real function for their users.

3 *Provide within the classroom the opportunity of developing and refining the skills of bilingualism – translation and interpretation – not only of language but of cultural experience.*

It is not just knowledge of another language which represents the skill of bilingualism. Being able to relate one language to another, and interpret one culture to someone from another culture, are also bilingualist skills. They are skills which begin to develop as an inevitable consequence of translingual and transcultural experience.

Children who listen to folk tales in their own language can translate these when retelling them to their English classmates, or when they plan, with their classmates, to act out the stories from the tapes. In the secondary school various projects can be developed which utilise the skill of the bilingual children for the benefit of the rest of the group.

For example, a comparative study of press handling of a story of issue – a popular enough study in humanities departments – can be broadened to take in a review of the way items are reported by the international press, or by the minority community foreign language press in this country. In addition to translating skills this could well raise, as points for discussion, the different kinds of bias that result from the way a newspaper perceives its readership, and cultural comparisons in terms of the kind of stories which predominate in different groups' popular papers.

4 *Provide language-learning opportunities, and the opportunity of becoming bilingual, to all students – even if a very small minority of English speaking students want to take up the option.*

Bilingual education materials in use in mainstream classes will expose majority language students to the fact that other languages exist, are just as useful as English, and that being able to *use* two languages is a skill which broadens the scope for work of those individuals who possess it.

In this situation some English-speaking children will want to learn some or at least one of the languages 'around' in the classroom. For pupils/students who want to do this there must be materials available. At infant level children are probably already teaching each other words and phrases. This work could be extended to include teaching each other the rhymes and songs which accompany playground games, for example.

At primary and secondary level a limited amount of basic language learning material can be stocked in school libraries and modern language departments: one tape and a workbook, just to start the student off. Obviously, at upper secondary level, the modern languages department should attempt to provide facilities for learning minority languages to the same standard as traditional foreign languages are taught.

5 *Never segregate the minority group for mother tongue learning. Always explicitly invite all pupils/students to join the group, even if only a few will.*

Whatever language maintenance provision is offered within the school, always allow and encourage majority pupils/students (and teachers) to join in. This means that the teachers employed, or who volunteer from the local community, must be prepared for mixed ability teaching, for beginners as well as advanced students.

6 *Preserve and defend the minority group student's rights to choose for her/himself the balance of minority and majority group language and culture which best meets the desired identity of the individual.*

Just as the bilingual education materials/courses are offered as options to the minority group students, so must they be offered as options to the minority group students.

At the moment the pressure for bilingual education is coming from the minority groups. Schools must meet their demands and recognise the languages which their children bring to the learning situation. But schools must do this in a way which involves and educates majority group students as well; in a campaigning way which will familiarise them with the benefits of bilingualism; in a way which will expose them to the beginnings of the process of seeing the world through another person's language and culture.

If our first halting steps in bringing minority languages into the mainstream of the education system can meet these six criteria then they may help in the evolution of a bilingual education programme which would both utilise minority languages to the benefit of minority group students, and help, rather than hinder, the growth of understanding and respect between the different peoples of our country.

Mother tongue: answering the critics

Critics argue that our education system will only concede the use of minority group languages in so far as doing so can serve the purposes of the system itself: these being to control and domesticate minority group communities, thereby assimilating them into society *as it is* and obviating the need for change.

This argument points to important warnings: schools should not use parents' first language solely as *one-way* channels of communication; parents should be made to feel at ease when talking to teachers through interpreters, either friends they bring with them or interpreters invited to school by teachers; as well as translating letters into community languages, schools should be prepared to translate parents' letters in other languages into English – whenever necessary.

Yet the assimilationist argument also signals possibilities for teachers, specifically, the possibility of moving on from discussing the use of minority group languages to issues of more general political importance. How accountable is the school, anyway, to the community it serves? What involvement, if any, do parents have in the decision-making processes of the school? How welcoming is the school to people in the local community who have special skills which are potentially valuable to the school?

Ultimately, a student's success in the school system depends on how well s/he performs in the mainstream of education provision, culminating in secondary school with set courses and examinations. Some people have argued that supporting bilingual students' first languages can result in organisational practices which lead to their being separated off from the mainstream of school learning – and therefore less likely to achieve by mainstream standards. This is a real danger. First, if mother tongue maintenance classes clash with other course options which a student needs to follow. Second, when the classes arranged to take place immediately after school, if their content bears no relation at all to what the students learn in the mainstream. In this case, the mother tongue teacher may be in competition with mainstream examination course teachers for a student's already scarce study time.

The main political effect of this is to leave the mainstream provision intact and unchallenged. Language policies in South African schools have been designed with this in mind. Critics fear that well-meaning teachers in British schools are instituting practices which, unintentionally, may be having the same effect.

Making the case for mother tongue support to be sited *in the mainstream* (to avoid the risks of ghettoisation) means taking the arguments to *all* teachers in a school. It will inevitably flush out a host of objections, some of which will be sincere and caring. Others will inevitably reflect ethnocentric, or even racist, attitudes. ('If English is good enough for us it should be good enough for them'.) Taking the mother-tongue argument to all teachers makes it possible to deal openly with such attitudes in staff meetings, and could well lead on to more general discussion of the way teachers' attitudes to their pupils can be affected by racist perceptions.

Some of those who argue in favour of schools using and maintaining the mother tongues of minority group children cite the EEC Directive on Mother Tongue Teaching to support their case. Critics have been quick to point out that the explicit purpose of the directive is to facilitate the mobility of labour in Europe. Children of migrant workers are encouraged to maintain the language and culture of their parents' country of origin. In time of slump, workers' resistance to being returned home will be lessened if they know that the children in the family will not face acute difficulties of reintegration. That is the theory. In practice, as one critic has pointed out, there is in the directive

> ... nothing about acknowledging and respecting the validity of other people's cultures, languages, identities. Nothing about enhancement of esteem and self-image. Nothing about the cognitive/emotional/social importance of keeping children's own languages going until fluency in English is achieved. Nothing about trying to find ways to enable them to gain the qualifications they so badly need in order that they should have opportunities and self-respect in an alien and prejudiced society.[4]

It is quite possible that minority group parents with real grievances may be lulled into acquiescence by a school's displaying its readiness to use community languages. They may take such a display as a sign that a school has a commitment to respecting cultural difference and to anti-racist teaching. So they may end up soft-pedalling on their complaint. The only way that a school can ensure that its policy of using community languages is not having this effect is to link it with a much broader programme aimed at expanding parental access and influence to decision making in schools *and* at giving students much more choice and power over their own learning.

References

1 Available from ILEA Learning Materials Service, Highbury Station Road, London, N1, for schools within ILEA. For schools outside ILEA, from the Commission for Racial Equality, Elliot House, 10/12 Allington Street, London, SW1. There are eight bilingual packs. Each one costs £3.00.
2 Adapted from the conclusion of an articles entitled 'Bilingualism in Education', first published in 1978 by ILEA Centre for Urban Educational Studies. Now available from *ISSUES in Race and Education*, 11 Carleton Gardens, Brecknock Road, London N19 5AQ, price £1.00 inc p.&p.
3 Adapted from the introduction to *Mother Tongue – Politics and practice*, originally written by the Issues collective, *ISSUES in Race and Education* No. 35. Price 50p + 20p p.&p. From Issues – address above.
4 Brockes, M., 'The mother tongue issue in Britain: Cultural diversity or control?', *British Journal of Sociology of Education*, vol. 1, no. 3, 1980

Chapter 21

ANTI-RACIST APPROACHES IN LONDON COLLEGES

Susi Rice (editor)

Kingsway-Princeton College is situated on three main sites in London. Its 3000 students, aged sixteen upwards, are drawn mainly from the London boroughs with a few from areas outside London. A wide variety of FT and PT courses are offered, ranging from vocational and pre-vocational through GCE, technical qualifications and general education. Extensive support services include workshops in language, numeracy, ESL and study skills; and careers counselling, welfare and personal tutoring.

North London College, the smallest of the ILEA colleges, is designated a 'Community College'. The catchment is mainly from local communities in the North London boroughs and includes many different ethnic groups. FT and PT provision has traditionally been aimed at the younger low-level student, but courses are also offered at GCE level, and for a variety of technical qualifications.

City and East London College is located on six sites in the ILEA boroughs of Hackney, Islington and Tower Hamlets. It offers a comprehensive range of FT and PT courses for all age groups with an increasing emphasis on meeting the needs of mature students and the many different ethnic communities in its catchment area. The levels of work are similar to those offered at Kingsway Princeton.

Susi Rice is Lecturer in Dress and Craft subjects at Kingsway Princeton and convener for the college Multicultural Education Committee to the Academic Board. She is a former Secretary of the London FE/AE branch of NAME.

Brenda McFarland is the LII for General Studies at North London College. She is responsible for student counselling at the college and is the Chairperson of the college Multi-ethnic committee.

Bryan Merton, now a Senior Lecturer at the new Haringey College of FE, was the Lecturer in charge of courses for youth, community and social work at Kingsway-Princeton where he was particularly involved with students from Afro-Caribbean and Asian backgrounds and, for a while, Chairperson of the Multicultural Education Committee.

Max Johnson and Phil Read are Course Tutors on the Race Relations Education course.

Verna Rosen is an LII in the Department of Applied Social Studies and General Education at City and East London, and Course Tutor for the access to HE course.

The background

London colleges probably contain the greatest mixture of culturally diverse students in the whole country. The need for Further Education to recognise and reflect such a multicultural population has been pointed out in several official documents, including three ILEA Reports,[1] two CRE publications,[2] a NATFHE policy statement,[3] and a survey by the London FE/AE Branch of NAME.[4] Several colleges have responded to such documents since the late 1970s with initiatives which were intended both to promote multicultural approaches to teaching, and to understand and deal with all aspects of racism.

This chapter will describe some of those initiatives. However, it is important that the reader should first consider the following differences between FE and other types of education, which affect all students, but which also have significant cultural implications.

Who chooses Further Education, and why

Below the age of sixteen, education is compulsory. It is the legal obligation of Education Authorities to provide facilities, and of parents or guardians to ensure that all children receive a certain standard of education up to secondary level. FE, on the other hand, is voluntary. The student who chooses it wishes to acquire skills and qualifications which may lead to Higher Education, or to a career. Some of the factors which will influence the choice of a college include the availability of specific subjects or courses; the locality of the college; advice from careers officers or teachers; parental aspirations; and recommendations from friends or relatives.

Students entering FE are therefore faced directly (possibly for the first time in their lives), with the need to make major decisions about their future. These decisions will be greatly influenced by many more people than was the case at school; further, these people will all hold and convey their particular *subjective attitudes about the relative status and role of class, sex and race.* This particularly affects students from ethnic minorities.

How admissions to educational establishments are decided

Admission to schools is dictated by a local catchment area. The choice of a school within a given locality is made on the basis of discussion between head teachers and the parents or guardians, and is concerned with relating the age of the child to an appropriate level of work.

Application to a college is made by the prospective student in person, who must deal with several different people, ranging from the office staff in charge of enquiries, to interview panels made up of management personnel and teachers. In addition, college admissions are not dictated by locality, but by the requirements of courses, which in turn are offered in response to such factors as local needs, demands of employers, or national trends. In many cases, admissions policies reflect the criteria set by Examining Bodies. As resources are allocated according to the above demands, colleges are more likely than schools to be selective about the students they admit.

The cultural implications here are, firstly, that the large number of personnel involved in college admissions will be making important decisions about young people from ethnic minorities, based on personal values about other cultures. Many of these people will have little or no expertise or training in the counselling or administrative skills which they need; also, they frequently lack understanding of different cultural expectations, with the result that prospective students may be given adverse advice regarding ways of achieving their aims.

Secondly, as most Examining Bodies and employers still tend to look for attitudes and values in their applicants which are based on Eurocentric ideas, there will inevitably be *ethnic bias built into entry requirements* for courses.

The curriculum
Educational provision in schools usually consists of a set combination of basic subjects, according to age and ability levels. There may also be some local variation, arising from the demands of a specific community. Decisions about the nature and content of the curriculum are the responsibility of the head teachers, and the degree of participation which they encourage will depend on the attitude of each individual head.

College provision varies in levels and aims across London. The range is set by the Education Authority, who try to offer a balance throughout the different regions. However, each college is free to decide its own priorities on specific courses and subjects. These are decided by the Principal and the Governing Body, through consultation with heads of departments and the Academic Board. Teaching staff are also frequently involved in initiating or developing aspects of the curriculum. As mentioned earlier, the acquisition of qualifications is such a major factor in FE, that much of the curriculum must reflect the requirements of Examining Bodies.

Culturally, therefore, the same implications relating to *ethnic bias* mentioned above, *will apply to the curriculum*. Even where colleges are providing multicultural perspectives in curriculum content and teaching methods, these are only effective where the college or subject has succeeded in influencing the Examining Body, and has direct involvement in the design and monitoring of syllabuses.

Personal relationships
Usually the pupils of one school live within a single area, which means that there can be frequent contact between the school, family and local community. However, college students come from diverse and far-ranging localities, so that home liaison is difficult. In many cases, parental involvement in college life may be actively discouraged by both students and teachers who see this period as a time to develop independence in ideas and behaviour.

School pupils form friendships within a largely unchanging group of classmates, who stay together for most lessons as a group, sometimes for several years. College students on the other hand are frequently with a different set of peers in every class; their courses of study will be shorter than at school, ranging from a few weeks to two years if they are full-time, and only one or two days a week if they are part-time.

In schools, there will be an adult focal point in the form of a class teacher, or Head of House, to notice and deal with personal problems. FE in London has no overall pastoral care system. In some colleges, the adult focus could be a course tutor or subject teacher. Other colleges form arbitrary 'tutor groups', where a teacher will be responsible for the personal welfare of a number of students, but will not necessarily have any teaching contact with these tutees. Other colleges again may depend entirely on one or two 'specialist' staff to provide counselling, careers or welfare advice for the whole student body.

Finally, whereas in school the pupil/teacher relationship is that of adult/child within a framework of authority and rules, students in colleges are more likely to perceive the teachers as contemporaries. This is one reason why the college atmosphere is often described by students as more informal and 'adult' than that of school.

The cultural implications to be considered relating to these points are: concerning their peers, students entering FE must adjust to losing the continuity and relative security of their school/home community, and form new relationships in an unfamiliar and fragmented environment. They therefore seek stability in a new peer-group identity through friends with common interests and experiences, such as a cult, or a *shared educational or ethnic background*.

At this stage, students are seeking a change from child to adult status, which to them means freedom from the restrictions of authority. This is a difficult period for all school-leavers; for young people from ethnic minorities, there are also often additional conflicts between the cultural expectations of different groups of familial loyalties, or the roles of the sexes, or sexuality. To succeed in bridging the gaps between the values of student, peers, home and different ethnic norms, requires that *adults working in FE* are *aware of their own attitudes* towards authority, different generations, *and other cultures*.

Some college responses to racism in a multicultural society

The following examples illustrate how some of the London colleges try to deal with the issues outlined above. The first step taken by several of them was to form multi-ethnic working parties or committees on their Academic Boards, which aim to initiate policies on multicultural Education.

Here is a description of the Multi-ethnic Committee at North London College, showing the wide range of concerns which such groups consider.

North London College Multi-ethnic Committee
(Brenda McFarland)
Following the publication in 1977 of the ILEA document on Multi-ethnic

education, the Academic Board established a working party 'to examine the role of the college with regard to multi-ethnic education'.

The working party made a number of recommendations concerning the collection of statistics of ethnic groups; the curriculum – whom we teach and what and how we teach; curriculum support – library and media resources; guidance and counselling services; staffing and staff development; and general college ethos. The recommendations were accepted by the Academic Board and a permanent Committee of the Board was set up to try to implement the recommendations and to act as a focus for multi-ethnic developments generally.

Although multi-ethnic education permeates all aspects of college life, a number of developments deserve special mention.

During the spring term of 1981, the College ran a staff in-service course in multi-ethnic education, one afternoon a week for six weeks. The topics covered in seminar sessions and workshops ranged from selection and admission procedures to racism awareness and a consideration of certain ethnic groups. The intention was to encourage staff to look critically at their own practices and to consider how they might improve them. It is hoped that in-service education in this area will continue to be college policy.

In addition, the college runs a course called, 'Understanding children from multicultural backgrounds' which is designed to aid greater understanding of the physical, social, emotional and intellectual development of children from different ethnic groups. The course runs one day a week for ten weeks, with a new course each term. It is thought to be useful for social workers, health visitors, house parents, residential care staff, nursery nurses, playgroup leaders, etc. Elements of the course include an examination of child-rearing practices in multicultural groups, with such factors as the effects of immigration on the traditional life-styles of other cultures. The aim is to identify areas where conflict with the host community may arise. Information about facilities and agencies specifically for multicultural groups is also available.

The college also provides for ESL needs. 'Operation Springboard' is an ESL work experience course, sponsored by Camden CRC and set up in response to the wishes of local communities to see their children established in 'quality' jobs and not confined to 'traditional ethnic sub-economy' jobs. The course is college-based for six weeks, with intensive language input, followed by one day a week in college while on work experience. A final two week 'pick-up' is available for those who have not been able to find full-time employment at the end of the course. Parents are visited twice a year, and there are 'open days'. Publicity for the course is circulated in five languages and the staff on the course make good use of the ILEA translating unit for both translation and interpretation. The course has been extremely successful, with most of the students finding employment.

There is also a 'pre-Springboard' course, funded by the college. This runs in the summer term, and is aimed at Easter school leavers. It provides an introduction to further education, jobs and careers.

Other ESL provision at the college includes an ESL link-course with local schools. Pupils spend two days a week in college, of which two half-days are devoted to ESL work and the rest of the time on skill sampling. There is also ESL servicing for a wide range of the college courses.

Another aspect of curriculum support comes from the library staff, who have been active in building up an excellent selection of international fiction and multi-ethnic non-fiction, periodicals, and teaching packs. The college playgroup, too, has a good selection of children's non-racist books.

Finally, an annual event which is much looked forward to is 'International Evening'. This is a multi-ethnic party, where food from many lands is prepared, eaten and enjoyed by both staff and students. A cabaret, reflecting the many cultures represented in the college, is performed by talented individuals within the college community. The evening usually ends with a disco, with music for all tastes. Students are encouraged to bring their friends, parents, brothers and sisters, so that the party-goers span all generations and cultures – both reflecting and helping to create the multi-ethnic ethos of North London college.

Of the many issues outlined, that of curriculum review has been tackled in a number of ways at different colleges. Brixton, Southwark and Kingsway-Princeton, for instance, have used various types of questionnaires, to raise staff consciousness of '... whom we teach, and what and how we teach ...'. The method used by Kingsway-Princeton multicultural working party was for representatives from each department to ask all subject areas the following four questions:
1 whether the subject includes courses which are specifically about a minority culture, (such as Black or Asian Studies);
2 whether any of their material is designed to meet particular needs of ethnic minority students, (such as language support for a specific group);
3 whether course content had been considered with a view to reflecting the backgrounds of minority cultures, rather than being Eurocentric;
4 whether any of the material is deliberately intended to educate *all* students to appreciate that they live and work in a multicultural society, and to demonstrate the equal value and importance of all cultures.

These questions provoked some remarkably honest replies, and also led to such initiatives as the introduction of various minority language courses, the development of ESL support across the college, and, most encouraging of all, to the organisation of a full staff conference on multicultural issues.

A further anti-racist initiative offered at the same college is a course about race relations, which was started as a direct response to demand by students, rather than staff. The following account was written by the team who designed and taught the course.

Kingsway-Princeton College – race relations education
(Max Johnson, Phil Read and Bryan Berton)

In September 1981 we initiated an extension class in race relations; that is, an essentially optional class for students who want to broaden their education beyond purely academic studies. The idea for this extra class came from the students themselves, mainly those who were already enrolled in GCE O and A level Politics classes. As part of the syllabus, they already study the history and politics of postwar immigration and subsequent race relations in Britain. In their lessons they had begun to ask for more time to discuss issues about racism than the syllabus allowed.

The extension was conceived not just as a chance for politics students to examine race relations in greater detail and depth, but for any interested student who was concerned to explore both the political and personal dimensions. Again, this demand came from the students who recognised that feelings, attitudes and behaviour were as much in need of scrutiny as facts and events.

In drafting the programme we consulted the students. We thought it important that the final version would be largely determined by what they wanted and needed to discuss. We proposed an inter-disciplinary approach that would combine, as far as possible, political, sociological and psychological perspectives. We decided to look initially at the period 1945–62 which provides an important background to the more familiar events of the last twenty years. For example, we considered it important to discuss the reasons for postwar immigration and the economic and imperial decline of Britain in order to understand white British reaction to black immigration. Then we turned our attention to the period 1962–81 which has seen the introduction of immigration controls, the passing of race relations Acts, the growth of race relations as an issue in party politics, and the apparent rapid decline, in some areas, of relations between the police and black British. The urban riots during the summer of 1981 would give added urgency and impetus to our discussions.

In the second term, we decided to supplement this perspective with a more explicitly psychological focus. We looked in particular at problems of identity, prejudice, discrimination and consciousness as they affect both individuals and groups. We assumed the interplay between the individual and the social, or the personal and the political. This meant that our discussions covered a wide range of issues, including the origins of racism, attitude formation and change, acculturation, family patterns, inter-racial marriage, male–female relations and race relations within the college. People had the chance not only to exchange views and experiences, but also to consider their social and political implications.

During both terms we used broadly the same teaching approach. We would start each class, (one and a half hours), with an input provided by a college lecturer, a visiting speaker, a film or a video. This would last for, at most, half an hour, and would be followed by discussion. We would try and leave ten minutes at the end of each session so that the main issues could be summarised.

The class started with about eighteen students, most of whom were from the social science area and black. By the end of the second term we were left with a core group of eight students all of whom were black. However, each class would be swelled by interested students and staff who might drop in on a one-off basis, and we rarely had a group of less than twelve. The size of the group meant that discussion was always lively and fruitful.

Although the major preoccupation was black-white relations, we did try to encourage a broader frame of reference. For example, in the second term we considered the issues of integration, assimilation and cultural identity, and, in doing so, invited a Jewish member of staff and a Rabbi to speak of the Jewish experience. We also enlisted an Indian evening student to offer his point of view which showed up interesting similarities and differences between the experiences of the Asian community and those people of Afro-Caribbean origin.

Because the discussions moved regularly from consideration of socio-political issues to more personal preoccupations and beliefs, the nature of the class at times seemed to change from that of a seminar to a more intimate group. The small size of the class and the continuing participation of a core group allowed complex powerful feelings to be expressed. This made for a challenging experience for both students and staff. It was always rewarding and friendly, and it has made us confident that this was an educational experiment well worth repeating.

A more formal approach to understanding the background to multicultural Britain has been taken by Hammersmith and West London College. They designed a CSE Social and Economic Studies syllabus for the MRFB in the early 1970s, on Africa, Europe and the Caribbean. (A copy of their submission appears at the end of this chapter.) The course was run at the college until 1981, when it was changed from an examination subject to an 'elective'. Although it has always been offered to the whole student body, the course has tended to attract mainly the black students.

The last example of anti-racist initiatives in this chapter illustrates an approach which relates not only to the curriculum, but also to another aspect of racism which was mentioned at the start of the chapter, concerning admission to FE. The ethnic bias built into criteria for entering FE applies equally to HE. There are many mature students from ethnic minorities who have the appropriate personality, intelligence and motivation to take up careers in several caring professions, such as teaching or social work. However, because they have not been able to acquire the qualifications or study skills necessary for a degree course, they would not normally try to pursue such professions. City and East London College recognised this, and in 1975 launched a pilot course aimed to provide access to HE for students from ethnic minorities, who – 'showed social work potential' – as described by the course tutor in the following paper.

City and East London College – Diploma and Social Work Course, including a Foundation Year of Education

(Verna Rosen)

This is a description of a full-time course with an annual intake of fifteen to twenty students, who must be aged over twenty. The duration of the course is one year at City and East London College, and two years at the Polytechnic of North London.

The ILEA course was set up as a pilot project in 1975 to provide alternative access to the Diploma in Social Work at the Polytechnic of North London for people 'who had an intimate knowledge of the West Indies' and who showed social work potential. It was presumed at the time that the absence of suitable applicants for social work training from the Caribbean was due, either to education interrupted by immigration and/or possession of language forms ('dialect interference') inappropriate for higher education. In consequence, it was proposed to run a foundation year of language and study skills, together with a basic introduction to some of the main social work subjects; sociology, psychology, social history and social policy. This was to take place at City and East London FE College and run in close conjunction with the Polytechnic of North London staff. The students are mainly mature women (very few men), aged between 20 and 50, with families.

No longer a pilot project, and no longer confined to West Indians, although these are in the majority, the present permanent course is closely integrated with the Polytechnic department. Students attend some lectures and seminars there and receive some joint teaching by CELC and PNL tutors. Wherever possible, they are familiarised with the Polytechnic course and its methods.

Since it was realised how much students supported each other on reaching the Polytechnic and how frequently even the most competent said that what they gained most from the foundation year was confidence, conscious efforts have been made to strengthen the student group and improve student autonomy. There has been a positive shift from tutor-organised sessions towards students making as many decisions as possible about their own learning. They arrange visits, speakers, plan subject content with staff. Many techniques similar to those described in David Boud's *Developing Autonomy in Student Learning* have been discovered and tried out by staff in the process of helping students to help themselves. Students listen to each other's essay plans, not to criticise, but to ask clarifying questions only; they work in pairs privately on spelling; they form triangles to elucidate complicated reading texts; and so on.

While some teaching sessions are fairly traditional in approach, there is in an eight weeks placement in social fieldwork agencies and much of the other work takes place outside the classroom. For example, a Welfare Rights Course is taught in the Welfare Rights Shop in Bethnal Green Road where students are in contact with members of the public seeking advice as well as meeting a variety of speakers from outside the College. There is a great deal of project work and visits to outside organisations: courts, social service committee meetings, schools, residential establishments, etc. These are often used as material for language and theory exercises in College. An example of an extremely valuable project is the one undertaken in connection with what started as a straightforward study of the nutrition of different communities in this country. It was recognised that students needed practice in organising themselves in groups and in negotiating with outside bodies. It was also believed that it is important, wherever possible, to start from what students are good at doing (in this case, domestic organisation). In addition to researching theory, students are asked to prepare social events, providing food from each of four cultures: Asian, African, English and Caribbean. This involves their organising themselves into a society to enable them to obtain finance, planning programmes in small groups, buying and preparing food, negotiating with college authorities, and inviting guests.

A residential course at the beginning of the year focuses on group processes. Sensitivity group sessions, run by an outside consultant and attended by students and some staff, take place weekly. These have been based largely on the thinking of Carl Rogers and have made use of many of the exercises in *Growth Games* by Lewish and Streitfield. The effect of these sessions has been described by students.

'The course is trying to highlight our hidden talents and, where they exist make them stronger.'

'These sessions have made me discover areas in me and other people I'd never have dreamed of.'

The presence of staff working on the same level as students has been instrumental in breaking down barriers to communication.

Students, like many people outside the course, are concerned about what it means to be on an all-black 'compensatory' course. They are ambiguous about it, but then they are, in this society, in an ambiguous position. When faced with the question of whether the course should continue they are adamant that it is needed. Their reasons vary from negative ones like:

'If it's the only way in for blacks, we'll take it to get into the system. You can't do anything until you get in and so you might as well use the system as it is set up.'

to positive statements, such as:

'I wish they had a course like this that was compulsory for black students on all courses. You have time to sort out amongst yourselves all sorts of sensitive areas.'

or:

'There's a bond, a commonness, amongst us which means you don't have to explain yourself all the time. In a mixed group you have to defend yourself from all different angles and that is where confusion comes about.'

Space is provided in the course for students to explore these and many other issues. Past students frequently stress the value of this space: to discover more about themselves: about groups; about their own strengths as a group; heightened consciousness of what is going on in the world. With these discoveries, they find confidence and with confidence they learn. Few fail to qualify as social workers. Many go on to further degrees.

To conclude this chapter, a comment must be made about the changing nature of FE in the 1980s. High levels of youth unemployment, especially among minority communities, mean that FE lecturers are faced with the need to teach a curriculum for which they may not have been trained, to students from backgrounds with which they are not familiar. In particular, colleges are now getting a lot of black youngsters who have nowhere else to go. These youngsters, though born in this country, still come from cultures where the 'open' and 'democratic' ethos of FE mentioned at the start of the chapter is not practised. Understanding the political background and dealing with the conflicts which such students bring with them, are additional factors which colleges must now face, if they are to effectively combat racism in the future.

References
1 ILEA – Reports on Multi-ethnic Education 1977, 1979 and 1983
2 The CRE 'A Second Chance', 1976; 'Further Education in a Multiracial Society', 1982
3 NATFHE – 'Further and Teacher Education in a Multicultural Society', 1979
4 London FE/AE Branch of NAME, 'Survey of Multicultural Policies in Colleges', 1981
5 David Boud *Developing Autonomy in Student Learning*, Kogan Page, 1981

Appendix: Hammersmith and West London College: A CSE Mode 3 submission to the Metropolital Regional Examining Board

Note of explanation
This syllabus, which is the first of a series, deals mainly with the people of Africa and their diaspora in the Atlantic Triangle that links this country with West Africa and the Americas – especially the Caribbean and the Southern States of USA. Future options within the series will include a syllabus dealing with the contrasts between agrarian economies in the Indian sub-continent and with industrial economies in Western Europe.

We believe such courses are needed to bridge gaps in our present curricula. The course should give students various background access to material on the basis of which they form a truer picture of their past relations, and a juster appreciation of the African contribution to human development than is possible on the basis of most existing syllabuses.

Social and economic studies:
Africa, Europe and the Caribbean
CSE Mode 3 Form of the examination and allocation of marks

PART I *An objective test*

Ten multiple choice questions on each of the four sections (A to D) of the syllabus, 40 questions in all.
Time: $1\frac{1}{2}$ hours.   Marks 20.

PART II

A paper of five questions on each of the four sections of the syllabus. Students will be asked to answer four out of these twenty questions, *one from each section*, and to get the highest possible marks should answer 4 questions, not more and not less.
Time: 2 hours.   Marks 60.

PART III *Course work*

EITHER a) From each of the four sections of the syllabus students should choose one subject and submit from 250 to 500 words on the subject chosen – a total of 1000 to 2000 words and four different subjects.

In addition, students should submit in respect of each subject chosen at least three items of relevant illustration in such form as maps, diagrams, date charts, drawings, photographs, cuttings from papers and magazines but not from books. Credit will be given for including some discussion and evaluation of facts presented in each section.

OR b) A *Project* consisting of not less than 2000 words, including pictures, photos, maps and diagrams plus an index and a short preface of 50–100 words saying what the project is about.

Syllabus

SECTION A

A1 *Early settlement – 1945:* The Roman Empire and the African presence in Britain.

Black presence since the fifteenth century: Britain as entrepot for slave trading with the Spanish and Portuguese Empires in the Americas; seaport settlements in England; official and other reactions to the black presence; the place of Africans in British society as marginal slaves, servants and freemen in the seventeenth, eighteenth, nineteenth and early twentieth centuries. Significance of the Mansfield Judgement. Short-term black residents – students, soldiers, etc.

A2 *Post 1945: Large scale*

Migration from Asia, Africa and the Caribbean; its causes – labour demands of receiving economy; excess labour in countries of origin, political and cultural factors.

A3 Patterns of the migration – numbers, areas of settlement, conditions of life, family patterns in the migration. Reactions of the indigenous community and restrictions on entry.

A4 Immigrant self-organisation and self-expression – political, economic, cultural.

A5 Images of blacks in the media in Britain, official and semi-official statements on the problems resulting from black immigration; failures and successes of official efforts to solve these problems; the creation of an institutional framework for improving race relations; the objective disadvantages experienced by blacks in education, housing, employment.

SECTION B

Atlantic slavery, the Slave Trade and its background

B1 Aspects of West Africa; the cultural continuum of Noke, Ife and Benin in Nigeria; the Kongo Kingdoms; Islamic penetration. European expansion; the first stage of European participation in slavery in West Africa – the Portuguese role therein.

B2 The New World: some aboriginal cultures of the Americas; their elimination and/or enslavement leading to the need for replacement labour forces both from Europe and, massively, from Africa.

B3 Mechanisms of slavery in West Africa; slave raiding; slave trading – forts, factories and barracoons; African participation, including the development of African states economically dependent in various degrees on the slave trade. The Middle Passage. Conditions, duration, numbers.

B4 Mechanisms of slavery in the New World; plantation and non-plantation slavery; slave resistance (the Maroons and the Haitian slave revolution); slave culture developing on the basis of memories of Africa.

B5 Europeans and slavery. The benefits to Europe; its impact on the British economy; French economic benefits; conditions and attitudes of working-class Europeans during slavery both in Europe and in the slave societies of the New World.

SECTION C

Abolition, emancipation and the post-emancipation societies of the Atlantic System

C1 How slavery and the slave trade were abolished between the late eighteenth and the late nineteenth centuries; factors – slave resistance; the growth of industrial capitalism in Europe and the new requirements of this system internationally: American and European humanitarianism and radicalism, e.g., the role of men like Clarkson, Robespierre, Wilberforce, Lincoln, John Brown, etc., the efforts of black abolitionists, e.g., Equiano and Frederick Douglass. The European working class response, e.g., continued emigration to the North and the support of the North by British factory workers during the American Civil War.

C2 Replacement of the slave trade in Africa by 'legitimate trade' and production of new commodities in West Africa.

C3 'The Scramble for Africa' – its aims, methods and effects. African resistance up to 1945.
C4 The growth of post-emancipation black peasantries in the Caribbean and the USA. Reconstruction in the USA. The importing of Asian indentured labour into Africa and the Caribbean.
C5 Some New World black responses to the post-emancipation situation. Resistance, e.g., the 1865 revolt in Morant Bay, Jamaica; the 'Back to Africa' movement and the founding of Liberia; migration in search of work.

SECTION D
Colonialism, anti-colonialism and independence
D1 The expansion of colonialism following the Treaty of Berlin; the establishment of direct and indirect rule; the sack of Benin; the dispersal of its art; the establishment of unequal trade in West Africa and of the forced labour system in West Central Africa; the extension of the enclosure system in East Central and Southern Africa.
D2 Anti-colonial responses and resistance, e.g., the Chilembwe revolt during the First World War; early African nationalism and Pan-Africanism including the Pan-African Congresses; the part played by European educational and religious systems in the colonial period.
D3 Independence – its meaning, political, cultural and economic.
D4 Two case studies against the above background.
and
Jamaica and Kenya – background, problems and prospects.
D5 Colonial background; variety of peoples and languages; the land issue; independence movements; current social and economic problems.

Anti-racist teaching policies

Introduction
Shaun Doherty

The chapters in this section describe existing school initiatives that are well in advance of the ILEA's delivery schedule, but none of the authors would regard this fact with complacency. A school policy is not something that is enshrined in a document; it is not 'holy writ' to be referred to when necessary. It is part of the daily life of the school. It has to be carefully monitored and adapted to the changing nature of the school and has to relate to all of its other initiatives and priorities.

No such policy has a constant progression. Given the present period of massive government cutbacks in education, schools have their backs to the wall. Teachers face unemployment, redeployment and insecurity about their futures while being pressurised by management to be more accountable. These are not ideal circumstances for their consistent involvement in new initiatives, however important these may be. Even in those schools where such initiatives are well under way there are periods of stagnation and even regression in their development. This is not always appreciated by the increasing number of education authority employees who are not practising teachers.

It is in this light that the ILEA's campaign should be examined. It is commendable and ambitious, but it makes a number of assumptions and assessments that merit comment. The Anti-Racist Statement makes the following claims:

> Another force is also available to the service. This is the strong tradition in British society of opposition to injustice in whatever shape or form.
> All employees of ILEA and users of the Authority's service are uniquely placed, if only they would seize the opportunity, to educate generations of young people free of racism and prejudice. (1.4, 1.5)

There is, however, another tradition and one which currently prevails in British society, of oppression and exploitation. The two traditions are in constant conflict and it is not a conflict that is going to be primarily resolved within education. Education alone will not free young people from racism even though it has an extremely important part to play; in the long run it is political and economic struggles that give people confidence to overcome racism and all of the other evils inherent in our society. In this respect the statement is deficient. It makes no real attempt to relate racism to our economic and political system and to explain how it is used both overtly and covertly to divide those who are capable of transforming this system.

This criticism of the ILEA's analysis should not, however, be used as an excuse for those of us in schools and colleges to opt out. The three chapters in this section are concrete and practical examples from practising teachers of how the objectives of the policies can be tackled and at least partially achieved. It is particularly encouraging to include the chapter on a primary school initiative which bears out the vast amount of positive work that can be done at this level in spite of the alarming evidence of racist ideas and assumptions in the minds of younger students. The way in which Martin Francis describes the students' own responses and ability to handle complex situations of conflict should be a valuable reminder to all teachers that we should never underestimate or undervalue the potential of students for self-activity. Too often teachers adopt a patronising, know-all attitude that stifles such activity.

These chapters encourage the right kind of optimism about the possibilities within schools to establish and carry through anti-racist strategies. In fact the best initiatives that have already been taken have come from the bottom up, not the top down. Those of us in the educational front line welcome the support the Authority has declared for the work already done and we are determined that this tradition should flourish and be extended.

Chapter 22

ANTI-RACIST TEACHING POLICIES

Shaun Doherty

> Holloway School is an 11–19 boys school in Islington with 1000 on the roll and a teacher/pupil ratio of 13.3. Its intake is predominantly working class and drawn from a diversity of ethnic backgrounds with a substantial percentage of students whose first language is not English. The school qualifies for Social Priority Allowance. Teaching is organised on a mixed-ability basis, though there is setting in some subjects.
>
> Shaun Doherty teaches English at Holloway School.

Holloway School launched its anti-racist teaching policy in February 1978. Five years later 'multiculturalism' has become part of the mainstream of educational life. In the intervening years there has been a multiplicity of initiatives on this issue. They are characterised primarily by a lack of any cohesion theory of racism and education and have arisen largely as the result of the activities of individual teachers or groups of teachers directed by the needs of their students and the demands of classroom teaching in a multi-ethnic society. They are increasingly being smiled upon, even actively encouraged, by local education authorities and government agencies because they can be seen as a possible response to what is perceived as a 'problem'. Andy Green describes the phenomenon in the following way.

> Multiculturalism, then, initially the name of an educational philosophy espoused by progressive teachers who sought, in support of the struggles of black students and parents, to oppose racism in schools, is also the banner under which the state intervenes with its somewhat different and contradictory objectives.[1]

In other words multiculturalism embraces a multitude of approaches, many of them contradictory. It has become a terrain on which these contradictions vie for hegemony. The response from schools nationally, however, needs to be put in sharper perspective; most of them are not engaged with this issue either because they do not regard it as relevant or because they are hostile to it. An increasing number pay no more than lip service to it, fishing out the required school 'policy' from the back of a filing cabinet when required. Thus the debate about anti-racist teaching necessarily relates to a minority of schools and education authorities, but is nonetheless important since it has implications not just for the whole of the education system but also for the society within which it operates.

In this chapter I will seek to give an account of the initiatives that we have taken at Holloway within the context of the policies of the ILEA and to examine critically the way in which they have developed. I will also seek to place these developments within a theoretical framework and to comment on the more recent contributions to the debate. The analysis and the narrative are my own, but I will draw on the collective experience of teachers at the school and hope to represent that experience as objectively as possible.

The Holloway policy

It is significant that the original policy was launched as a direct result of events in the world outside schools and in particular as a response to the political activities of the National Front. In 1976 the Front were encouraged by their showing in the GLC elections and sought to project themselves as a respectable party with serious electoral pretensions. They sought to obscure the fact that their leaders were firmly within the political tradition of the German National Socialist Party of the thirties and they attempted to project a populist image that used policies of racial segregation and repatriation to play on the fears of disaffected white workers whose aspirations for full employment and the abolition of want had been betrayed by successive governments. Black people were presented as the scapegoats for this betrayal. During the latter part of 1977 and the beginning of 1978 the National Front directed their propaganda at multi-ethnic schools and 'red' teachers in an attempt to recruit young whites. Through their youth paper *Bulldog* and through leaflets like *How to Spot a Red Teacher* they hoped to set students against teachers and whites against blacks. This campaign, by the Front's own admission, was a failure. They were faced with hostility from within schools as students and teachers responded to the challenge of racism and outside schools the success of organisations like the Anti-Nazi League was able to stem the advance of the Front both on the streets and through counter propaganda.

Holloway School was a part of this opposition. When a National Front leaflet was found in school we decided to formulate a policy to combat racism. The headteacher, George Spinoza, presented a document to a staff meeting and after there had been a sharp and extensive exchange of views, not all of them favourable to the initiative, there was a consensus for the adoption of the policy. The school's initiative received widespread publicity including two reasonably favourable reports in national newspapers and the lurid headline 'Head Canes Racist Poison' to a front page article in the local Islington paper. The response from the ILEA was not unfavourable either and the head received a number of congratulatory phone calls. When we drafted the policy document we were anxious to find a peg within the cloakroom of the Authority's overall philosophy on which to hang it and we managed to find a tenuous one in the document from the Schools Sub-Committee *A Multi-Ethnic Education*[2] which made a tentative reference to the possibility of 'providing positive teaching against racism'. This provided the initiative with some legitimacy even if the arguments presented in the policy document would not have respectability instantly conferred upon them.

Obviously there was not a common theoretical position on the staff, though individuals did have their own analysis, but it is fair to describe the policy as both interventionist and integrationist. It was interventionist in that it sought to counter any manifestation of racism in school and it set out a number of guidelines and argued for the adoption of a number of proposals that sought to further this end:

> We should seek to undertake a campaign of education in assemblies, in lessons and during form periods. Such a campaign should seek to achieve the following:
> a) Impress upon pupils that discrimination against people because of their colour or place of origin is wrong.
> b) Explain why black people, Cypriots and Asians have a right to live in this country. This is particularly important because of the numerous myths that are perpetuated about immigration.
> c) Prevent any racialist abuse occurring inside the school wherever we possibly can. For example if epithets like 'coon', 'nigger', 'wog', 'yid' or 'paki' are heard they should not go unchallenged. We should explain why they are offensive and prevent them becoming common currency within the school.

It argued for the confiscation of racist literature and an accompanying programme of education to explain why such action was necessary. The document also recognised that schools were a reflection of society and that wider events inevitably impinged on their life. It tackled the argument that we would be accused of bringing politics into schools by explaining that schools and education were already subjects of political decisions, that their existing function was founded on political assumptions and that it was the National Front that had decided to turn them into political battlegrounds on the question of racism – which decision demanded a response if multi-ethnic schools were to survive.

We did not imagine that the adoption of this policy meant that it would be carried out consistently by all members of staff; neither did we imagine that even if it were that it would make anything other than a modest contribution to the wider struggles against racism. Those teachers most committed to the initiative were aware that the roots of racism lay in the nature of British society and its imperialist past and that unless the social and economic base of society were transformed there would always be the possibility of racism being used as a weapon to divide workers. We took the view that racism should be opposed wherever it raised its head and that if manifest in schools teachers and students had an obligation to respond to it. This interventionist stance is in direct contrast to the 'liberal' views of multicultural education that have since been put forward by writers like Robert Jeffcoate and Michael Banton. I will look more closely at this contrast later in the chapter.

The second characteristic of the policy was that it was integrationist. This is a clumsy word, but it attempts to convey the view that a theory of anti-racist teaching is in effect a theory of education as a whole. It is not an appendage, something tagged on as a benevolent afterthought, but an integral part of the school curriculum. A multi-ethnic perspective has clear implications for the internal organisation of the school, for selection of teaching groups, for pastoral care, for examination syllabuses, for the school library and the development of resource materials. If it is to mean anything at all it must permeate the whole life of the school.

There is no doubt that this aspect of the policy, particularly that which relates to the design of the curriculum, is the most difficult to implement and monitor. Not all departments, during the five years that the policy has been in operation, have responded to requests to outline how their curriculum reflects the school policy and even those departments that have responded would admit that their attempts were often unsystematic in design and uneven in operation. I have outlined some of these initiatives elsewhere and will give more consideration to them later in this chapter. Before doing so it is necessary to examine how the initial launch of the policy was followed up and how attempts were made to implement those aspects not directly related to the formal curriculum.

Central to this examination is some understanding of what might be termed the ethos of the school. Holloway is a single-sex, multi-ethnic, working class, inner-city comprehensive school. (What is 'comprehensive' about a school claiming those attributes is a question that should be directed elsewhere!) It is fair to say that there are no serious racial tensions among the students and that the staff are generally well disposed towards the anti-racist teaching policy. In this respect it has a number of advantages over schools which such a description would not fit and where the hierarchy are either indifferent or hostile towards such a policy. When the policy was introduced to the students in assemblies and form periods it was well received; in a sense the staff were externalising a mood which already existed among the students. Parents and governors responded similarly when the policy was represented in the school booklet. The circumstances for the development of the policy were relatively favourable.

It was obvious that the initial momentum of the launch of the policy would not be sustained, but there were various attempts to ensure that it was not lost altogether. An in-service training course was established on a series of evenings after school in an attempt to acquaint the staff with the history and cultural traditions of the Caribbean. Since attendance was voluntary, those who attended indicated some commitment to the policy and there is no doubt that they did learn something from the course. It was, however, marred by being presented largely from a black separatist standpoint that involved an analysis of racism that was in many ways antipathetic to the involvement of schools and teachers in the fight against it. This analysis has been admirably dealt with in Andy Green's article and I do not intend to devote any time in this article to an additional criticism of it. Suffice it to say that teachers who had been actively campaigning against racism, some of whom were committed socialists, were understandably irritated at being described as a significant part of the problem they were trying to face.

To monitor the impact of the policy a multi-ethnic sub-committee of the school's curriculum group was set up and in the initial stages it met periodically and reported back to the larger body. Some of the problems that it faced are reflected in the response to a questionnaire which it distributed to all staff two years after the policy had been launched. Twenty-four replies were received (about a third of the staff) and a digest of these replies was compiled. It considered three main areas; the extent of racist remarks and abuse, the appropriate response to these and an assessment as to whether there had been an increase in the extent of the problem during the two years of the policy. Some teachers were obviously more aware of manifestations of racism than others and these would be the same teachers who would be most likely to respond to them. Students soon became able to identify these members of staff and to modify their behaviour accordingly. In this way the problems were disguised rather than eliminated, but at least it was established that racist remarks were not respectable in the school. The problem of non-intentional racist abuse was raised, for example the reference to Spurs' supporters as 'Yids', a term they themselves began to embrace. Some members of staff were unsure whether or not this constituted a breach of the policy and were less confident in dealing with it than with intentional abuse. Of course the question of intent does not determine whether a term is racist or not, clearly 'Yids' in the example above is, but it does have a bearing on the way in which a response should be made. Many replies drew attention to the fact that sexism and sexist remarks were a much bigger problem in the school and this perception has lead the staff to develop a specific policy on this issue.

The second part of the questionnaire looked at the nature of our response and one comment in particular stood out:

> I find it difficult to introduce anti-racist attitudes in a way which allows the kids to see the contradictions for themselves. I think merely being didactic reinforces prejudices.

This comment emphasised the importance of curricular provision; our response should not primarily be reactive, though such a response is inevitable, but should be based on a curriculum designed to introduce the issues in a more positive way. A common thread running through the replies was the need to respond to each case individually and not to have a uniform response. In particular it was emphasised that it was dangerous to characterise whole groups of students, for example skinheads, as racists. This kind of cultural stereotyping would encourage the creation of an organised racist presence in the school when none had existed previously.

At this stage it may be useful to look at some examples of remarks made in my presence, usually in the classroom, and outline my response in each case. Not that I would wish to suggest that my reactions were in any way exemplary, but it is useful to have some practical examples of responses to an issue that is all too often clouded by the mists of theoretical abstraction. Since the context of the incidents is important I have attempted to provide a very brief summary of the background.

1 *A second year class was writing a story. There was hardly any conversation and most were engaged with the act of writing. One of them lunged towards an Asian student in the front row, 'You fucking Paki curry eater. I'll kill you'. The outburst was not provoked in any discernable way.*

This was obviously an extreme example combining racist abuse with the threat of violence; it certainly took me by surprise. I immediately stopped the lesson and called the offender out to the front letting the rest of the class know that I was angry. The main motive initially was to protect the victim and let him know that I was not 'neutral' in the face of such abuse. I then explained to the class why the remarks were doubly offensive. The offender apologised and in a discussion after the lesson I was able to reinforce the points I had made by asking him how he would have responded to a similar attack. The irony was that he was West Indian and had been on the receiving end of similar verbal abuse if not the physical threat. This incident does not have a happy ending; it had such an unsettling effect on the victim that shortly afterwards he asked to be transferred from the school.

2 *A sixth form Asian student came into a fourth year lesson with a message for me from another teacher. As he left, one of the class asked in a conversational tone, 'What did the Pak want?'*

It was a casual, gratuitous comment, not intended maliciously, but had it been left unchallenged would have helped to contribute to an atmosphere which legitimises off-the-cuff racism. I took the opportunity of explaining that not all Asians were Pakistanis (the sixth former was in fact a Ugandan Indian) and that the epithet 'Pak' was offensive. The point was taken, but I am not confident that in different circumstances the offender would have changed his use of language. The point is that the remark was not allowed to go unchallenged.

3 *During a form period discussion with a fifth year group the question was asked, 'Sir, don't you think this country is overcrowded?'. In the same discussion came the confident assertion from another student, who had friends in the National Front, 'It's obvious what the problem is; there are two million blacks in this country and two million unemployed – if we kick them out we could all have a job.'*

The first question was not explicitly racist, but did make implicit racist assumptions. It led to a lengthy explanation about the nature of immigration and the way in which immigrants settled here and how they had in some areas established their own communities. To have responded without such an explanation would have been guilty by omission. It was in the event a good opportunity to implement one of the objectives of the policy. The second question was obviously connected to the first, but was much more explicitly racist in its formulation. It led to a difficult argument in which I attempted to explain that black people did not cause unemployment and that they had in fact been invited to this country in the fifties to fill a vacuum in the labour market. It must be stressed that these points were not just made by me – the teacher – thankfully they were taken up by other students in the class and their contributions were no doubt more effective. I was able, however, to establish the context within which these contributions could be made.

4 *Passim, 'Sir, heard the one about the Irishman ...?'*

Given my own Irish ancestry this usually occurs as part of an attempt to poke fun at me and it is important to avoid a paranoid reaction to it. But I do point out that Irish jokes are in society as part of a political attack on the Irish as a direct result of the situation in Northern Ireland and when questioned about my own attitude to that situation I have always tried to explain my point of view as honestly and as simply as I could. Yes of course Irish jokes are racist, but often the best way to deal with them is to disarm the teller rather than to beat him round the head. There is no doubt that anti-Irish attitudes are more acceptable among students partly because they are so much a part of the common currency of television comedy shows and tabloid journalism. It is important that they are not exempt from the school policy.

5 *After a particularly unpleasant incident the white victim is in tears and shouts out, 'I hate that black bully.'*

One of the dangers of the response of teachers in schools that have adopted an anti-racist policy or that are sympathetic to such a policy is that it will be governed in instances like that outlined above by feelings of guilt rather than considerations of justice. It has to be pointed out to the victim that the offender is not a bully because he is black and that there are white bullies as well, but it is equally important that he sees that justice is done if he has been the victim of violence or extortion. Teachers rightly resent the reluctance of heads and governing bodies to take action against students who are guilty of serious acts of violence simply because they are black. Far from assisting the anti-racist cause such reluctance engenders resentment among white students who feel that double standards are in operation. An anti-racist policy is a policy for white students as well.

Those are a few examples of incidents and my response to them. In the more serious cases they would also be accompanied by a letter home and an interview with parents. I am aware that in print they may appear to be rather trite and it is impossible within the constraints of this article to give a sufficiently detailed account of all the nuances involved in any response, but I hope they do serve to illustrate some of the points that were contained in the school policy.

The questionnaire went on to consider whether racist incidents had increased or decreased during the two years that the policy had been in operation. The most obvious problem in making this assessment is the fact that the policy itself had made staff more aware of the problem and whereas in the past an incident may have slipped by unnoticed, now it would be remarked upon. The most significant response to this section drew attention to the shifting political developments outside school. The National Front suffered a humiliating defeat in the 1979 general election, the Conservative Party stole most of their votes, and this marked an end to their attempts at political respectability. After a period of internal feuds both the Front and the British Movement became more overtly 'Nazi' in their political stance and became more openly committed to violence. This led directly to a series of racist attacks on blacks both at home and in the streets and there is no doubt that some school students were attracted to these organisations because of the prospect of a 'good punch-up'.

The role of the media also came under scrutiny in some of the replies and attention was drawn in particular to the *Sun*'s coverage of the 'Four hundred pound a week Malawi Asians at a Heathrow hotel'. Ironically this was the very paper that the students chose for the school library.

The list of recommendations that arose from the questionnaire and subsequent meetings of the sub-committee is interesting to look at in retrospect. While a few still look wildly ambitious, others have at least been implemented in some measure. They were:

1 Publish an updated policy which includes returns from all departments.
2 Discuss the best way of publicising this policy with students and parents.
3 Produce a resource list of materials that have proved successful.
4 Involve the Multi-ethnic Inspectorate in discussions about new initiatives.
5 Set up a committee to consider our response to sexism in the school as a matter of urgency.

It is only now that 1 is being implemented through a revised version of the policy, though a version was included in the school booklet for parents. Recently a display of materials has been put together for the school's quinquennial review; the display includes examples of students' work as well as resource material from different departments. The inspectorate were involved in discussions with the sub-committee and with individual departments and the final recommendation has led to a one-day conference and the preparation of a school policy on sexism.

At present we are concentrating on the production of an up-dated policy statement and the involvement of all departments in the school in the establishment of proper provision in the curriculum. The provisional draft for the revised statement reiterates our interventionist stance:

> We have a responsibility to educate our students for life in a multiracial society. The racist attitudes and prejudices present in our society have a detrimental effect on students in school and the climate in which they learn. The only way in which we can carry out our responsibility is by making a firm stand against racism in whatever form it presents itself.

It also acknowledges that there are many racist aspects of society, that we, acting simply as teachers, cannot directly influence and it attempts to describe some of the ways in which these aspects have changed over the last seven years.

State racism is now more firmly entrenched than ever with the new Nationality Act joining existing Immigration Acts on the statute book; with police harassment of young blacks unabated despite the demise of the 'Sus' law and the apocalyptic warnings of the inner city riots and with unemployment, the principle breeding ground of racism, the cornerstone of the present government's economic policy.

It also highlights the one aspect of the original policy that has proved the most difficult to implement. The curriculum innovations that we have managed to establish are fragmented and unsystematic, but some departments have made a start. The History department has revised the unit of the third year syllabus on African and Caribbean History to include the following:

1 Dispelling misconceptions concerning the 'primitive' state of Africa prior to the coming of the Europeans, and developing awareness of the complexity of traditional African societies.
2 Examining the economic basis of racism.
3 Introducing the methodology used by African historians.
4 Studying Jamaica as an example of a multicultural society.
5 Reviewing the causes and the problems associated with migration.

The fourth and fifth year has a general syllabus title, 'World Affairs 1919 to the present day'. It includes units on: 'Aspects of Apartheid in South Africa', 'Population and Race in South Africa', 'Genocide', 'The Road to the Second World War' and 'Civil Rights in the USA'. The Sociology department has introduced a course unit on population and immigration and has organised the viewing of a number of films with the third, fourth and fifth years including, 'Last Grave at Dimbaza' (a documentary filmed illegally in South Africa with a chilling insight into a racist society) and 'Divide and Rule – Never!' (a film which captures the mood among young people at the Anti-Nazi League carnivals of the late seventies).

The English department has embarked on a number of initiatives that are worth a mention.

1 The school's language policy document makes this point:

> 'The language of examination and instruction in schools is Standard English. The natural language of nearly all our students is some form of non-standard English.'

The most recent survey of linguistic diversity at Holloway highlights the number of students for whom English is not their first language. In the current first year 38 per cent come into this category. We have sought to establish that there is some attempt at mother tongue-maintenance in the classroom. The educational arguments have already been outlined in other case-studies in this book, and in documents from the ILEA and the NUT. It is interesting that in a mixed ability classroom the effect on the whole class can be beneficial. For example, Bengali speakers are seen by their peers not just as learners of English, but as experts in their own language. In addition

it is clear that the use of mother tongue and translations can have a dramatic effect on the student's development of narrative, one of the most important ways that we make sense of the world.
2 The use of autobiographical writing is an obvious way of establishing the sense of personal history and identity of all students. In a multi-ethnic school this kind of writing is a marvellous exemplification of Chris Searle's phrase a 'World in the Classroom'.
3 There are numerous class readers that we have found useful in exploring themes that enable discussion to focus on the questions of racism. *East End at Your Feet*[3] by Farouk Dhondy has led to work on immigration and *Long Journey Home*[4] by Julius Lester has produced work on slavery. Amrit Wilson's *Finding a Voice*[5] led to first year students empathising in writing with the numerous Asian families that have been victims of racist attacks in recent years.

We recognise that a great deal of work still has to be done in the area of curriculum innovation and we can obviously learn from the practice of other schools.

The Holloway document has often been held up as an example of what schools should be aiming at, but we would always seek to emphasise that a document is not a policy. A genuine policy is the practice of the school. The above account has sought to demonstrate that there is a world of difference between the two.

Political intervention versus the liberal tradition

Recent developments in the theory of multiculturalism have sought to resurrect the liberal child-centred tradition of education and to bury the attempts of those of us who have emphasised that anti-racist teaching is part of a wider political fight. In this respect the Rampton[6] report came as a pleasant surprise. It argued that teachers should be prepared to examine their own attitudes and actions and be prepared to take a stand against racism.

> In short we are asking teachers to play a leading role in seeking to bring about a change in attitudes on the part of society as a whole towards ethnic minority groups.

Although the ILEA has welcomed the report, the principal teachers' union, the NUT, reacted very defensively to the notion that teachers might have racist attitudes. The government reacted in a more hostile way by sacking the chairman of the committee. Whilst it is important to reject any attempt to situate the roots of racism within education and teachers' attitudes, it is clear that the education system reflects the society within which it operates and as such is far from being immune to the problem. Rampton argues for an unashamedly interventionist position, but there are those who would attempt to espouse the liberal tradition of the development of every student to her/his maximum potential while at the same time rejecting the idea that teachers should look for a political explanation for the failure of this potential to be realised. This view has been most recently advocated by Michael Banton who argues:

> The liberal objective has been and is parity of esteem as individuals for all children irrespective of their appearance, family background and preferences about styles of living in the private domain ... it is undesirable to assign children to cultures. They should be as free as it is possible to decide their own affiliations and the fluidity of group identities must be acknowledged.

Yet he himself points out that prejudice in society is rarely directed against individuals as individuals, but against individuals as members of a social or ethnic group. To put it more bluntly, when Gulam is beaten up on the way home from school it is not because his attackers are prejudiced against him as an individual (they probably don't even know him) it is because they are prejudiced against Bengalis and all others that they identify as 'Pakis'. Banton castigates the 'radicals' for attempting to explain this racial prejudice in terms of the socio-economic basis of the state; yet he himself does not seem to acknowledge those aspects of our society that are clearly racist and which seek to foster racist attitudes in order to divide and rule. He reduces the fight against racism to an attempt to alter the attitudes of individuals and ignores the need to tackle its roots. At least Banton makes a number of valuable comments about the dangers of 'cultural romanticism' and he draws attention to some of the problems presented by the word 'multiculturalism'. Those who argue that we should respect the cultural traditions of all groups in society ('let a thousand flowers bloom') over and above any other considerations find themselves facing a number of contradictions. For example the practice of arranged marriages is anathema to those who are committed to the struggle for women's rights. Similarly the demand from some of the elders of the Muslim community for religiously segregated schools plays into the hands of those who would like to establish segregated schools as a prelude to the advent of a more general apartheid.

Banton's views seem to echo the much cruder position advanced by Robert Jeffcoate in *Positive Image*.[8] This book has been given a prominent place on many initial and in-service training courses for teachers when it should more justifiably be placed in the nearest dustbin. Jeffcoate begins by placing himself 'within the much maligned tradition of middle class white liberalism'. If it has been maligned then it is not without cause if this is a typical evocation of that tradition:

> ... curtailing the National Front's legitimate entitlements is of the same order as trying to gag white racism in the classroom – ideologically and strategically dangerous – and young white racists have as much right to attentive adult ears at school.

To allow the expression of racist ideas to go unchallenged in the classroom or elsewhere in school is to adopt a political attitude that will encourage the abuse of ethnic minorities. It is to abdicate the very responsibility that Rampton placed on the shoulders of teachers. It is also rather shoddy to equate the organised, adult expression of racism in racist organisations like the National Front with remarks and attitudes expressed by students in school. In the latter case it is often possible to challenge those views successfully through discussion and debate. With the former, debate is futile and counter-productive. Even the most cursory examination of the examples given earlier in this article will show the folly of failing to respond to the expression of racist views in the classroom. Imagine the effect on a West Indian or Asian student in the classroom if in response to the remark, 'I think we should kick out all the blacks 'cos they're taking all our jobs', the teacher replies, 'Ah, that's an interesting comment – now let's move on.'

It would be inappropriate to conclude this section without some consideration of the methods of combating racism in schools being adopted by those local authorities that have demonstrated a genuine commitment to the task. The strategies being implemented by my own authority, the ILEA, give rise to real concern. Those who now have political control of the authority believe that change in society and therefore in schools can be brought about by manipulating the existing machinery of the local state. They do not recognise that this apparatus is incapable of delivering the goods on this or any other reform; they are convinced that with the right leadership permanent reforms can be instituted. Hence they show their commitment to an issue by creating a bureaucracy around it and advertising a series of highly paid managerial jobs to staff it. This is exactly what has happened with the ILEA's commitment to multi-ethnic education and the GLC's programme 'Dismantling Racism'. The pressure for anti-racist teaching came initially from black parents and students in the early seventies and subsequently from the convictions of classroom teachers, often in the face of unsympathetic heads and colleagues. The impetus for the Holloway policy did not come from a progressive local authority, but from within the school's own experience. In my view it would be preferable for the ILEA to provide money for the provision of supply teachers in schools to allow practising teachers some time off to develop anti-racist teaching programmes. There is enough expertise inside schools if only teachers had the opportunity to organise it and spread it. The appointment of highly paid advisory teachers mitigates against this valuable do-it-yourself approach by creating 'experts' to do the job instead. Classroom teachers are forming the distinct impression that the creation of a new layer of advisory teachers is not designed to help them, but to keep them on their toes! It is difficult not to regard the creation of these new posts as an attempt by the authority to demonstrate to black parents in particular a public face for their multi-ethnic commitment. Much more convincing would be the direction of resources into schools so that they could engage with the problem themselves and initiate programmes of anti-racist teaching that went beyond a superficial declaration of intent.

This is not to say that the ILEA has not undertaken numerous initiatives in addition to the creation of this new bureaucracy that are of real value to teachers in schools. But even an authority with a record of such initiatives must not be regarded as above criticism.

References
1 Green A., 'In defence of anti-racist teaching: a reply to recent critiques of multicultural education, *NAME Journal*, Spring 1982
2 ILEA 'A Multi-ethnic Education: Joint Report of the Schools Sub-committee and Further and Higher Education Sub-committee, 1977'
3 Dhondy F., *East End at Your Feet*, Topliner (Macmillan), 1976
  Lester J., *Long Journey Home*, Knockout (Longman), 1978
  Wilson A., *Finding a Voice*, Virago, 1978
4 See *TES* 29.5.81 for extended summary of the Report
5 Banton M., *Race, Prejudice and Education, Changing Approaches* for Royal Anthropological Institute, 1973
6 Jeffcoate R., *Positive Image*, Readers-Writers, 1978

Bibliography
Multicultural Education: Views from the Classroom, BBC 1981 (Chapter 10)
'Combating Racialism in Schools' Union Policy Statement: guidance for members, NUT 1981

Chapter 23

ANTI-RACIST TEACHING IN THE PRIMARY SCHOOL

Martin Francis

> Normand Park Primary School has a roll of 200 and an average class size of 25. Its intake is drawn from Fulham. The majority of pupils are white working class, with 10–20 per cent British born black and a number from other ethnic minority groups. All classes are mixed ability – some contain two different age groups.
>
> Martin Francis is a class teacher at Normand Park Primary School and is also in charge of library and resources. He is a member of ALTARF and has contributed to many of its publications. He has also published articles in the journals *Educational Fightback, Cambridge Journal of Education, Teaching London Kids, Radical Education* and the *Times Education Supplement*.
>
> This article first appeared in the *Cambridge Journal of Education*, Easter 1982.

The innocence of youth?

My work on anti-racist teaching has developed as part of the collective practice of the Primary Workshop of All London Teachers Against Racism and Fascism. There is plenty of research to show that racist attitudes begin from an early age. One of the early objections that we were faced with was the one that sees children as essentially 'innocent'. If they come out with racist remarks this must merely be a reflection of their parents' views. This view may at first seem attractive: it lets the child off the hook, and it also reduces the importance of the child's racism to the level of yet another parroted opinion and denies that children make sense of their own world in the same way as adults do.

If anti-racists have this 'innocents' approach it severely limits what they do. Anti-racist teaching becomes the rescuing of innocents from the wicked racists who wish to infect their vulnerable young minds with the disease of racism. Anti-racism teaching becomes a moral or religious act aimed at 'cleansing' children's attitudes.

In contrast, our view is that children are engaged in a continuous process of building up a picture of their world and making sense of it. Their accumulation of experience and knowledge enables them to explain their position and also to predict their future. Now of course, some of the information that they build into their scheme may be wrong, or onesided; their experience itself may be limited. It may also be that the information they have and their experience is so conflicting that they end up confused and their actions become arbitrary and contradictory. All the same they are actively working at understanding things and are not passive recipients of parents' views.

Teacher's role
Given this model the role of the anti-racist teacher becomes different. It is her/his job to make an intervention in the child's process of understanding racism. This is not done by taking away the active role of the child but by feeding into the process information and experiences that contribute to an understanding that will go beyond the scapegoating explanations that racists will give of current economic and social ills; and will also go beyond what can easily seem a morally correct but (to working class pupils) essentially middle class do-gooding anti-racism that is totally unaware of political realities that face the children and their families.

Strategy for a wider school context
Taking this model as our starting point it became clear that anti-racist teaching was not possible without a general framework of good primary practice in the classroom or the school. In March 1980[1] we summarised this as involving:

1. a) organisation of the school and classroom in mixed ability groups.
   b) the 'atmosphere' of the classroom – encouragement of discussions, exchange of ideas, openness to others.
   c) teachers' awareness of childrens' attitudes, reaction to namecalling, racist remarks etc.
   d) organisation of resources so that they are available for independent use by children as well as teachers.
2. Development of specific areas of the curriculum which are particularly suitable for anti-racist teaching: e.g. environmental studies;
   a) use of classroom language/personal history resources (parents and children);
   b) language work (particularly discussion, of local issues in which children may be involved);
   c) ILEA's *Explore A Story*, other biographies, childrens' own news, etc.;
   d) discussion of current affairs, TV programmes; drama including role play about current/historical/fictional events followed by discussion.

It should be recognised that an across-the-board multi-ethnic approach can be developed into anti-racist teaching where the teacher sees this as viable, correcting misinformation or ignorance over other cultures that come up in assemblies, school meals, religious observance etc. To make anti-racist teaching a part of the school's practice rather than something happening in one classroom is quite a slow process. You can begin to prepare the ground for this by: putting your own class-made materials into the general resources pool or library for all to use, with explanations to guard against misuse; presentation of your classes' work in school assemblies; display in the corridors; holding staff meetings in individual teacher's rooms so that they can talk about their work in that particular room; arranging cover so that time is set aside for teachers to visit each other's rooms. Eventually a unity of approach can only be achieved by adopting a school policy on racism. This has already been done in many secondary schools but is only just beginning in primary schools. Later in this article we'll look at the outline of what a school policy should be.

A personal approach

Meanwhile I'd like to return to my own practice. I currently teach fourth year juniors, most of whom I also taught in their third year. There are a number of children of West Indian descent in the class but most of them come from a traditional white working-class estate just across the road from the school. In terms of the framework outlined above I have been able to get quite a long way. The atmosphere of the classroom is one where we have lots of discussion and the children have gradually learnt to listen to each other and accept the need to be able to offer evidence for the opinions that they express. This has been quite a hard process. Our discussions are usually held in a circle and a stone is passed from child to child. You can only speak when you are holding the stone. This gives all an equal chance to speak, to some extent curtails male dominance and stops duologues being set up. I obey the same rules as the children but am not 'neutral', i.e. I express a point of view if called upon, which children may, and often do, argue with. I have also tried to indicate through the displays and resources in the classroom an acceptance of other cultures. So we have materials showing black people, our artwork is multicultural, we have both multicultural and anti-racist books. Similarly the curriculum has an anti-racist component. This is not a separate area dealt with in a little box but is part of the general curriculum and comes up in language work, geography, drama, environmental studies, history and music. I seldom do specific projects on a multiracial theme and this reflects a concern that I have about treating other cultures in an 'exotic' way – projects on food, dress or music can often do that without adding to children's understanding of racism. Indeed by making other cultures strange, albeit colourful, they can reinforce racism. As the authors of *Unpopular Education*[2] suggest, to make the content of education relevant we need to make the fundamental conflicts that face pupils the subject of study in school – not in order to resolve them but so that pupils have a few more tools with which to begin to understand them. In this context our foci should include the divisions of race, sex, class and age within our society and internationally our relationship with the Third World. These conflicts will often be evident in the pupils' immediate experience of family and community and in a more distanced way in the press and television coverage of the issues. A further distance is provided by similar experiences earlier in history or in other countries.

Over the last two years this is the way the issue of racism has been tackled in our classroom – beginning with items closest to the child's experience and becoming more distant.

1 School
1 Discussion of racist abuse in the school and the steps that can be taken to combat it.
2 Discussion about activities of one class member who took part in NF activity with older gangs and wore a swastika armband to school.
3 Design of anti-racist posters followed by a few people making up a comic, with their own anti-racist 'Superman' sorting out 'NF' thugs.

2 Community
1 Tape/slide show of local estate including the issue of racist graffiti produced by environmental study group. It included discussion of what the graffiti made black people feel – and who was responsible for it. This was shown in assembly to the whole school;
2 Complaint by environmental study group. It included racist graffiti on park benches – taken up with council officials and cleaned off;
3 Discussion of housing policies locally – including possibility that after the riots black families were being moved to particular blocks; a workman's statement to black pupil that new houses he was working on 'weren't for blacks', issue of 'sinbin' estates;
4 Invitation to parents to visit exhibition about Grenada as part of open evening.

3 National
1 New Cross Fire Massacre, examination of press coverage and the follow-up Protest March. Comparison with press treatment of neo-nazi riot after Chelsea football match (this was taken up later when pupils visited Chelsea Football Club and asked officials what they were doing about racist elements in crowd).
2 Writing and artwork on Notting Hill Carnival;
3 Discussion about the summer 1981 'riots';
4 Discussion (in light of riots) of how children saw their future: employment, housing, 'the bomb'.

4 History
1 Visit to Ashanti exhibition at Museum of Mankind, background work on British in Africa – artwork, modelling and creative writing;
2 Story of Harriet Tubman – writing and presentation of play about Tubman's life;
3 Paul Robeson, study of his life and music;
4 *Diary of Anne Frank*. Story read to class and creative writing about feelings aroused by the story. Background on rise of Nazis and Second World War;
5 *How We Used to Live* (Yorkshire TV), covers years 1938–1953 includes scenes showing Blackshirts – discussion of present day parallels.

5 International
1 Study of press reports and poems from the children involved in Soweto. Class, imagining they were Soweto children, wrote letters describing feelings about strike and having to flee.
2 Discussion and interview initiated by the pupils themselves about the child killings in Atlanta;
3 Link with school in Grenada, West Indies, following my visit there. There are a number of Grenadians at our school and several in my class. Pen friend writing to be followed by joint projects. Aim to educate our children about problems faced by single crop Third World country, and Grenadians about our lives and particularly the problems faced by black people in London. Production of book about our school to send over which (again at pupil's initiative) includes section on graffiti and the NF.

This is only a small number of the things that have been covered and probably appears haphazard. This is partly because most of the items slotted into other things we were doing and weren't isolated items. For example the Soweto issue followed work done on the Burston school strike but also reflected questions raised in class about children's dissatisfaction with the education they were being offered.

A growing perception

The various levels of this approach feed into the child's growing awareness and understanding of racism. When the child mentioned above wore a swastika into school it was white children who objected. During the subsequent discussion they drew on community, historical and international sources to oppose the boy's ideas, while an Asian boy drew on his personal experience: 'It's people like your friends who beat up people in my family.' Eventually the boy withdrew from the NF and was *admired* by his classmates for doing so. They realised what a difficult process he had gone through:

X (the boy in question)	When I tried to leave the NF they beat me up for no reason. They always do that.
Teacher	Did you explain why you were leaving?
X	They were too violent and they were beating up people and stabbing them and all that. They just started beating me up. They were calling me 'chicken' and 'nigger lover' and all that.
Teacher	Do you think it took a lot of courage for X to say that?
Chorus	Yes.
K	They could have killed him for all you know.[3]

An issue for all schools

Later in a local radio interview the children attributed the boy's change of mind to the regular discussions that we had in the classroom. One pupil, Saul, transferred to an all white school in the country (he himself is white) and wrote to us that 'there is a lot of racism in this school. I think it's because they don't know any black people.' That 10 year old was still constructing his view of racism despite being removed from the immediate atmosphere of discussion. He now chairs the school debating society. He put his finger on a key aspect of anti-racist teaching: i.e. that it is important for 'all-white' schools. Although such schools don't have the advantages of the first level above, particularly in terms of pupils' individual experiences, they can do a certain amount at community level, a considerable amount at the national level, and they have equal access to the historical and international levels. Certainly at these levels it should be possible, through creative writing, role play, etc. to enable the children to get some idea of how it feels to be in a minority so that the *emotional* area is touched as well as the *informational*. There are now quite a few books that describe the experiences of minority groups in England. *Our Lives*, available from the ILEA English Centre, Sutherland Street, SW1 includes pupils' accounts of their lives in England and positive and negative experiences.

Saul recognised the contribution that all-white schools have to make when pupils are growing up in a multiracial society – even when their immediate first hand experience is monoracial. Do we?

Towards a school policy

It is obvious that this sort of approach cannot take place without it being reflected in the school generally. 'Democracy in one classroom' will soon produce other tensions inside the school. Children taught to look critically at the media are also likely to be sceptical about the utterances of teachers. Children taught to discuss controversial issues openly and produce evidence for their views are unlikely to think much of a 'because I told you to' approach by other teachers. This is where a school *policy* becomes important. The difficulties involved are immense but the possibilities are exciting. A recent edition of *Issues In Race and Education*,[4] pointed to the danger of policies becoming just another piece of paper and stated 'the need for a policy must be presented in the context of the real problems our schools face. Each school should examine what is going on in its own background and uncover the extent of racial harassment and abuse in the school and the community and examine the attitudes of teachers as well as pupils. This means that a debate has to take place in each staffroom'.

One North London primary school recently discussed what the ingredients of a school policy should be. Their framework included the following.

1 A general statement on the school's opposition to racism and racist groups and a commitment to cater for *all* its children.

2 An outline of what a multiracial/anti-racist stance means for various aspects of the curriculum – language, history, geography, social studies, etc.
3 Guidelines on dealing with racist incidents that are operated by both teachers and auxiliary staff.
4 A commitment to examine the remedial, disruptive, and ESL provision in the school for racial bias.
5 An examination of books and learning materials for bias and a commitment to providing positive materials.
6 An examination of the role parents play in the school and suggestions for making this more contributory to the school.
7 Establishment of links with local community groups, the local law centre, etc.

The government has recently expressed some disquiet about the activities of racist groups in schools and the document *Nazis in the Playground*[5] listed some of the evidence about that activity. Schools and LEAs were roundly criticised for doing little about it. The NUT has responded with its own document on racism and schools.[6] It is now up to LEAs and individual teachers and schools to move into action. Ideally LEA policies should give schools the educational (and financial) backing to put anti-racist teaching into practice. Equivocation will serve the racist cause.

References

1 *Race in the Classroom: Teaching Against Racism in the Primary School*, All London Teachers Against Racism and Fascism, Unit 216, Panther House, 38 Mount Pleasant, London WC1.
2 *Unpopular Education: Schooling and Social Democracy in England since 1944*, Education Group – Centre for Contemporary Cultural Studies, Birmingham, Hutchinson.
See also *Issues in Race and Education*, Autumn 1981, for elaboration of Unpopular Education ideas in context of race and education (available from 11 Carleton Gardens, Brecknock Road, N19 5AQ).
3 Transcript published by West London NAME, March 1981.
4 Issues, May/June 1981: 'Every Child must know where we stand'. Available as above.
5 *Nazis in the Playground*. Centre for Contemporary Studies, Shoreditch High Street, London.
6 Available from NUT, Hamilton House, Mabledon Place, WC1.

Chapter 24

A COURSE ON RACISM

Ilona Aronovsky and Carolyn Sikorski

> The authors are a community education worker and a community worker who have worked for several years in multicultural areas in London and the provinces. Both have been active in anti-racist organisations including ALTARF.

The East End of London has traditionally been an area of low wages, poor housing conditions, uncertain employment prospects and high immigration. Despite its close historical connection with the trade union and Labour movement, it has had also a related history of racism, fascism and racist attacks. Racist and fascist views are still manifested today with the main target being the Asian community. The main perpetrators of racist violence and abuse are young people of school and college age.

Expressed racism at school and particularly in the classroom is obviously of concern to teachers, but racist attitudes and actions are not easily dealt with. The experience of teachers who spontaneously take up the use of racist terms in a class is that polarisation between the teacher and white pupils quickly develops with the white pupils making racist assertions on their terms. The teacher can try either to counterpose her/his own arguments or to use authority to silence the pupils. Frequently the teacher is left with the feeling that all s/he has done is to harden racist attitudes.

In 1981 we became increasingly concerned at the overt racism expressed by white fourth year pupils taking part in a programme of community courses. A day examining racial prejudice in a structured way was included in the programme. We recognised that the development of polarisation during the sessions would be counter-productive and also that the pupils needed to be presented with hard facts if racist beliefs were to be challenged. We started the day with 'Bafa Bafa'[1] a cross-cultural simulation game which enables pupils to experience the hostility and paranoia often felt in an alien environment. The fact that such strong feelings developed in a short space of time amongst people who knew each other was discussed after the debriefing and its relevance to life in the East End explored. We then followed with *Our People 2*[2] (part of a Thames TV series on racism) which gives facts and figures to debunk racist myths surrounding black people in this country.

The discussions following the film indicated that some pupils were questioning previously held beliefs and allowed others to express anti-racist views. Generally a 'them and us' situation did not develop between the adults and pupils. Pupils with hardened racist attitudes showed little movement in their views, but they were often questioned by others in the group. It was clear that previously the young people had come across very little to counter the pervasiveness of racist attitudes and assumptions.

Whilst recognising that a one-day session was unlikely to achieve any lasting change in attitude we felt that the approach of confronting racist views directly, logically and systematically could be used in the classroom, and that it was vital that schools tackled the issue. Fortunately we were developing links with teachers who were desperately searching for a constructive approach to the issue of racism in their teaching and who were prepared to invest time and energy.

Pilot course and development of a teaching pack on racism

A working group consisting of ourselves and teachers from two schools therefore developed and tested out an extended course on racism[1] in 1981. It was used effectively with third formers in a predominantly white working class school and with stunning success with fourth formers in a multicultural school. We re-edited the course and distributed it to all social studies departments in the Borough at a launch conference supported by an Adviser. A number of multiracial schools have since successfully used the pack. However, since there is little to challenge a dominant racist ethos in majority white schools we wanted the method to be more systematically tested out. In such schools taking up the issue of racism in the classroom is far more difficult but particularly necessary.

Two social studies teachers in such a school approached us about using the course with fourth year groups, timetabled simultaneously. We offered to work with them in order to offer support and to assess the suitability of materials and methods. This article will deal with the experience in that school.

The school and the classroom situation

The catchment area of the school is a mainly white lower middle class/working class area, adjacent to the heart of docklands to the west and to a multicultural area to the north. A higher percentage of children are from owner occupier families than the adjacent white working class areas, where chronic unemployment and long-term destruction of the industrial base precede the current recession. However, these trends do affect the whole area.

The teachers told us that the predominant ethos of the white pupils was unquestioningly racist. Racist abuse of a particularly unpleasant nature aimed at black classmates was not uncommon. They felt that the school had yet to take up the whole question of anti-racist policies and curriculum and that the issue of racism was ignored by the majority of the teachers including the headmaster.

The environment supported their view – British Movement graffiti was daubed on the back gate at the school. No attempt was made to remove it in the time we were there. In the library a copy of Basil Davidson's *Discovering Africa's Past* stood next to Peter Gibbs' 1956 biography of Cecil Rhodes from the *True Books* series which describes how Rhodes saw the 'great empty spaces of Africa' and later 'sent his men to take Rhodesia from the native savages' with the result that the country was 'tamed and civilised and cultivated'.

The lack of development of anti-racist education in this school must be understood in the context of a LEA which, compared with many others, has only just begun to look at policies and resources for multicultural education, let alone to develop clear anti-racist guidelines.

The teachers were keen to use the course because there was a dearth of adequate materials available on the topic of racism. Standard sociology texts often reinforced racist assumptions. They decided to put the twelve-unit course into a seven week slot of two double periods a week as part of a syllabus which was already meant to cover racism. One class averaged 30 including one Afro-Caribbean and three Asian girls. Desks were arranged in rows, so even when working in smaller groups only a minority of pupils actively participated in discussion.

As a result discussion in the class was generally between a small number of vocal pupils and the teachers. The most racist pupils remained silent and withdrawn apart from two occasions when they contributed vociferously but were neither supported nor challenged by their white classmates. The norm was racist and the arguments were worked through with the teachers counterposing an anti-racist analysis.

This rarely resulted in a strong reaction from the pupils and often the feeling was one of 'what has racism to do with us?' The black pupils did not take part in discussion but their written work showed that they were involved in the course.

The contents in brief and preparation

The course initially takes the pupils through personal prejudice and stereotyping. This is followed by the history and role both of the British Empire and of black people in Britain. The pupils are then introduced to national statistics of jobs, housing, education and crime. Local information follows, bringing the subject closer to home. The final part of the course looks at racism and fascism in the East End and its causes and consequences both in the past and today. The course is ready to use and each unit contains an outline of the aims and objectives: suggestions for teaching methods and possible pitfalls, extra information for the teacher, fact sheets and work sheets for the pupils, back-up and source information and local newspaper cuttings. The introduction explains how the course should be used and is intended to prepare the teacher for problems s/he may encounter during the following weeks.

The teachers read the course through and familiarised themselves with the content and the approach before embarking on the teaching.

Although both of us could not be present all the time, wherever possible we discussed progress at the end of each session and how the next one should be tackled. We had two longer meetings to assess the materials and response to them. The rest of the article examines the progress of the course in the class in which one of us was always present.

It was made clear to the pupils that they would be participating in a special course. We did not start with any attitude assessment, as to embark on a course aimed at reducing racism by allowing pupils the freedom to express prejudices against black people would be extremely negative. Instead the course was kicked off by the always successful 'Bafa-Bafa' an event which sensitises the pupils and prepares the ground for the rest of the course. At the end of the course the groups filled in confidential questionnaires to ascertain how much they had absorbed and what their views were.

The pupils' response to the course

A few practical problems during the playing of 'Bafa-Bafa' did not affect the outcome of the game and the class focused on the topic of prejudice against strangers and a fear of the unknown. Whilst they agreed that racial prejudice created barriers between black and white people they felt that this was just a fact of life.

The concept of stereotyping and its consequences for different groups of people was then introduced by the viewing of *Why Prejudice*[3], a video produced by sixth formers in North London. The video examines the stereotyping of people, particularly black, with examples ranging from the present day *Mind Your Language* to the childhood gollywogs in Enid Blyton books. The pupils grasped the idea of stereotyping but contested whether or not it does greater harm to the lives of black people than those of white.

The pupils then studied slavery, the contribution of black people in Britain, the Empire, colonialism, neo-colonialism and imperialism and migration. This unit, No. 3, which took three sessions, is a key one, as it should give pupils a basic understanding of the historical and economic relationship between Britain and black people. It shows the exploitation of the Empire by the British ruling class and looks at the way black people in Britain have been 'written out' of history.

The method is to use information sheets, one on each topic. The pupils examine a topic in small groups and then report back to the whole class for discussion. The sheets are supplemented by *Our People 3* which documents the history of the British Empire and includes original footage of black soldiers in the Great War.

Most of the information contained in this unit has been completely new to all the pupils who have participated in this course, regardless of which school they attend, and from previous experience we had felt that the unit needed more time.

On this occasion the usual difficulties were combined with typical classroom disasters. The wrong film was screened and the school technician lost the key sheet on imperialism. As a result the majority of the class did not develop the basic knowledge necessary. This has not been the case in other groups.

The worksheet on slavery is an historical account of the development of slavery. It shows how slaves were treated, their resistance to the slave owners and that slaves were first and foremost merely a commodity. That ideas of racial superiority can be traced back to the days of slavery and have been used ever since to justify imperialism and racism was appreciated by the pupils. However, in the discussions after the report back from the small group they had to be heavily prompted to develop an analysis of slavery in terms of economic exploitation of black people and its relationship with colonialism. In contrast groups from multicultural schools have had little difficulty with such an analysis. An important part of the unit gives a balance to the slavery section by looking at the long history of black people in Britain. It gives details of black people who are conspicuous by their absence from most history books, despite their important contribution to British history.

It turned out that the group who reported to the class on this section contained one of the most overtly racist girls in the class. She reproduced the information from the sheets and reported back accurately, but then she stated vociferously, that she did not believe any of it, and her father would back her up. She claimed that black people were not 'fighting for Britain' in the Falklands. Her classmates neither supported her nor challenged her on this and we introduced information on black regiments into the discussion. *Our People 3* with its original film of black people fighting on the side of the British was subsequently screened.

Only a small number of pupils appeared to develop a realisation of what the Empire was and in whose interests it operated. The close connection between the development of industrial Britain and the consequent destruction of the economies of the countries of the Empire was not absorbed. That the Empire benefited the British ruling class rather than the British working class, was crucial to the development of British capitalism and certainly did not benefit the working class of the colonial nations was not understood by most pupils.

Assimilation of these ideas was hampered by the pupils' poor understanding of twentieth century history (some pupils thought that the First World War was the same thing as the Second World War) their lack of sense of their own history and of the basic concepts of class and inequality. We felt that this resulted in a mechanical listing of facts rather than an understanding of the issues in the reports back.

As a result there was some pressure to, in future, omit this unit. However these issues are key – without an historical understanding of racism it can be reduced to a purely psychological phenomenon with the solution being to persuade white individuals to relinquish their prejudices. Racism then becomes only a matter of individual white responsibility and arouses guilt, hostility or even indifference. White working class pupils in contrast to a growing number of black pupils have internalised a notion of history which completely excludes their own. Without this it is difficult for them to draw parallels between themselves and black people and to discover the common roots of racism and the exploitation of working people.

Subsequently, we have taken the unit much more slowly and shown *Our People 3* a section at a time with explanation and discussion after each section. This approach has enabled the pupils to grasp the basic theme which, combined with a discussion about who features in history books and who doesn't (women, the working class, black people) gave a much firmer base for the rest of the course.

The core of the course, units 5–8, covers employment, housing, education and crime and looks at the results of the discrimination shown against black people.

Unit 5 questions commonly-held views on the effect that black people have had on the position of white people in Britain. The unit revolves around the film *Our People 2* which, through the use of well-presented factual information music and old footage of pre-war British slums, explodes myths associated with post-war immigration.

The three subsequent units look at each topic separately. Through the use of the appropriate part of *Our People*, worksheets and local newspaper cuttings, the issues are brought right to the pupils' doorsteps.

Chronic housing shortages are contrasted with the area's falling population; the steady decline since 1900 in employment opportunities arising from factory and dock closures is documented and the coverage by the local paper of a 'riot' in 1981 headlined 'Black Fury' is contrasted with a black youth's first-hand account of the action of the police during the incident.

The teachers were encouraged to collect cuttings in the weeks leading up to and during the course to ensure that the information was up-to-date. This also reduced the effect on the pupils of the outmoded flared trousers worn by the young people in *Our People 2* which can give pupils the impression that the whole subject is shrouded in the history of 1978.

This part of the course was taught fairly formally. The need to work through the information systematically to some extent conflicted with the need to explore the views of the class. The pupils however grasped the reasons for unemployment in the area 'because the big firms are moving away ...', 'government cash cuts ...', 'factories and docks are closing down ...' were representative points of view, although some still thought also that the population was increasing. There is no doubt that the majority of the class will face unemployment when they leave school. That fifteen out of a class of twenty-one now believe that this is not because, to quote a commonly held myth, 'black people are taking the jobs' is a significant step forward. In the words of one pupil 'I thought the blacks took all the jobs and houses etc., in

Britain, but they haven't.'

. On the whole housing proved a more difficult area. The class generally fell into the owner occupier bracket so inadequate housing was not within their personal experience nor had they previously covered the subject at school. Consequently it was difficult to develop, in the short time available, a basic understanding of, or interest in, the relationship between housing and class inequality. At the end of the course it emerged that the majority of the pupils had little social or economic concept of class and, despite their obviously working class backgrounds, perceived themselves as middle class. The description 'working class' was considered denigrating.

Despite the lack of personal investment in the topic the major racist outburst occurred during the session. Two pupils who normally did not participate in the discussion announced that the information on housing was 'all lies'. They cited examples of black people buying large houses. The teacher, they maintained, was brainwashing them. This view was not supported by the rest of the class but the pupils obviously had support at home as the headmaster received letters of complaint with racist statements from parents. Unfortunately the teacher in turn was afforded little support from the head.

The questionnaire showed that whilst some of the pupils had absorbed the main factors which influence housing, others identified this section as being the least interesting of the course.

The information in the crime unit was of more immediate interest to the pupils. Media bias though not such a familiar topic is always an interesting subject to raise, and is examined in the section.

The unit looks at the role of the police in the area in respect to their relationship with the black community. Information from the local Police Monitoring Group and the Home Office statistics on the incidences of racist attacks can be compared with the coverage in the local paper of incidents involving young black people.

Most of the white pupils were of the opinion that the police are racist. Brushes with the 'law' are a commonly reported experience for white young people in our area so the pupils identified with the experiences of black youths. They quoted instances of being stopped or moved on by the police, the distorted way newspapers write about teenagers in general was related to racist reporting of incidents between black youths and police.

The last units examine the rise of fascism in the 1930s, both in London's East End and Germany and the history of racist and anti-racist action up to the present day. They span the history of racist incidents in the East End, from the attacks on the Hugenots and the Irish to the racist murder of an Asian man in a High Street by teenagers on a shopping day. The anti-racist movements and the key role played by black people in contemporary history are examined.

Background material is provided for the teacher to inform her/himself on current fascist propaganda. This should not be used in the classroom but it often already influences the pupils' thinking. The teacher is able to understand

and therefore respond appropriately to oblique comments from pupils which have had roots in the current propaganda.

The units expose the Nazi ideology of regimentation and a 'hang'em and flog 'em' approach to the disciplining of young people. Many course participants perceived a day in the life of a privileged Hitler youth as considerably more unpleasant than a day in a modern Detention Centre. This provides a contrast with the efforts that present-day Nazis have made to appeal to young people.

Some teachers may be reluctant to cover these areas, particularly when there are members of fascist organisations in the class. In our experience such pupils are taken aback by the information on NF leaders' views on how delinquents should be dealt with, particularly if they are also involved in delinquent activity themselves. Unless the views of racists or fascists are confronted directly with reference to past and present society, the practical application of the information covered in the previous units will be lost. Our experience has been that because the course content has logically led up to the looking at the views of the people who use and perpetuate racism that less confrontation actually takes place in this unit than might be expected. The approach puts these views in their historical and political context and demonstrates the positive alternative.

Many young people in this area come into direct contact with fascist organisations or their propaganda. Many are already uneasy about the role of these groups without being clear as to their true nature. These pupils believed that some young people join the NF and BM 'because they have nothing better to do, but some because they hate coloured people . . .' Fifty three per cent of the two classes thought the NF should be banned, others thought not as 'they are groups for people with racist views to belong to.'

In predominantly white groups from schools in the Docklands area, pupils were often initially in favour of fascist organisations. Exposure to the information produced a correspondingly stronger reaction against these groups.

The effects of the course on attitudes

The groups were asked to complete questionnaires at the end of the course. It was made clear that it was not an exam, and that we were interested in the pupils' opinions of the course. The questionnaires were designed to find how much information the pupils had absorbed and whether or not they felt that their views had changed.

The answers to the questionnaires showed, overall, a positive change in attitude amongst white pupils. Fifteen out of twenty-one felt that the course should be taught to other classes in the school because:
'Most children are prejudiced and they don't know the facts and proper figures of blacks in Britain.'
'We did not know the facts till now, we took blacks the wrong way.'

'It may change the views of people, therefore creating a better relationship.'

The responses of seventeen out of twenty-one to open ended questions on what they thought they had learned showed they perceived themselves as less prejudiced and changed in their views as a result of the course. These answers all included comments that black people were not the cause of unemployment and other social problems.

'My views have changed in the way that they don't take our jobs and I used to think they did all the muggings, but now I know they don't.'

More personally some commented,

'I have realised that they have got feelings like us and that they have had a hard time in this country.'

Many pupils also wanted to learn more from black people themselves and felt that the course could have been improved by 'Asking more blacks what they think of the whites.' (White pupils in multicultural groups have commented that they had learnt much from hearing the views and feelings of black classmates.)

There were still areas of confusion; for instance whilst virtually all agreed that there was discrimination of black people they were not convinced that it needed to be eradicated. The majority grasped the reasons for unemployment and poor housing in Newham, but had not linked the causes of inequality with racism. This explained the feeling that sometimes came over in discussion that racism was not a problem for white people. However it was obvious that the course had succeeded in refuting many of the common racist arguments and black people were no longer seen as the cause of many problems.

Only four pupils, including those responsible for the racist outbursts showed no attitude change whatsoever, although one wrote:

'I think Hitler should not have been brought into this course, as we should be forgetting him, not remembering what he done.'

The four black pupils did not participate in discussions. Their questionnaires showed a positive response to the content, and also the difficulty of having to deal with a dominant racist ethos:

'Which part of the course did you find interesting?'

'I found this part interesting where the truth was given. Like we are not responsible for unemployment.'

'Your own views on discrimination ...'

'I think all blacks and Asians get discrimination from whites ... especially at school we get picked on by whites. We get racial attacks and the teachers get abuses by older pupils.'

'Should the course be taught to other classes?'

'Yes and No. If this course has to be taught to other classes the white people shouldn't say things against them because that causes arguments and this course can teach people the truth.'

These responses indicate the pressure upon black pupils in predominantly white, racist schools.

General conclusions

Both teachers were pleased with the results of the course, through using it they gained confidence and developed their own understanding of racism. Crucial to its success was the commitment of both to anti-racist teaching and their willingness to experiment with teaching methods, including the use of open-ended discussion. We all found the process emotionally demanding but the results in the end were worthwhile. It is impossible to challenge racist views without discussing them openly; the course structure ensures that such discussion takes place on anti-racist rather than racist terms. In schools of this nature there are few pupils who are equipped to or are willing to take an immediate anti-racist stance, certainly in a large class. It may happen in smaller groups where informal relationships with teachers can be established.

In multicultural schools where discussion is obviously more balanced in the class as a whole, pupils are able to learn from each other, and a high level of debate much easier to achieve – exhileratingly so ...

A black pupil from a multiracial school suggested that the course should 'Discuss how and why riots break out. What is being done to keep kids off the streets. I would like to have discussed why the government builds nuclear weapons instead of helping unemployed people ...'

Our experience shows that a slot which tackles racism directly, needs specific preparation and follow up, and indicates what these areas of study are. A major reappraisal of the curriculum in terms of an anti-racist analysis is also needed. Teachers have commented that using this course has revealed the ethnocentrism of the school's curriculum and how it can be changed.

Developing anti-racist teaching needs anti-racist policies and a commitment to change both within schools as a whole and by the LEA. If teachers using the course communicate the results to other departments our approach could be used to develop both policy and practise with schools. It indicates to the LEA the need for clear anti-racist guidelines, resources, support and encouragement for teachers, in an area of fundamental change for British education. Anti-racist education, after all, challenges the whole basis of the content and practice of British Education.

References

1 'Bafa Bafa' now 'Rafa Rafa' available from Christian Aid, PO Box no.1, London SW9 8BH, price £2-00
2 *Our People*, Film/Video, Guild Sound and Vision, Woodston House, Oundale Road, Peterborough, PE2 9PZ.
3 *Why Prejudice*, Video, Concorde Films, 201 Felixstowe Road, Ipswich, IP3 9BJ.

Conclusion

The case studies

These case studies show how important it is for educationalists to start thinking about ways in which they can eradicate racism from the processes of learning with which they are involved. We must take responsibility for showing how this might provide possibilities for the development of a future based on education of its citizens for a multicultural society. Throughout the sections on playgroup and nursery, primary and secondary, resources and teacher training and anti-racist education the emphasis has been on the importance of combating racism as an insidious enemy of learning. We must expand the curriculum of students and teachers to ensure that it is not based on the need to justify the position of any particular country class or sexual group. For this reason the book has case studies which try to challenge the racism of covert and subtle attitudes derived by the very young from negative attitudes. The hypocrisy of 'doing good by doing little', often involves seeing children as 'innocent' in a society which is far from innocent. We have attempted to show how in playgroups the positive images of ethnic differences should counter the negative effects of covert racism (chapter 1). In primary schools anti-racist approaches and policies should involve parents, governors and staff in a determined effort to ensure that school supports the eradication of wrongs in the community to which pupils and parents belong (chapter 3). Secondary school, world history and world studies approaches should promote an understanding which effectively explains the existence of Britain as a nation-state, with its own imperial and colonial legacy. Anti-racist education must be developed by an approach to geography, for instance, which does not separate social, political and economic forces which influence the development of human beings in relations between Europe and the Third World (chapter 6). The development of anti-racist whole school policies at primary and secondary level is a step forward in the idea that schools can have corporate aims, and as a result, carry forward collective reforms across the curriculum (chapter 3, 5 and 22). All subjects including maths and science, can in combination with other subjects contribute to the exploration of political divisions based on class, gender and racism. This often presents difficulties for teachers when a divided curriculum needs to be re-orientated by a new emphasis, for instance, on world/peace studies which are neither ethnocentric or Eurocentric. In addition to the human resources of teachers and pupils, we have recourse to learning resources of various kinds. We have tried to show how important it is for resources of all kinds be they television programmes, library resources, texts, bilingual packs or special courses, to be used positively rather than as a *deus ex machina*. All resources are biased; stereotypical symbols and images are used by everyone in making sense of the world. In fact, teachers really are intermediaries who must contextualise their resources rather than simply hide behind them. Anti-racist teaching, central to a clarification of all of these issues, implies a political stance since it challenges unfair and unequal power relations and is most effectively supported by whole school policies on racism which unify the efforts of teachers across the school and the curriculum – overt and hidden.

In compiling these case studies the editor has been conscious of the need to make our position clear to those who see a distinction between the various terms used. We are also aware of objections raised by critics of 'multiculturalism' who see this as merely tinkering with the curriculum, e.g.

> According to the Institute of Race Relations the development and promotion of multicultural studies has done nothing to tackle the fundamental issue of racism. It is this issue that must be given the highest priority. 'Our concern ... is with anti-racist education (which by its very nature would include the study of other cultures). Just to learn about other people's cultures, though, is not to learn about the racism of one's own. To learn about the racism of one's own culture, on the other hand, is to approach other cultures objectively[1].

Multiculturalism and anti-racism

Until recently many innovators have taken a stance based on the idea that respect for ethnic cultures ought to be put within a multicultural perspective to achieve social harmony within society. This view depends on mutual respect for social diversity. All cultures are valued for their own sake and in terms of their own intrinsic value to the whole – hence both multi-ethnic and multicultural developments. While we acknowledge the debt that we owe to this perspective, we feel that it involves a form of liberalism which does not challenge the stratified society in which we live.

Recent debates about social perspectives which inform 'multiculturalism' have highlighted contradictions in the way in which education may be affected. Critics who see multicultural education as a gesture aimed at appeasing black and white militants castigate this 'celebration of multiculturalism' for its uncritical acceptance of the very status quo which perpetuates social divisions, economic oppression and racism. (See Mullard '81 and Carby '82). Rejecting an integrationist approach identified with 'multiculturalism', they understandably pour scorn on the notion that all cultures can be presented in such a way that they are equally valued whilst outside educational institutions a stratified society maintains systems of inequality and injustice. We believe that anti-racism is a more appropriate political standpoint for educationalists. We do not see 'multiculturalism' as having the potential for integrating society into social and ethnic groups on a 'separate but equal' basis (which would amount to a form of apartheid). On the contrary we suggest that anti-racist education for a multicultural society should shift the emphasis from an obsession with compensatory measures which locate deficiencies in the ethnic and class communities to a thorough-going analysis and eradication of institutional racism in the social structure and its negative and destructive potential.

As Andy Green points out:

> There is at the moment, within writings on the sociology of race, a growing tendency to stigmatise black family structures and forms of black culture, and in so doing, to trace the cause of black oppression and subordination in society back to the black community itself. The result is generally to obscure the way in which racism subordinates ethnic groups, and thus to sidestep the most important political issue.[2]

Readers will, of course, be able to identify in this collection of case studies the many and varied positions which teachers hold in response to the situations they face, the pupils they teach, their catchment areas, the kind of schools they work in and the support they receive in their schools, particularly from 'the powers that be. In some of the case studies writers show the concern that schools might feel about various aspects of their involvement with the community, political education, language and linguistic development of second language users, cross-curricular development and collaboration between departments. As Peter Mitchell points out, it is clear that in all schools but particularly in secondary schools, where the overt curriculum operates as a collection of disciplines or where the hidden curriculum of schooling is insufficiently scrutinised, curriculum innovation is unlikely to have a real effect. In these cases the tendency is then for multicultural curriculum development to be based on a 'do-it-yourself' tinkering with subjects, courses and programmes as they stand. Curriculum development depends on the conditions in which teachers operate in the school as well as on external constraints. Parental and community expectations, governors, local political parties, local schools, timetables, department and pastoral systems, rules and responsibilities, allocation of scale points etc. are all important considerations. It is, however, very easy to draw comparisons between the multicultural model with piecemeal curriculum developments based on cultural pluralism and the more ambitious anti-racist perspective which calls for a more radical approach.

The school

Tuku Mukherjee's training course (Chapter 19), involved creating a 'subtly racist school'. This was a painful but revealing exercise for participants even though it was conducted in the relatively safe and neutral area of a teacher training college. For staff and pupils facing the task of developing a common approach to anti-racist education in real schools the difficulties are enormous. What is frequently referred to as the 'ethos' of the school, or in my terms, the combination of the effects of both the overt and hidden curriculum, has characteristics which are peculiar to each school. I would argue that this ethos must be examined with the systematic scrutiny that one would apply to an examination of one's own conscience and attitudes. The aims of the school should be formulated on principles that promote anti-racist and anti-sexist education across departments and pastoral systems. For this reason we would urge schools, in keeping with Berkshire and ILEA's policies to seek for whole school policy development, all the better with LEA backing. This enables the staff as a whole to examine its curriculum and procedure using the usual channels e.g. working parties, staff and departmental meetings, conferences etc. as well as INSET. This scrutiny will enable schools to find the means of enabling students to learn about the societal aspects of racism across the curriculum. Cross-curricula collaboration is absolutely essential for this process since the programme involves teaching which doesn't fall neatly into the subject boundaries. Indeed so clearly will schools need to signal their anti-racist stance it would be invidious for any department, student or staff member to be left out of this process.

Schools cannot afford to turn a blind eye to the living conditions of their pupils and parents. For this reason, a dramatic transformation, already widespread in certain LEAs in Britain needs to be affected in the relationship between parents and schools in joint attempts to eradicate inequalities created by racism, sexism and class in the school and the community. Complex institutions e.g. secondary schools and colleges require greater efforts in order to engage actively with social and political issues across the curriculum and within the community.

The hidden curriculum mirrors certain forms of institutional racism and classism in society. These concepts are difficult to grasp since they are the results of collective practices which escape the control, and often, the attention of individuals. These practices are, however, resisted vigorously by the people who feel the oppression most strongly. A culture of resistance of the kind which manifested itself in response to poor housing, unemployment, harassment by police and educational disadvantage in the riots of 1981 will eventually seek forms of solidarity within schools where racism and other forms of inequality are ignored. Certain schools were activated by a common concern felt by community agencies and parents over the political effects of the Nationality Bill. On occasions when teachers felt impelled to declare opposition to racist attacks, demonstrations and distribution of racist propaganda, staff have engaged in political education and action with community support. In so doing they have thereby demonstrated that protestations of concern for equality ought to be consistently linked to political practice if anti-racist stances are to have an impact on the community and wider society. The neutral stance advocated by some educationalists in their anxiety to avoid taking sides presents schools with no opportunity to back up their policies with support for the communities to which their pupils belong.

References

1 Sivanandan, A., *Roots of Racism*, Institute of Race Relations, 1982 (from

Race, Sex and Class; Multi-ethnic Education in Schools, ILEA)
2 Green, A., *In defence of antiracist teaching: a reply to recent critiques of multicultural education* NAME Journal, Vol 10, No. 2

Bibliography
Schooling in Babylon, Carby H., in *The Empire Strikes Back* by the Centre for Contemporary Cultural Studies, Hutchinson, 1982
The Social Context and Meaning of Multicultural Education, Mullard C., in *Educational Analysis*, Vol. 3, No 1, 1983